Interrogating the Image

Movies and the
World of Film and Television

Del Jacobs

Kathy, Dick —
Thanks so much
for your support of
Film at SCF.
Del Jacobs

UNIVERSITY PRESS OF AMERICA,® INC.
Lanham • Boulder • New York • Toronto • Plymouth, UK

Copyright © 2009 by
University Press of America,® Inc.
4501 Forbes Boulevard
Suite 200
Lanham, Maryland 20706
UPA Acquisitions Department (301) 459-3366

Estover Road
Plymouth PL6 7PY
United Kingdom

Library of Congress Control Number: 2009928967
ISBN: 978-0-7618-4632-1 (paperback : alk. paper)
eISBN: 978-0-7618-4633-8

All images courtesy of Photofest

Cover photo: Lawrence Woolsey (John Goodman) in shadow with camera from *Matinee*

Contents

Introduction

This Introduction offers an orientation that is hopefully beneficial to both the film enthusiast and the casual moviegoer. A brief overview of the various generations of spectators as well as a short and selective history of film consumption follows in Chapter One. This mapping also gives a longitudinal sense of the expansion and eventual diversity in media forms using moving images. There are also some thoughts regarding the differences between consumption of cinema and television. Arguably, distinctions here tend to favor cinema, elevating its status as interrogator. This result is that films are produced that become more dystopian in outlook as cinema loses its grip as the primary purveyor of the moving image. The majority of the text is a detailed analysis of several films and the interrogative stances evidenced in their narratives. Separate chapters are dedicated to movies considered reflexive/reflective, critical, and ironic, and the manner in which the work of both theorists and practitioners can inform our appreciation of them. An Epilogue offers some considerations for the future regarding the interplay between the audience and the moving image.

Writer-director Paul Schrader was asked by his publisher, Faber and Faber, to write a book detailing the canon of cinema, a film version of Harold Bloom's literature-focused *The Western Canon* (1995). In attempting to construct the text and canon, Schrader found the fragmentation of film culture working against him. There were simply too many niches and special interests that needed to be acknowledged to signify a balanced canon. Schrader's difficulty was connected to the explosion of cinema culture in the latter decades of the past century. Not only did he note the many and diverse ways that cinema was used and various interests served in the last century, but he anticipates an erosion of that role in the next. Schrader writes:

Motion pictures were the dominant art for the 20th century. Movies were the center of social mores, fashion and design, politics—in short, at the center of culture—and, in so being, dictated the terms of their dominance to the other art forms: literature, theater, and painting were all redefined by their relationship to cinema. Movies have owned the 20th century. It will not be so in the 21st century. Cultural and technological forces are at work that will change the concept of 'movies' as we have known them. I don't know if there will be a dominant art form in this century, and I'm not sure what form audiovisual media will take, but I am certain movies will never regain their prominence they enjoyed in the last century.[1]

This book is about the slow unraveling of the control movies held when they "owned the 20th century," and how they tended to portray the incursion of other media onto their interpretive turf. Cinema provides the grounding for emerging technologies that employ the moving image, as well as the theoretical basis for understanding its structure and composition. Movies, however, have never stopped morphing. Technology and social context have both defined the art of film and led us to 21st century models of production, replication, distribution and consumption of televisual images.

As other forms of media using the moving picture proliferate (video-on-demand, Internet, cell/picture phones), cinema intensifies its interrogation of them. The result is a heightened self-awareness of mass media and its influences on society and, concurrently, critiques of those emergent structures and their influences. The single film has proven a capable vehicle for noting the relationship of itself to the larger society, and it persists in further exploring the effects of media spawned by cinema. It carries the case that the pervasiveness of the moving image shapes the general inculturation or enculturation process, for better and for worse. In cases where the omnipresence of visual media and the accompanying potential for obfuscation has occasion to undermine the free will of its citizen-viewers, cinema can expose the dilemma and also suggest ways of relief.

Film directors have been known to both romanticize and authenticate the process of movie making. Orson Welles called cinema " a ribbon of dreams" and Jean-Luc Godard noted that the movies reveal "truth twenty-four times a second," a reference to the number of single frames of film that run through a projector in that time. In exploring narrative movies about the moving image—those that situate their stories and characters within the worlds of film and television—certain claims are made about media and its impact that the filmmaker feels especially empowered to address.

The contemporary trend of an obsession with a critique of media and its influence in society is evident in *Redeeming Modernity: Contradictions in Media Criticism* (1990) where author Joli Jensen contends that:

" . . . the media, so widespread, ubiquitous, and appealing, have been accused of misleading individuals, misrepresenting reality, commercializing feelings, and, in general, corrupting contemporary life. Our ambivalence about our own participation in popular forms of communication stems from the demonic image that dominates discussions of the role of mass communication in society—an image of the media as a monolithic, and malevolent, force."[2]

Jensen further considers media commentary "inevitably cultural and social evaluation, and thus it is always political."[3] While mass media can serve as scapegoats for modernity, in that they can be blamed for what is wrong with modern life, for not saving us from its negative repercussions, as well as even causing some modern evils, if we recognize media criticism as a "displaced critique of modern life"[4] then perhaps a redeeming approach can arise.

Films themselves have presented this kind of media criticism, turning the camera on the very process of creating and consuming movies and television. Film represents itself as dreamer and truth-teller, a rhetorical device that reveals much about itself and television. Director Wim Wenders acknowledges cinema's power to affirm and/or transform in that, "It can either confirm the idea that things are wonderful the way they are [or were], or it can reinforce the conception that things can be changed."[5] As such, they can enable the possibility of what Jensen calls " . . . redemption by cultural purity. The unchallenged assumption is that there are certain kinds of cultural fare that are in-and-of-themselves worthy—these are forms that are seen to have an automatically ennobling and uplifting influence on us."[6]

As movies represent themselves through the experience within the space of cinema, they are inherently reflexive. When television and competing media arise, the movies that interrogate their producers and audiences become more critically and ironically observant. Furthermore, when political, corporate and media structures more intensively coalesce and integrate in the latter part of the 20th century, the movies tend to observe the media-making tools and their results as dystopian and ideologically self-serving.

In tracing the representations of these relationships, certain tendencies re-occur in the films selected for study. All display reflexive elements befitting Jay Ruby's definition of "reflexivity":

To be reflexive is to structure a product in such a way that the audience assumes that the producer, the process of making, and the product are a coherent whole. Not only is the audience made aware of these relationships, but it is made to realize the necessity of that knowledge. By sabotaging the traditional illusion that we are watching unmediated life, reflexivity signals that films are created, structured articulations of the filmmaker . . .[7]

The films set during the period from the 1930s to the 1960s, when cinema more or less dominated the media landscape, employ historical depiction infused with nostalgia. They celebrate a loss of innocence with the sacred space of the cinema as a key setting and player in this rite of passage. If cinema can be perceived as a maternal force in these texts, there frequently exists a paternal one represented by a mentor or father-figure that shepherds the lead character through some growth or socialization process; he is usually associated with the making of movies or media, often portrayed by a film director, theater owner, actor or colleague. Youthful characters in *The Last Picture Show*, for example, traverse adolescence in a small Texas community of the 1950s under the watchful eye of a town elder, who also happens to own its only movie theater. This is an era when television begins to displace the movies as a primary means of moving picture presentation.

A central reason to examine movies that feature film (or television) as part of our cultural history and as something important in their characters' lives is that this kind of reflexivity prompts *reflection* about film or TV in our lives. Despite the movie's title, the closing of the Royal Theater in *The Last Picture Show* is a relatively minor and unimportant event in the narrative. Yet director Peter Bogdanovich chooses this as a metaphor with which to characterize the changes that have beset the lives of these characters. The presence of the movie theater in this tiny, one-street rural town of Anarene, Texas, said something about their connection to modernity and the ability of Hollywood movies to deliver images of escape and inspiration. We witness the emergence of television as a replacement system, as well, and the popular music of the time as additionally important to the historical frame. But Anarene is losing its picture show, and that connotes something even more profound about the loss and passing of this time and this culture. Bogdanovich insinuates that the abstract villain in *The Last Picture Show* could well be television:

> " . . . The sociological fact, the closing down of the picture shows and the predominance   of television was definitely creating a more insular society. Just like drive-in theaters were against the idea of 'theater.' Theater means a kind of coming together of an audience. There isn't anything more wonderful than an audience. To take that away from pictures and theater removes a certain experience, not only from the audience, but from people who make the thing. Because to not experience a lot of people laughing or crying just doesn't do it. It doesn't do it to say it's in 40 million homes."[8]

When television usurps cinema's role as the primary provider of moving images, a trend accelerating in the 1960s, films that scrutinize TV's ascendancy become critical about its increasing dominance. Emboldened film directors and writers—some actually trained in television and documentary

(Sidney Lumet, Paddy Chayefsky, Haskell Wexler) and others emergent in the film culture of social criticism (Oliver Stone, Spike Lee, Tim Robbins, Warren Beatty)—embrace the mantle of "truth-teller" and likewise utilize reflexive devices and narratives that often incorporate mentors or father-figures. In these stories, however, warning signs are highlighted that illuminate the faults and shortcomings of television: its propensity to sanitize and limit choices (*Pleasantville*), its celebration of dysfunction and the notion of celebrity (*Natural Born Killers*), the complacency of TV audiences and the willful manipulation by producers (*Bamboozled, Network*), the blurred line between what is real and manufactured in television news (*Medium Cool*). Additional films acknowledge the impact of media forms interrelated with conventional television. These include advertising, political campaigns, newsgathering, and reality TV. The movies critique these structures and provide adaptive strategies, often employing a latently ironic outlook.

Filmmakers may approach a dissection of competing media forms with some myopic crankiness. Surely, the economic impact that television had on the movie industry in the 1950s and 1960s invited a jaded perspective on the tube's role in society. In the ensuing decades, however, the consolidation of media control has grouped major film studios with other outlets for filmed product (TV, home video, cable) so that a significant or negotiable part of the financial return goes back to the film producers no matter what the forum for audience consumption. It is this consolidation, frequently engendered by political and industrial desire for establishing oversight and resting control in the hands of a few powerful conglomerates, which continues to inspire filmmaker truth-tellers to provide narratives that offer resistance strategies.

In *Life the Movie: How Entertainment Conquered Reality* (1998), Neal Gabler recognizes cinema as the most pervasive, powerful and ineluctable force of our time—a force so overwhelming that it has metastasized into life. In fact, cinema was almost larger than life at the turn of the 20th century. When movies burst upon the scene, they were an unprecedented phenomenon because they could be easily reproduced and replayed, and they reached people as groups rather than as single individuals. Other late 19th century media such as newspapers and books, for example, found their target audiences of literate persons one by one. Theatre could be reproduced but only with greater expense and effort. Moreover, movies reached viewers indiscriminately, regardless of their educational level or language spoken, and without the customary intervention of gatekeepers such as the state, church, school or family. Eventually, social controls would affect content and access, and film audiences would fractionalize. These developments would indeed accelerate our reliance on moving images in our lives.

Today, the moving image is interactive, multiplied, magnified and miniatur-
ized as an experience for audiences who, 100 years ago, were less likely to feel
its omnipresence. Like all art forms, cinema persists as reflector, mediator and
interrogator of the human experience. And when it turns its lens on itself, movies
clarify the way filmmakers envision the roles of artist and of audience.

The films explored in this text investigate the culture of the moving image.
Beginning with narratives where cinema itself is the focus, the movies affirm
traditions with mostly conservative, restorative impulses. When television
replaces cinema as the dominant carrier of the moving image, films about
TV culture are mostly critical of television's power and influence; they offer
alternatives to guide viewers in an understanding of a world where cinema
and TV now coexist. Often cynical, ironic, and alarmist in tone, these films
suggest a rejection of the world/worldview sustained by a media environment
that is subject to coercive manipulation by its creators, even as its audiences
are unknowingly or willingly manipulated.

At roughly the halfway point into the motion picture era, the mid-20th
century, Americans went to the movies almost 100 million times a week.
A popular, influential art form and commercial industry unified the country
into a mass audience. Television soon emerged to eclipse the dominance of
cinema, but the moving image was central to both media. The omnipresence
of "pictures that move like living people" (a tag line that promoted early
flickers) is taken for granted, not only to entertain or edify, but as a necessary
means of negotiating life.

In asking the question "Why do movies matter?" it is helpful to suggest
that in order to understand the culture of the time and those who inhabit it,
historians and social critics must consider the experience of a dominant medium during that place or time. So, to understand the Greek culture, we turn to
their tragedies and epics, their architecture and philosophy; for 15th century
Florence, look at the paintings; for medieval France, trace the development
of architecture, especially cathedrals; for Elizabethan England, the theater;
for Victorian England, the novel. These art forms flourished and embodied
a particular historical moment. If one wishes to gain some sensitivity of
the life and times of the 20th and 21st centuries, then the movies and their
offshoots seem an appropriate place to focus. Indeed, a Ball State survey in
2005 revealed that the average person spends about nine hours per day using
some type of media; television is the dominant media device, with computers
and their expansion from text to more sophisticated visual, moving pictures/
graphics catching up fast.

The moving image captures and illuminates the drama of its time. If movies matter, then it seems movies that train their sights on this very apparatus
should *especially* matter. They provide significant reflections of how film-

makers and audiences helped shape these times. This text is an exploration of the image-makers and receptors, using the movies themselves as a tool of interrogation. The relationship between those who create and those who consume the moving image has evolved against a backdrop of social and technological changes. When film became such a commonplace cultural force—accelerating in the 1920s and reaching higher peaks of influence in the 1940s—filmmakers almost by necessity included movie-making and movie-going as part of their subject matter. But beyond that, filmmakers have also been fascinated self-consciously and often obsessively with film, its history, and its power as a medium. Later, as will be shown, film also becomes preoccupied with the cultural role of television.

At first, the movies competed with television for audiences, but filmmakers soon realized a spirit of cooperation was necessary since both relied on the moving image. Even as they share audiences, each medium remains unique in some properties and capabilities. As films interrogate this relationship, they sometimes do so at a time of contention; other films do this in a revisionist fashion, returning to a past era from their contemporary perspective.

While examining films about the role of media in society, other issues emerge that have been the subject of study in literature, music, art, journalism, advertising, and other realms of discourse. Like those fields, the movies provide a window through which we may observe and understand what is potentially confounding about our world. Cinematic themes include the function of nostalgia in evoking an emotional or aesthetic appreciation, the changing perception of gender and racial identity, the engineering of a "celebrity culture," and the collusion among political, media, and corporate forces to contain dissent or limit dialogue in a free society. These and other aspects of modern life are dramatized and critiqued in the films explored in this text.

As filmmakers characterize, romanticize, or criticize the role of television, audiences have become more self-aware and sophisticated through their experiences of film-going and television-watching. An analytical framework of "stances"—reflexive/reflective, critical, ironic—is offered as an organizing conceit in this text. Films that deal with film and television can be grouped three ways. First, there are films that are "reflexive/reflective" in depicting the images and markers of media in our culture; these tend to be nostalgic and historical. Then there are films that are critical of the role of media in society. While, unsurprisingly, these are more focused on television, they also offer insights into the attitudes and ethos of film; these tend to provide a critique of media and society. And finally, there are films that deal critically with film and television and its representations of modern society itself; these tend to employ a critical/ironic posture where reflexivity is heightened.

Consider these stances as tendencies, characterizations, or perspectives that inform a filmmaker's point of view, and likely, can be appreciated by the viewer. Cinema utilizes reflexive/reflective, critical, and ironic stances to ask how the moving image both examines itself and the ways it has transformed culture. In exploring the narratives and implications of several films that deal with media-making from the 1930s to today, these perspectives are utilized by filmmakers and audiences to create dialogue and understanding of life in the 20th and 21st centuries.

The reflexive/reflective stance grounds both filmmaker and spectator in a self-awareness of media-making. It assists in developing or enhancing other perspectives. So, reflexivity becomes celebrated as a rite of passage that, initially, affirms the status quo but can lead to reconstructive or rejective tendencies. Movies about movies consecrate cinema as a repository of memory, with elements of nostalgia, reverence and regret. The experience of making and/or watching movies is frequently romanticized or idealized. A significant shift occurs in 1970s as the movies become more critical of their own apparatus and history in films such as *Day of the Locust* (Schlesinger, 1975) and *The Last Tycoon* (Kazan, 1976), both set in the 1930s. By the 1990s, both established and independent filmmakers were skewering the process of movie-making in *Barton Fink* (Coen, 1991), *The Player* (Altman, 1992), *Swimming With Sharks* (Huang, 1994), and *Living in Oblivion* (DiCillo, 1995). Until the 1950s and on occasion thereafter, when cinema examines itself their narratives tend to be comforting and restorative. Transitional films such as *The Bad and the Beautiful* (Minnelli, 1952) and *The Big Knife* (Aldrich, 1955) anticipate some of the cynicism of the aforementioned movies about movies.

So, although some films examined the moviemaking process from a critical stance, it was the advent and acceptance of television that generated a wellspring of critical movies about that new medium's impact. On the one hand, TV usurped cinema's role as a manufacturer or marker of history and as a conduit for the audience's understanding of it. But on the other, cinema usually attempted to reveal and critique rather than honor TV's techniques of manipulation. Television's omnipresence since the 1950s has served as both an obstacle to and an enhancement of the critical stance. Movies invite the critical interpretive stance with regard to television, as well as when regarding other institutions reliant on TV for their stability; these include systems of organization that are political, corporate, social, and familial. In movies about television, this critique is usually presented by concentrating on the roles of the professional media practitioner/player and the participating audience. These films infer implications for society at large and offer opportunities for re-envisioning or reconstructing those systems or structures.

The ironic stance is evident in movies that grasp the irony—the discord between appearance and reality—in media-making. Television, once again, provides the most fertile ground for creating and disseminating texts to influence interaction with political, corporate, social and familial systems. Movies dramatically and satirically illustrate how TV and other media forms can both expose and conceal truths that impact those systems. These films are warnings to a media-saturated culture and frequently conclude with a rejection of the world revealed in the film.

There have been several academic and popular press publications related to the motion picture experience, various interpretive strategies, and their applications in intellectual discourse. Many of these are referenced in the following pages and have informed the author's own sense of cineliteracy, which is defined as the critical understanding of the moving image developed through the processes of reading and writing the screen. Two seminal works are worth mentioning. James Monaco's *How to Read a Film* (1978), originally published by Oxford University Press, has expanded its title in the 30th anniversary edition to *How to Read a Film: Movies, Media and Beyond*; Monaco's astute observations on cinema provide a grounding for analyzing the moving image in the digital multimedia age. Leo Braudy's *The World in a Frame: What We See in Films* (1976), originally published by The University of Chicago Press and now in its 25th edition, considers popular American film as one of multiple histories—visual style, genre, characterization, and within a cultural context.

The American Film Institute has a long-standing tradition of educational commitment since 1967. The Film Foundation, established in 1990 by acclaimed filmmaker Martin Scorsese and fellow film directors, sponsors an ongoing program called *The Story of Movies* that is "an interdisciplinary curriculum introducing students to classic cinema and the cultural, historical, and artistic significance of film."[9] Designed to teach audiences how to "read" the visual language of film, *The Story of Movies'* project highlights six underlying objectives:
Understand the historical and artistic development of American movies

Understand the social, cultural and artistic significance of film
Think critically about social issues, such as racism, politics, democratic ideals, war, history and culture, as depicted in movies
Use film as a cultural shorthand that speaks across the multi-ethnic, multicultural world in which we live
Think creatively and critically, not only in the movie theater but in all aspects of our lives, and certainly with all artistic communication

Embrace the American multi-cultural experience and achieve a deeper understanding of our own place in a diverse national culture. [10]

This book exists in the traditions of those authors and educators aforementioned. *The Story of Movies'* objectives inform this excursion into movies
that investigate the role of the moving image in our lives.

The movies explored throughout this text invite us to use the structures of
film and television as a means of reconstructing society; this entails a turning
outward and a focus upon what surrounds us. It also provides a means of reconstructing self; this requires a turning inward and taking inventory of what
inhabits us. These stories and their characters are our guides.

NOTES

1. Schrader, Paul. (2006). "Canon Fodder." Film Comment. Vol. 42, No. 5.
Sept/October 2006. 35.

2. Jensen, Joli. (1990). *Redeeming Modernity: Contradictions in Media Criticism.* Newbury Park: Sage Publications, Inc. 12.

3. Ibid. 16.

4. Ibid. 192.

5. http://www.brainyquote.com/quotes/authors/w/wim_wenders.html

6. Ibid. 183.

7. Ruby, Jay. (1977). "The Image Mirrored: Reflexivity and the Documentary
Film" from *New Challenges for Documentary.* Berkeley: University of California
Press. 65.

8. Bogdanovich, Peter. (1999) "Adapting and Directing *The Last Picture Show*";
Scenario, Vol. 4, No. 4, Winter 1998-99. 96.

9. http://www.film-foundation.org

10. Ibid.

Chapter One

Audience

In examining the several films that follow, a common feature is that they include characters and representations of the audience. Critical exploration of these films often positions that group of spectators or viewers within the narrative text as stand-ins for an overall audience for film or television at a particular time in history. The moving image is backdrop to the dramatic play of their lives in these films. As cinema evolved, its relationship with its audience also changed. And as other vestiges of the moving image became dominant, particularly television, that relationship changes further.

A BRIEF HISTORY OF "WATCHING"

One would be hard-pressed to locate a living person not acculturated through the mechanical or electronic moving image, with the exception of remote tribes and island dwellers. Today, movies are acknowledged as a re-creation or a representation of reality, as light and shadows on a screen. In *How a Film Theory Got Lost* (2001), Robert Ray notes that filmmaking has always been shaped by answers to a set of fundamental questions: "How do we make sense of a film? What happens when we encounter a movie segment for the first time? How do we process cinematic information?"[1] Most viewers, indeed, make meaning with some acknowledgment of what Bertolt Brecht defined as *apparatus* matter—where production, distribution and consumption influence that meaning. Thus, a concerted understanding, or reading, of a particular film invites an inquiry into its manufacture (when? why? how? by whom?), its dissemination (through what means? with what effect?), and its reception (by critics/historians and spectators). The moving image has been welcomed as a tool of modern communication.

In the past 110 years, artists and audiences have created and consumed cinema in various ways indicative of their own times. Cinema that began as a public spectacle with the Lumière Brothers' Cinematographe in Paris (1894) and Robert William Paul's Theatrograph in London (1895), presented the first wave of film audiences with a novel experience, albeit one for which they had been conditioned to perceive largely through other forms (theatre, carnival, circus, Wild West shows, etc.).

The first generation of film audiences experienced the sheer novelty and power of watching pictures that moved. From 1895 through the 1920s they witnessed the birth, development and consolidation of an art form and industry. Indeed, most in that first wave audience consumed movies that were silent, or accompanied by piano players, organists or other musicians, even symphony orchestras. Complete films could be 30 seconds in length, as were the first Lumière and Thomas Edison works, or an evening's worth of entertainment such as D.W. Griffith's feature-length *The Birth of a Nation* (1915). Some films were tinted or hand-colored. Some experimented with the size of the image and the potential for multiple images using split-screen effects. Some were even synchronized with audio recordings. Most of the genres celebrated today were established and experienced early codifications during this period: historical and contemporary drama, romance, western, crime, animation and comedy. Sometimes a film, like Buster Keaton's *Sherlock, Jr.* (1924), combined self-reflexive notions of the movies, special effects, genre conventions and narrative play in unusual ways; here, Keaton plays a meek theater projectionist and amateur sleuth who literally penetrates the silver screen and lands in the action.

It was around this time that the growing influence of film initiated a modern culture of celebrity. Picture players such as Charles Chaplin, Mary Pickford and Douglas Fairbanks—some of the first "stars" of movies—became flesh-and-blood magnets for mass audiences who flocked to see them in screen stories or in personal appearances at the cinema. Their personas were used to sell more than movies. As trustful spokespersons, these stars rallied support for war bonds and assorted commercial products. While other mass media forms contributed, it was in the movies of the first half of the century where many popular personalities found their desired presence most felt by audiences. Even entertainers who initiated their careers in vaudeville (Al Jolson), radio (Jack Benny), or clubs (Paul Whiteman & His Orchestra) found their appearances in early films an essential means to connect with audiences.

Then as now, the chance encounter with a movie can and did change lives. In *The Grey Fox* (Borsos, 1982) a real-life character named Bill Miner, played by Richard Farnsworth, is released prison after a sentence of 33 years for robbing stagecoaches. It is 1903 and he is working in the mining fields of the American northwest. Bored with his lackluster job, he wanders into a tent-showing of *The Great Train Robbery*, and director Philip Borsos recreates an oft-recounted moment when early century viewers became so engrossed in the action and gunplay on the screen that more than one drew his pistol and fired in response to the flickering images! Miner, meanwhile, gets inspiration from the film narrative for his next vocation—robbing the trains that replaced the stagecoaches.

By the time sound pictures became an industry-wide reality, the first generation of audiences was giving way to the second generation. As audiences viewed more and more films, the comfort and reliability of that experience as a leisure pastime helped usher the reflexive/reflective stance. Awareness and cross-referencing of "the film experience" would be celebrated in films made during this period, as well as those that followed that were set during this time. The years from the late 1920's through the early 1950s comprise Hollywood's Golden Era. The studio system was firmly established and its factory-like output to a mostly homogeneous audience set a worldwide standard for quality, making American movies the desired import in most foreign countries. After a relatively freewheeling and candid series of films during the early sound era, the movies came to grips with their role as a moral arbiter that dodged or encrypted certain volatile issues and representations after establishment of the Production Code of 1934. The young viewer who saw Lon Chaney, Sr., in *Phantom of the Opera* in 1925 or Fredric March in *Dr. Jekyll and Mr. Hyde* in 1932 would find these characterizations tamed somewhat by Claude Rains (*Phantom of the Opera*, 1943) and Spencer Tracy (*Dr. Jekyll and Mr. Hyde*, 1941) in the Production Code era, when scripts were submitted for review and each finished film was awarded a seal of approval in order to play in the studio-owned theaters around the country. Hollywood films provided both illuminations of issues as well as escape during the Great Depression. In the years of World War II, there was general agreement that films should bolster home front morale and parallel the intentions of the War Department. It was during this time that attendance at American movie houses reached its all-time high, with about 95 million tickets often sold weekly during the war years.[2]

Second generation audiences speak wondrously of the year 1939, considered to be the most "golden" of the golden era. The production output was certainly vigorous that year, with 476 U.S. pictures released. Contrast this with 143 films released in 1971, one of the lowest before production titles increased due in large part to emerging video and cable markets of the 1970s.[3] Two movies from 1939, both from the same studio (Metro-Goldwyn-Mayer), crystallized the period for many of that generation. *Gone With the Wind* is, adjusted for inflation, the most financially successful American film in terms of box office gross revenue.[4] Its audience was pre-sold by the popularity of Margaret Mitchell's novel on which it is based, as well as the cast and high-quality production values. The film won eight Oscars and was reissued frequently before its eventual release to television and home video. If *Gone With the Wind* is about the mythic American past, then *The Wizard of Oz* is a counterpart that also gives us a parallel world of fantasy complete with its own mythic underpinnings. *Oz* became a perennial favorite on television screens before *GWTW* was released for broadcast, and thus probably initiated many second and third generation audiences in the moving picture experience and in the fear of flying monkeys! After 1945 and the acceleration of postwar institutions such as suburbia and television, a third generation of film audiences was emerging from the baby boom.

Third generation audiences, in the period from the early 1950s through the mid-1970s, incorporated the phenomenon of television into their viewing experiences. In 1948, only 58 American cities had TV stations and they broadcast to 1.6 million sets. People watched TV communally—in a bar, a bowling alley, at the home of someone who could afford a receiver that was often more furniture than screen. But by 1954, there were 32 million homes with television and Hollywood knew it had a competitor. Attendance at theaters confirmed this, with weekly ticket sales at about 47 million in 1957, half the wartime peak. As the decade ended, 90 percent of homes had television.[5]

Hollywood reacted with fear, hostility and innovation towards the new medium. Movies themselves could be outright critical of television in the course of their narratives. The film industry also supported an ad campaign called "Movies Are Better Than Ever" throughout the 1950s with a series of presentation gimmicks, some of which proved short-lived and others long-lasting. Widescreen processes, the curved screen of Cinerama, stereo and multi-track sound, 3-D movies, and more carnivalesque ploys such as Aromo-Rama, Duo-Vision, Emergo, PsychoRama and others enhanced the nature of film spectacle, right up through Sensurround in the 1970s.

While narrative often played a secondary role to spectacle or sensation, the movie screens themselves in the early 1960s actually became smaller. The large, urban cinema palaces of the silent and early sound era suffered attendance drops during the 1960s and 1970s, and many were demolished, abandoned or retrofitted as multi-screen showcases; some gave themselves over to programming for inner-city audiences since the core middle-class filmgoers preferred suburban outlets for movies that were closer to their homes. Drive-ins proliferated in the 1950s; more than 4,000 were operating by mid-decade, when they accounted for about one-quarter of U.S. box office revenue.[6] In June 1957, there were nearly 6,000 drive-in theaters in America and one week their attendance actually superseded that at indoor theaters

An audience in 1953 enjoys a 3-D movie, one of several film exhibition techniques experiences by spectators in the 1950s that could not be accomplished on television screens. Others included stereophonic sound, color and widescreen projection.

for the first and only time.[7] By the early 1960s, multiplex cinemas began to dominate exhibition practices. The film audience, once unified by choice and design at the single-screen theater, now fragmented into niches so that even families could choose different films on a night out, much like they selected programs on the television sets in their rooms at home.

Besides the diversity in technologies and in the screening venues, there was the content of cinema itself that distinguished itself for third generation audiences. American movie directors, at first influenced by the Italian Neorealists and then practitioners the French New Wave, began to make more expressive, personal films in the 1950s and 1960s. As in other periods of history, the popular arts during this time experienced a reevaluation of their boundaries of expression. This included forays by Elvis Presley and Little Richard in popular music, Hugh Hefner in the magazine publishing world, Jack Kerouac in modern literature, Jackson Pollack and Mark Rothko in the art world, and Andy Warhol in popular fashion. The sociohistorical scene was ripe with tensions that fueled inspiration for filmmakers in this generation—the Cold War, McCarthyism, civil rights, Vietnam, feminism, generational conflict, the drug culture, political assassinations, identity politics, environmentalism and more. Movies may have become more diverse, but annual attendance diminished to an all-time low during this period, with 1971 the nadir of a 25-year economic decline after the peak year 1946.[8] This is not to imply that engaging and ground-breaking mainstream motion pictures were not being made. The year 1967 produced *2001: A Space Odyssey, Bonnie and Clyde, The Graduate, Rosemary's Baby*; 1968 showcased *Midnight Cowboy, The Wild Bunch, Z, The Producers*; 1969 presented *Easy Rider, Butch Cassidy and the Sundance Kid, Medium Cool, They Shoot Horses Don't They?* and 1970 brought *M*A*S*H, Catch-22, Little Big Man, Five Easy Pieces*. Inarguably, films during this period—late third generation—became more youth-oriented as the older, "lost audience" preferred television.

What is the demarcation point between third and fourth generations? As with the junctures that came before, it is less easy to point to a specific moment in time than to a collection of events in roughly the same period. In the film content arena, there emerged the importance of the "blockbuster" movie that could reach a mass audience, invite repeat viewings, engage watchers through some new parity of story and spectacle, create synergy with other consumer products, and perhaps spin off sequel films that instigate further products. First, *Jaws* (Spielberg, 1975) and then more precisely *Star Wars* (Lucas, 1977) epitomized this strategy. Blockbuster movies became "experiences" and cultural phenomena. Also significant as markers of the fourth generation were two technological occurrences—the convergence of cable TV systems, with special attention to Home Box Office (HBO) as a premium service in the mid-1970s, and the market penetration of the videocassette recorder (VCR) shortly thereafter.

The blockbuster action film is the movie as a theme-park ride. The narrative and spectacle of a film such as *Star Wars* viscerally engages the viewer, prompting further discourse in other ways that engagement builds upon that first move through the turnstile. Along with watching franchise films, audiences become part of the franchise, due largely to marketing strategies and licensing agreements for several types of consumer goods that exist as "tie-ins" to the movie. Blockbuster film experiences bind viewers to other viewers in place and time; later, the uninitiated can also come aboard with little effort but cannot be acknowledged as an original player. When young fans lined up to see *Star Wars: The Phantom Menace* (Lucas, 1999), a full 22 years after the original was first released, many spoke wistfully of not being able to have had the opportunity to be present when *Star Wars* first opened. They had likely seen the first film, perhaps on video, and now take opportunity to interact with a big-screen representation in the cinema space.

If the third generation encountered the tension between the movie experience and the television experience as one of competing and coping, the fourth generation of audiences saw the boundaries between the two mediums become both blurred and porous. Video became the primary means by which audiences experienced the moving image of narratives originally termed "film." Annual revenue from video cassette sales and rentals outdistanced film box office receipts for the first time in 1987.[9] Since then, when considering all video-on-demand services, video games which incorporate narrative and spectator strategies, and home video as a secondary market for movies, more people "go out and *get* a movie" than "go out and *see* a movie" during any given week. Yet, the big-screen experience is still the launch-point for many films that become successful in their secondary market exposures. In the fourth wave, undoubtedly, viewers have more choices and venues when contemplating the moving image. The three-year old child who witnesses her first moving image, with full recognition thereof, may do so on MTV (perhaps a music video of Michael Jackson's "Billie Jean"), followed by a McDonald's commercial (where she identifies the icon of Ronald McDonald with her food experiences) that ties-in with a Disney movie which her parents eventually bring her to watch in her first visit to a traditional cinema.

A screening room in a private home where current theatrical releases would be played was formerly the purvey of Hollywood movie moguls, members of the jet-set, or the occupant of the White House. But since the 1970s, recent feature films have been delivered to homes wired for cable and subscribing to HBO, Showtime, and several other movie channels. The box in the corner that formerly delivered mostly G-rated fare for the entire family now brought films and comedy specials geared to more mature and varied tastes. Coupled with the videocassette, a consumer product that earned its market penetration as much with adult films (i.e., pornography) as with programming for other niches (exercise videos, sports programs, music videos), consumers began managing their own presentations in their own private spaces that fit their own schedules. The affordability of home video camcorders unleashed a renewal of amateur or neophyte moviemakers who could capture reality on their own and then instantly replay the images. Since the 1920s, amateur movies (mostly referred to as "home movies") had been economically feasible for some consumers. The emergence of 8mm and Super 8mm film, and then the videocassette and digital tape, provided the impetus for many to "write with light" in the latter decades of the 20th century. Doubtless, many in the fourth wave witnessed their first moving picture experience as home movies, starring themselves. There are ramifications, it would seem, of growing up in an environment of empowerment regarding the ease with which one can create film recordings and collect them as self-representation (of performer and/or photographer); it confers a kind of immortality, or at least legitimizes interest in a subject since it has been documented and preserved. At the very least, most persons have become increasingly more comfortable with the language of the moving image, its use, and applications in everyday life. This is "cineliteracy" and like any tool of empowerment, it both creates and deconstructs. A commercial culture of hyper capitalism champions the continuous creation more than deconstruction, however. To pause, ponder and deconstruct, would mean there is less time for consumption of created goods.

Along with the blockbuster movies that became cultural events during this period (including *The Godfather* films, *Titanic*, and *The Sixth Sense*), there were reactionary forces. The laws of physics play out in the arts as well, although the reaction here is more opposite than equal, at least in terms of financial revenue. The rise of independent cinema in the 1980s and 1990s afforded a platform for low-budget films, formerly marginalized topics, and allowed maverick moviemakers to enter the game. The multitude of multiplex screens, cable channels, and video stores beckoned new producers who, while rarely reaching the blockbuster status, were able to gain notice and perhaps access to a larger professional film arena than ever before. When not able to create spectacles due to budget constraints, they often relied on quixotic narrative techniques, making cult films in the process. The least expensive and often innovative strategy to employ is a creative editing strategy that disrupts the linear narrative flow. *Reservoir Dogs* (Tarantino, 1992*), Run Lola Run* (Tykwer, 1998) and *Go* (Liman, 1999) from the 1990s have given way to further structural ruptures in recent films such as *The Rules of Attraction* (Avary, 2002), *Memento* (Nolan, 2001) and *Irreversible* (Noe, 2002). When oft-repeated, however, these techniques become clichés and/or part of the collective language of producing and understanding moving pictures. Another low-budget technique that distances independent film from blockbusters is the very "look" of the movie, accentuated through production values in the shooting. *The Blair Witch Project* (Sanchez, Myrick, 1999), a pseudo documentary, is purposefully shot in grainy 16mm and on videotape. Filmmakers such as Spike Lee in *Bamboozled* (1999) began using digital video, and that technology is slowly working into the blockbuster mentality; *Star Wars: Attack of the Clones* (Lucas, 2002) was photographed and, in some cases, projected in digital video. *Collateral* (Mann, 2004) alternatingly uses a mixture of 35mm film and digital video.

The moving image is ubiquitous and omnipresent for the fifth generation of audiences. For them, the difference between celluloid and digital video may be a moot point. Purists will continue to argue about the warmth of film stock versus the sterile sheen, graininess, or low contrast of video. In many cases, the kind of narrative can dictate the recording media of choice. "Films" such as *Bloody Sunday* (Greengrass, 2002) and *28 Days Later* (Boyle, 2003), which are documentary-like in topic lend themselves to video use in capture and reproduction. *Diary of the Dead* (Romero, 2007) and *Cloverfield* (Reeves, 2008) openly acknowledge that video camera recordings are the film source. While the quality of image will matter in many cases, the ease with which images can be created and called up will be most significant for the fifth generation. An Internet platform such as YouTube.com, for example, permits anyone to upload and share moving images and sound with anyone who has access to a computer screen.

Two technological delivery systems have revolutionized the way all generations today consume the moving image: the Internet and the DVD (known as digital versatile disc, but more commonly digital video disc).

Brief, flash-animation on website pop-ups that momentarily or permanently draw the eye away from content a user/viewer is seeking are interruptions that Internet surfers frequently confront. There is a constant process of reviewing and rejecting/accepting detours from the original query of engagement. At another level, feature-length movies or programming can be streamed or downloaded from the web for attentive viewing. Live web-cams also offer moving images in a continuous, uninterrupted stream. These represent the breadth of moving images on computer screens—from a few seconds to feature-length to ongoing—with a variety of other styles and dimensions persisting between them. Mainstream studios and distributors are partnering with Internet sites to offer film and television products directly to audiences, frequently with little time between their premieres in cinemas or on television; one such operation is hulu.com, which provides streaming movies (from studios such as Columbia and Universal) and TV shows (from networks such as NBC and FOX). In addition, the opportunity for both legitimate and illegal "file sharing" brings a further array of choices when engaging audiences through the Internet. A thorough exploration of the fifth generation of audiences for the moving image must begin, if not center upon, the home computer screen as a point of initiation and primary engagement.

Since 1997, the DVD player began to reshape the way film was experienced. The movies were a natural data field for the DVD and that technology has changed not only the ways that movies are made but also the ways they are watched. Two decades earlier, a movie on videocassette was about the size of a paperback book. Indeed, when Akio Morita of Sony Corporation instructed his engineers to devise what was to become Betamax tape, he requested it be the relative size and shape of a book, the better to be collected and placed on the shelves of consumers' libraries. The film itself was, in content terms at least, identical to that same film projected in theaters. Nothing more, sometimes less. Three decades ago that version of a 35mm "film" would be encircled on metal reels holding about 20 minutes each, with a feature encased in two steel canisters containing three reels each. The film weighed 40 pounds or more and, in some theaters that were highly unionized, could only be carried to the projection booth and screened at the hands of a union projectionist. For many, part of the mystery and magic of movies incorporates the fading of house lights in the cinema, the strike of the projector's arc lamp, then evidenced by the beam of light that flooded out from the projection room portal and gave screen life to the celluloid images. Today, not only are the secrets of moviemaking revealed ad nausea on selected DVD commentary audio tracks and supplements, but the fortification of the "home theater" has turned middle-class consumers into varying levels of audio-video technophiles who orchestrate the presentation. They are no doubt wowed by spectacle, collectability, and, hopefully, some deeper appreciation of narrative content.

In some ways, the film storyteller has surrendered to the market force of narrative packaging in this war for the audience's attention. Is a viewer more, or less, empowered when she is able to literally stop the film and freeze the frame—for whatever reason? Perhaps to answer the telephone, go to the bathroom, explain a plot point to a less involved viewer, or maybe even ponder the jitterless image of the picture-perfect frame in this pause mode, freezing and breaking into it in new ways. The storyteller no longer controls the ball, as they say in sports, at least not in the way s/he once did in the screening space of the cinema. The work of art/artist is now subject to manipulation as much as the spectator in the audience.

Television, and more increasingly, the DVD now mediate several aspects of moviemaking once guided by the relationship of viewer to film. These include pace of editing, shot composition and selection, sound design, music scoring, choice of performers, durability ("Would you pay to own this and view it again and again?") and other factors. As storytellers strive to continue to make frames worthy of watching, audiences have amped up their own strategies for maintaining or breaking a relationship with them. Returning to Robert Ray and his reflection on the postmodern experience, we note that "the art object no longer controls our reading of it."[10] Postmodernism has recognized that formalism in and of itself cannot signify meaning, and thus certain "encrustations"—to cite Brecht again—inform or dominate a reading of the film text. These include, but are not limited to, gossip, editorial commentary, promotional discourse, social levitation, and synergistic play of all sorts. The fifth generation of spectators will have difficulty, it seems, viewing art for art's sake.

FILM AND TV: MANNERS OF APPROACH

In examining these films that follow, it is helpful to keep in mind the differences inherent in a viewer's approach to the cinema screen and an approach to the television screen. Characters are presented in these movies that have a relationship to the screen, one that is generally understood by audiences of the films, and customized and enacted by the actor-players in the different films. Understanding the manners of approach—i.e., how the directors of these films have their characters "use" the media—provides an underpinning to the themes and purposes of their cinematic works.

Consider our preparation undertaken to engage in the ritual of cinema-going. There is the stirring of consciousness and raising awareness of a given film, perhaps even before that picture is made. The release of a John Grisham novel might invite speculation as to who will be cast in its film version and what material will be deleted or embellished, perhaps years before the movie is watched. Publicity is generated as the film begins shooting and this is carefully managed to exploit interest but not reveal too much information, ideally, so that a state of anticipation is reached in the weeks or days before the movie's release. Most feature film releases now favor web sites so that anyone with a computer can be privy to information via electronic press books and miscellaneous links. Previews begin appearing in theaters, online and on television; perhaps early critical reviews are posted in print and online. Internet coverage, especially through fan sites, stokes or extinguishes interest. And in the days leading up to the release, persons connected with the film will likely be seen on national and local TV talk shows promoting the picture. Television, once thought to be a second-rate competitor to movies, is now the primary means of selling first-run movies to the public, as well as promoting their eventual release on home video. Today the TV monitor, not the cinema screen, is the dominant space for watching most moving pictures.

It is Friday night and a choice has been made from several films in many possible multiplex locations, with starting times that are usually frequent and convenient. If the viewer prefers not to stand in line that evening, a ticket can be ordered online and printed at home or have waiting at the box office upon arrival. En route to the cinema, there can be discussion with a companion concerning the film about to be seen. One feels like they are approaching uncharted territory—mentally and emotionally, if not physically since the viewer has likely visited this particular theater before. The viewers park their car in a nearby parking garage or lot alongside the multi-screen cinema, and perhaps enter it with some measure of awe. A degree of efficiency surrounds the people moving on the ticket line and in front of the concession stand. Refreshments are purchased; the usher is handed a ticket to allow admission.

Viewers make their way into their selected auditorium and sit with other like-positioned, like-prepared patrons.

These are the moments of intense anticipation. They may be accompanied by small talk, observations of those surrounding, meditation, or even distraction by the pre-show "entertainment" that some spectators feel sullies the purity of the ritual. Soon, the lights dim and the screen comes to life. A gathering of commercials, promotional announcements, and previews likely precede the main attraction, which then is revealed. To be sure, a measure of exhaustion can set in when too many previews contain too many of their film's high-octane moments, so the beginning of the feature film may come more as a relief in the ritual these days. The logo-credit of distributors is purposefully understated today, perhaps because two or more are often responsible for a major film and some equitability is sought. Maybe the boisterous confidence of old school introductions is passé, and the modest start will indeed look and sound better on the smaller home screen where most will view the film. Nevertheless, the emphatic roar of the MGM lion and the heralding drum beat of the 20th-Century Fox fanfare or the brass sounds that accompanied a Warner Brothers picture were moments of audio bravado that unquestionably "announce" the feature is about to begin.

Once the film commences, the spectator surrenders control and becomes one within a community. Approximately two hours later, the collective experience at this 7:45 p.m. screening is concluded and being digested by a couple of hundred people. Some remain in their seats through the closing credits, watching for information or perhaps listening to a musical selection reprised from the film. Some patrons head for the exits, just like people who leave church services before the final hymn is completed or students who close their notebooks and gather personal belongings in a classroom as the instructor commences to conclude a lecture. Of course, some closing credits can extend for seven or eight minutes. Compare the current extravagance—in technique and/or time-span of both opening and closing credits—with the no-nonsense approach of older Hollywood movies where opening credits were a few titles cards and the closing credits may only have listed key cast members or a simple "The End." Some filmmakers, Woody Allen in particular, are known for their austere approach in this area even today. Still, the closing credits are part of the movie's denouement, a time for viewers to catch their breath and prepare to return to the lobby, the car, and the home.

Most movies employ a three-act structure in their storytelling and movie-going, as well, resembles that. The second act in a screenplay is traditionally the longest and contains the most complications. In an oversimplification of the screenwriting process, Act One presents a would-be hero in an ordinary world from which he or she must journey in order to affirm heroic status. Act

Two contains several tests, defeats, alliances and difficulties met along the way which inform his or her tenacity to succeed, which is usually accomplished in Act Three and is often referred to as "the journey home."[11]

Now, consider the activity of attending and consuming cinema as something compartmentalized into three acts. Act One is the physical approach to the cinema, accompanied by certain emotional and psychological sensations. Once the viewer has settled in the theater and the film begins, so does Act Two, which is the film itself. For spectators, the participation in sense-making occurs during the film at an immediate level but continues when they leave the theater and begin fully processing the film just seen. Viewers then speak or think about the film, process it so that the film works on and with them, and perhaps they even question some feelings or interpretations. This is the journey home and a cinemagoer's Act Three. Now, it would be disingenuous to say that this proverbial third act ends upon arrival back home or at the next planned activity; it could likely continue into further hours or days, especially after having consumed a confounding film. *Mulholland Drive* (Lynch, 2002), for example, is a film that invites multiple interpretations and challenges the processing capacities of viewers. The ritual process of cinema-going in physical terms has boundaries of time and space. Television is less restrictive, as will be discussed below. The physical process of cinema-viewing is mostly linear. There are clear, cause-and-effect relationships that elicit a pattern of attention/reaction in an uninterrupted flow. Although the narrative of the film being watched may be nonlinear and convoluted, it is still unreeling in the moment and the spectator in the theater is helpless to stop it.[12]

That momentum and pacing over which the spectator has little control is a distinguishing characteristic that separates cinema from television. A few years ago, a button was worn by some cineastes that read, "Film is Art, Television is Furniture." While acknowledging that TV is the preferred method by which a majority of consumers observe moving pictures, we must also consider the differences in ritual engagement. A movie screen can dominate approximately 70% of one's field of vision depending upon where you sit in a theater. A 27-inch television set, on the other hand, might cover 15% of that field. Consider, also, the visual distractions that surround the TV set—other furniture, windows, wall art, lamps, perhaps a wayward cat that jumps atop the monitor. There are audible distractions as well—telephone, street noise, doorbell, home appliances, other conversations. These are often accepted or incorporated into the ritual of watching TV, or the control of them must be managed somehow.

Consider broadcast or cable TV viewing as a ritual, in comparison to that of attending the cinema. Going to the video store to rent a movie shares some of the elements of choice, journey, monetary exchange and even the possibility of shared post-film reaction with others that are associated with the cinema visit. Likewise, the viewer must schedule a screening. Conventional TV viewing, especially since the advent of cable, VCRs and time-shifting variants such as Tivo, has become more accessible, more choice-laden and less eventful as a ritual. Please remember, this is not about program content, but the process and apparatus-as-ritual.

In the 1950s and 1960s, audiences could set their watch or calendar by television. If Uncle Miltie is on, it must be Tuesday night. *Bonanza* begins and it's about an hour before bedtime on Sunday night. Radio and television was programmed into "day-parts" which carved up the broadcast day into segments geared to specific markets (housewives, children, news watchers). Reruns, then syndications, of popular series were implemented, as independent stations and those slots in off-network times sought to be filled with what was attracting viewers, regardless of who was traditionally watching at those times. The 24-hour channels, niche marketing in specialty stations, and the VCR/DVD-R made adherence to anything resembling day-parts less a con-

Television at first united, but ultimately fragmented, the mass audience. By 1954, there were 32 million television homes in the U.S. and TV would soon become film's chief competitor for viewers.

cern. Television was now everywhere and anytime. It enabled and ennobled rootlessness as a characteristic of post modernity, usually for a monthly fee.

Television spectators consult printed program listings or an on-screen guide to consider what show to watch. Or they can merely recline on the couch and graze through the channels until something catches their interest, watching parts of many wholes. An uninterrupted flow occurs, with programs emanating from worldwide origins—a Jerusalem street one second, an icy New Hampshire hamlet the next, downtown Tokyo another. The sense of power and dislocation converges in a whirlwind fashion until a choice is finally made, a commitment to view for a time, perhaps an hour or less. Of course, commercial television will provide planned interruptions.

The mini-narratives known as commercials are placed within the larger program-story and constitute a double distraction. First, they invite the spectator to interact with a new body of characters as they promote their products—the distraught gardener and her knowing neighbor who has just the right plant food, an elderly man who needs to confirm an ailment he thinks he has thanks to the power of suggestion, pesky kids who won't eat their soup, a dog with fleas. These mini-narratives present a quandary, then a commodified solution—product or service-based—that is purchasable. The viewer processes his interest, need and demand for the solution, and mentally files that away or makes note to act in response before being allowed to rejoin the main narrative. Second, they force segmentation of the main narrative that may not have been the preferred manner of presentation. In other words, the scriptwriter in commercial-supported must allow for dramatic breaks or pauses at specific intervals, forcing plot points or character revelations into compressed bits or juxtaposed against advertisements. If a theatrical film that initially played without commercial breaks is sliced and diced without attention to the segmenting demands of broadcast TV, then its cinematic pacing, rhythms of editing, and framing and composition, are ill served. Additional distractions come from corner logos, pop-up promos and text crawls at the edges of the screen, frequently teases for upcoming programs.

Repetition is essential to the economic foundation of television. It not only reinforces the commercial messages but also conditions its audience to the world of certain TV narratives to which they regularly return in order to receive an imprint of its sponsor's message. Theme music and opening credit sequences are the most immediate and identifying invitation that cues the viewer's engagement and ensures comfortability (which, in turn, invites a receptive impulse towards commercial messages). Consider some of these introductory moments: Marshall Matt Dillon doles out western justice in a gunfight on the main street of Dodge City in *Gunsmoke*; images seem to float in outer space—a door opening, the crashing of a window pane, an eyeball,

the notation "E=mc²", a free-floating body and a ticking clock—and Rod
Serling announces that "you've just crossed over into *The Twilight Zone*"; *All
in the Family*'s Archie and Edith Bunker at the piano singing "Those Were
the Days"; Tony Soprano driving on the turnpike and through his New Jersey
neighborhood with shots of toll booths, skylines, refineries, restaurants, and
open lots as A3's "Woke Up This Morning" plays on the soundtrack. Credit
sequences, usually less than a minute, quickly orient/reorient the viewer to
the performers, setting the tone for the show to follow. Films, on the other
hand, unless they are sequels or part of an ongoing franchise, need to take
more time to provide orientation, to light the audience's fuse so to speak, and
to condition it for narrative and thematic reception. Hence, the movies can
offer pre-credit sequences of action related to the story.

Once the TV watchers have completed the piecemeal viewing experience,
two choices are faced. Like their cinema-going counterpart, they may elect
to disengage from the set and contemplate the narrative just witnessed. If the
program was viewed with another person, they could likely discuss aspects
of the show. This, however, can also occur during the unfolding of the TV
narrative, a communication exchange not normally tolerated to much extent
in cinemas although the conditioning of consumers with one medium (talking
allowed with the TV set on) has affected their behavior when experiencing
the other (conversations between patrons in the cinema). Ironically, a perversion of the "silence is golden" mandate in cinema—or even the belief that "art
speaks for itself"—is the running commentary on DVD audio tracks that can
be deployed during home viewings.

It is likely that the spectator of TV programs, having completed his narrative journey, will allow himself to be ushered into another narrative with no
cause for pause or alarm, barely processing what was just watched. There are
several instances where end credits of sitcoms and dramas are rushed, their
soundtrack lowered or images partitioned and squeezed so that other information can be placed in the frame—a voice-over teaser for the 11:00 news or the
newscaster seen via picture-in-picture in the corner of the screen, some clips
announcing the linkage of one character from the program to another upcoming show, a plug for the weekend football game on this network. This flood
of sounds and images is meant to make recollection and reflection recede in
favor of maintaining attachment to the TV medium.

Marie Winn has called television the "plug-in drug." [13] While its addictive and ritualistic manner of use can be seen as variations on pill-popping,
joint-rolling, and syringe-filling, there are other attributes—many also shared
by cinema—that surround TV spectatorship. It costs the viewer something
in terms of money and time. It is readily available and always there when
needed. Despite what has been noted about repetition, the varieties in its

menu of content-offerings can mentally and emotionally transport viewers to other realms of experience and affect their consciousness in different ways. It is, more often than not, consumed by an individual alone or in a very small group. Until the innovations of the VCR and other forms of video-on-demand and personal archiving, the consumer was dependent on concentrated models of production and distribution for his TV fix. Because of its welcome presence in the living rooms and bedrooms of our homes, television was seen as a soothing and friendly force by many, and then as a necessary appliance. As it further melds with the computer screen, it will become more apparent as our window to the world. Winn originally focused on TV programs and the negative effects of television on children's play, imagination and school achievement. While there are several, important considerations on how TV spectatorship has shaped us—and continues to do so—as a species, here we will concentrate on some key narrative film texts as they assess the making and/or consumption of TV. But before proceeding with movies about television, it is helpful to consider movies about movies and the manner in which they condition a reflexive/reflective posture toward the moving image.

NOTES

1. Ray, Robert. (2001). *How a Film Theory Got Lost and Other Mysteries in Cultural Studies*. Bloomington: Indiana University Press. 23.

2. Knight, Arthur. (1979). *The Liveliest Art*. New York: Macmillan. 290.

3. Bogdanovich, Peter. (1985). "The Best American Films of 1939" from *Pieces of Time: Bogdanovich on the Movies, 1961-1985*. New York: Arbor House. 159.

4. Box Office Mojo. www.boxofficemojo.com/movies/?id=gonewiththewind.htm

5. Thompson, Kristen and Bordwell, David. (2003). *Film History: An Introduction*. New York: McGraw-Hill. 328.

6. Ibid. 334.

7. Karney, Robyn, ed. (2000). *Cinema Year by Year, 1894-2000*. New York: Dorling Kindersley. 460.

8. Corey, Melinda and Ochoa, George, eds. (2002). *The American Film Institute Desk Reference*. New York: Dorling Kindersley. 97. Weekly attendance at theaters in 1971 averaged 15.8 million patrons per week. A current, healthy box office tally averages 28-30 million per week (Source: National Association of Theater Owners).

9. Thomson and Bordwell. Ibid. 680

10. Ray. ibid. 58.

11. Volger, Chris. 1998. *The Writer's Journey: Mythic Structure for Writers*. Michael Weise Productions: Studio City.

12. *Mulholland Drive*, for example, is one of the few mainstream DVD releases to be released without chapter stops. These markings allow viewers to skip around and navigate through a film at their own discretion. Director David Lynch refused to

allow this option to be encoded on the disc, so *Mulholland Drive* unfolds as a thriller with the filmmaker's narrative flow thwarted only by the home viewer's ability to pause, fast-forward or rewind.

13. See *The Plug-In Drug: Television, Computers and Family Life* by Marie Winn, originally published in 1977 and revised in 2002.

Chapter Two

Movies About Movies:
The Reflexive/Reflective Stance

In *The Last Picture Show* (1971), director Peter Bogdanovich tells the story of a small Texas town and its people in the early 1950s. It is a wistfully nostalgic look back at a time and culture that by 1970, one could no longer find. The spaces of west Texas had changed, albeit slightly, and no one had yet preserved so eloquently in commercial narrative cinema the experiences of youth and coming of age among this mid-century, rural population. *The Last Picture Show* began a wave of films (*Summer of '42, American Graffiti, Animal House, Diner*) geared towards a young demographic that mixed nostalgia with bittersweet adolescent experiences, acknowledging character interplay in a modern world where mass media—including cinema—is a significant part of the social landscape.[1]

Aside from its telling title that signifies both place and a kind of finality or passage, *The Last Picture Show* immediately and deliberately makes the viewer aware that s/he is watching a movie. Bogdanovich chooses to tell this story with black and white film. In 1971, most television programming was in color—save for older movies and much archival newsreel footage—and network audiences, especially, were immersed in the rich, hyperrealism of color images. The choice of palette is a double clue to the viewer that the content of *The Last Picture Show* is stark and darkly realistic, and the story is ethnographically real. The viewer engages in a cinematically-created telling of the story where the temporal and historical location of these events would be marked by and viewed in a past that was created and historicized through mediated storytelling in black and white. This choice to enjoin the viewer in the artist's self-consciousness of a text as a movie illustrates Jay Ruby's definition of reflexivity. Ruby contends that reflexivity is "the capacity of any system of signification to turn back upon itself, to make itself its own object by referring to itself." It is with this notion and realization that we begin to understand what it means to be a spectator of cinema.

In fiction film, Jay Ruby categorizes reflexive elements found in (1) comedies that are satires and parodies about movies, TV and media-makers; (2) dramatic films that contain subject matter of movies, TV and media-makers; and (3) modernist and postmodernist films concerned with exploring the parameters of form, sometimes exploring conventions such as blurring of fictional and nonfictional events. *Blazing Saddles* (Brooks, 1973), *Matinee* (Dante, 1992), and *Network* (Lumet, 1976) would conform easily to Category 1, while *The Bad and the Beautiful* (Minnelli, 1952), *Cinema Paradiso* (Tornatore, 1989) and *The Majestic* (Darabont, 2001) are Category 2 films that celebrate the production and presentation process. *The Player* (Altman, 1992), *Bamboozled* (Lee, 1999) and *Wag the Dog* (Levinson, 1997) can fit comfortably into either Category. Several films such as *The Purple Rose of Cairo* (Allen, 1985)—and others including pseudo documentaries such as *Zelig* (Allen, 1983), *This Is Spinal Tap!* (Reiner, 1984), *The Battle of Algiers* (Pontecorvo, 1966), *Medium Cool* (Wexler, 1969), and *Bob Roberts* (Robbins, 1992)—address the parameters of form and belong to Category 3; to these we can add several of the other movies explored in this text and not yet mentioned, including *Bulworth, Natural Born Killers, Being There, Pleasantville,* and *The Truman Show.*

This chapter deals with films that in one fashion or another explicitly make the presence of film-going in our personal and cultural pasts a central feature of the story and characters within. In *The Last Picture Show*, as well as each of the following cases, at some points we are watching the characters as audience-members who sit in a theater. The films they observe are usually movies or the kinds of movies that can be recognized as significant in the history of cinema. For at least this reason, the movies treated here are favorites of film buffs, not surprisingly, and there seems to be some delight among people who are self-conscious about the art form itself as a kind of "inside joke" with the producers of the movie regarding their shared love of movies. In addition, there are many references to other films and film-going in general.

These movies reflect that the audience of film has become trained and specialized in the population, so that a film may specifically point to that role and activity of watching and say "Here are people living their lives through film-going, and you know what kind of meaningful activity that is." Thus, in examining *how* film constructs and depicts the audience, and how important film experiences are to characters with which the audience identifies, certain perspectives or stances are revealed that inform the themes of these movies. Films about film, especially those directed by persons nurtured by a culture of cinema like Bogdanovich and others in this chapter, may even be a kind of "expert testimony" about the influence of film on our lives. In subsequent chapters, a similar position can be taken regarding films about the television experience, several of which are directed by persons who worked in that medium. The films explored here, however, are set in periods before TV was a mass medium (*The Purple Rose of Cairo*), when TV was just emerging as a competitor with the movies (*The Last Picture Show, Cinema Paradiso*), and as it steadily began to overtake cinema as a dominant method for consumption of moving images (*The Majestic, Matinee*). In this chapter, most character-spectators are keenly aware of the movies' value to the real lives and they express this through word and action.

Reflexivity is enhanced in several ways that the spectator can link to real life and "reel" life representations. The elegiac mood of *The Last Picture Show* comes from a sense of melancholy about the human condition, which applies in varying degrees to *Cinema Paradiso* and *The Majestic* as well. It also comes from the idea of the passing of a generation, the passing of time, and the loss of innocence. These films are about the places where life and cinema connect, which in the narratives are the Royal, the Paradiso, the Majestic, the Strand and the Jewel, but also our own consumption of *The Last Picture Show*, *Cinema Paradiso*, *The Majestic, Matinee* and *The Purple Rose of Cairo*. The connection is also felt in the actor-icons used in these films. Giuseppe Tornatore enlists Brigette Fossey, famous as the child star of *Forbidden Games* (Clement, 1952) as his mature Elena in the extended director's cut of *Cinema Paradiso*. It is a reflexive choice for a film dedicated to cinema heritage, just as Peter Bogdanovich taps Ben Johnson to portray Sam the Lion. The Royal even has a poster on display for *Wagon Master* (Ford, 1950), in which Johnson has a leading role. Johnson was a member of director John Ford's stock company and a familiar face to moviegoers of the 1940s through 1970s, usually in supporting roles. He brings a resonance with the past and the kind of supporting characters he usually portrayed were dedicated to duty, were loyal and traditionalist, reserved, respectful and mature.

Major studio releases of Hollywood's Golden Era, the period of the 1930s through the postwar era, also exemplify Jay Ruby's assessment of reflexivity as a state where the audience assumes that the producer, the process of film-making, and the product are a coherent whole. In both *The Jolson Story* (Green, 1946) and *Jolson Sings Again* (Levin, 1949), not only is the audience made aware of these relationships, but also made to realize the necessity of that knowledge. *The Jolson Story* and its sequel presents the life story of Al Jolson, noted musical entertainer and movie star whose later career was marked by a fear of modern audiences not accepting his performance style, which was rooted in minstrelsy, vaudeville and Tin Pan Alley song making.

The release of *The Jolson Story* was instrumental in reacquainting the postwar public with the legend of Jolson and afforded his career a rebirth. The final twenty minutes of *Jolson Sings Again* is a dramatization of the making of *The Jolson Story* as the actor portraying Jolson, Larry Parks, is coaching the actor Larry Parks in his screen portrayal of Jolson. Primitive split-screen techniques allow Parks to portray both Jolson and himself. *Jolson Sings Again* captures the mechanics of moviemaking and climaxes at a film premiere where the audience in the theater, the moviemakers, and viewers of scenes from *The Jolson Story* within the outer film *Jolson Sings Again*, acknowledge both the championed entertainer and the means by which he is revealed.

So, an awareness of the behind-the-scenes process of narrative film construction is a significant part of the reflexive process. This mindfulness accelerated with the dissemination of French New Wave production techniques in the late 1950s—such as hand-held camera work, a dominance of location shooting, untraditional protagonists and storytelling structure, and an improvisational tone—which gave cinema a presence, accessibility and invitation to both reveal and become further understood by its audiences. By the 1970s, cinema entered academia full force with the introduction of film and media studies programs at several universities; the movies and television were now career-oriented goals within a curriculum that invited students to create programming and/or critically deconstruct it. A heightened awareness of the process of making moving images also became part of the popular film experience thanks to the explosion in home video formats and *Entertainment Tonight*-style "infotainment" television shows in the 1970s and 1980s. Today, digital video is a means of affordable production of the moving image, and also a primary means of consumption.

Perhaps one cannot help but invoke reflexive tendencies today because its reminders and applications constantly surround audiences. Whereas studios formerly partitioned their moviemaking mechanics from the spectator, and filmmakers tended to be more like magicians who rarely discussed the tricks of their trade, the manner in which movies are made and sold today invites an active participation by explaining how many of the production decisions fit together. The self-consciousness of filmmakers who create "art" within an industrial setting inspires viewers to themselves ascertain the influences on those directors and writers, thereby informing the film—and the film spectatorship experience—with greater resonance through reflexivity. Peter Bogdanovich in 1971 easily incorporated this reflexive consciousness into *The Last Picture Show,* while the characters within the film (set in 1951) have barely begun to acknowledge it.

Woody Allen's *The Purple Rose of Cairo* retreats further into the past, yet it provides a fanciful extension of the reflexive/reflective process. Here, a character named Cecilia literally penetrates the world of the film she observes at the theater, and conversely, a character from the fictional world of the film is allowed to enter the real world of Depression-era New Jersey. The confinement experienced by Cecilia in *The Purple Rose of Cairo* suggests the limits of reflexivity as a sole and singular stance.

A film possesses what may be termed a "signifying image" that can be isolated and explained as a key to part of the larger theme represented by the filmmaker and understood by the audience. The signifying images in these selected films incorporate the tactile representations of cinema—theater facade, projection equipment, movie screen, and celluloid itself—into the frame that allows the visual to evoke the thematic. In *The Last Picture Show*, the signifying image is Sam the Lion saying goodbye to Sonny and Duane while they sit in the front seat of a pickup truck on Main Street in Anarene, the Royal Theater in the background. The camera holds on Sam a few seconds longer than is expected, as he looks at them. The boys are off to Mexico for some carousing and, when they return, they discover that Sam has unexpectedly died of a heart attack. As owner of the Royal and moral conscience of the town, he tried to live and to display the dreams that could sustain adolescents through difficult times. The movie house will soon close, and one of the boys will pick up the mantle of Sam, passing the torch if not the flame. This shot foreshadows the disappearance of Sam and his influence, as well as the transference of that potential to Sonny.

In *Cinema Paradiso* the signifying image is illustrated in a medium shot of Alfredo the projectionist, Toto his boy-helper, and a large arc-lamp projector that, itself, is an icon-as-character. In a scene from the film, this image intercuts with shots of the audience in the cinema and the projection of movies onto the screen. *Cinema Paradiso* illuminates the relationship of spectator to screen image through the mediator figures of projectionist Alfredo and later, film director Toto/Salvatore. The audience at the cinema actively participates in the engagement process, sometimes cheering or booing at scenes, sometimes imitating the actions they see on screen. When they are denied their images through projector malfunction, they scream at Alfredo. He is the keeper of the flame, the carbon-burning rods that brightly reflect against concave mirrors which allow for illumination of the spectators' fears and desires either in the Paradiso or when projected outside in the town square. Salvatore is brought up to respect the power of the flame, first as cinema and then as romance. Alfredo will mentor him through both processes.

The Majestic presents Luke and Adele in a romantic clinch behind the theater screen, while the film projected as backdrop to their kiss is *The Day the Earth Stood Still* (Wise, 1951). Their embrace signifies an acceptance of amnesiac Peter Appleton as the long-lost Luke, but the movie that underscores this Prodigal's return is a warning of Cold War threats couched in the text and iconography of the science fiction film. When Peter's memory returns, he faces a subpoena for alleged Communist leanings expressed in the films he wrote while in Los Angeles. Appropriated as a signifying image of *The Majestic*, this moment embodies its most significant themes.

In *Matinee*, two images follow one after the other. Film director Woolsey stops to explain the origin of horror movies to young fan Gene, using the allusion to primitive man and his construction of cave-drawings; then the pair walk into a movie theater as Woolsey conveys all the enchantment and wonder of buying a ticket and walking into the modern equivalent of the prehistoric cave. The audience has come to expect something spectacular, he knows, and Woolsey is determined to deliver. In *Matinee*, Woolsey will succeed beyond his wildest dreams.

And in *The Purple Rose of Cairo*, Cecilia is seated in the Jewel Theater, transfixed by the image of Fred Astaire and Ginger Rogers dancing in a 1930s escapist musical film. Although she has experienced a temporal transformation when she entered the world of the interior film, she finds herself eventually relegated back to the reality of her drab existence. Only the vocalizing of these movie stars offers her the faint hope of a romance that is like ." . . heaven, where my heart beats so that I can hardly speak."

It is the sensation, emotion, and note of recognition that initially ratify the reflexive. Familiarity breeds intent. The notion of a signifying image—-whether a shot or a brief scene from a movie—-informs the appreciation of a cinematic work that is comprised of hundreds of shots.

As we interact with these film narratives, it behooves us to consider the etymology of the word "entertainment." It comes from the Latin *inter* (among) and *tenere* (to hold). Art provides what the Greeks called *ekstasis*, which means, "letting us stand outside ourselves." However in most modern applications, entertainment—*inter tenere*—usually pulls us *into* ourselves, and can deny us perspective by providing a prescribed one.[2] Both applications certainly pertain when considering the reflexive/reflective stance of the spectator, especially when s/he is both producer and consumer of movies as is Salvatore in *Cinema Paradiso* and Peter Appleton in *The Majestic*, Peter Appleton. Other characters explored via films in this chapter—Gene in *Matinee*, Cecilia in T*he Purple Rose of Cairo*, the patrons in *The Last Picture Show*—are singularly spectators. The prescribed perspective of entertainment in the films within these films is escapist. However, this should not deny the tension that can emerge when we apply reflexive tendencies that relate to them as "art."

It will be observed how reflexivity in these films becomes a tool for organizing their presentation and assists in the process of interpretation. (1) The reflexive stance grounds the spectator. (2) It prepares him or her to develop strategies of interaction with film. Tracing through these movies we acknowledge Salvatore and Peter, for instance, as consumer/creators who are made whole again through reintegration with their respective pasts and with film as a mediator. (3) Reflexivity, then, can assist some characters/ spectators in a reintegration and renewed purpose. Gene, in another example, is a young viewer enamored with the apparatus of production, accepting fantasy projections as escape. (4) Reflexivity is celebrated and harnessed as a rite of passage. Cecilia is a spectator overwhelmed by the apparatus of production, especially celebrity markings, who transcends reality only to realize it cannot be remade by cinema fantasies. (5) Reflexivity, then, can encourage a restorative strategy to affirm the status quo but also instigate other postures—critical and ironic—that allow for films and perspectives that can be reconstructive or rejective of the status quo.

CINEMA PARADISO (1988)

Cinema Paradiso, like *The Last Picture Show*, uses the tension of nostalgia and decay to engage the audience. More so than *The Last Picture Show*, *Cinema Paradiso* employs the space of the cinema and the process of presenting, consuming and, ultimately, making movies, for its dramatic backdrop. Its director, Giuseppe Tornatore, delivers nostalgia that is equal parts regret and resignation, while Bogdanovich works to affirm the need to persevere despite the loss. *The Last Picture Show* posits the unending conflict between love of life and despair in living as a crucial component of its drama. The unavoidable future is faced squarely in both films, with *Cinema Paradiso* embracing cinema and *The Last Picture Show* releasing us from its spell.

With more persistence than *The Last Picture Show*, *Cinema Paradiso* celebrates and eulogizes the movie theater as a character and a space for establishing community. Audiences at the Paradiso in the 1940s and 1950s would likely not consider their engagement in cinema metaphorical; viewers of *Cinema Paradiso*, however, can discern those implications from the films unveiled therein, such as the neorealist dramas and genre pictures. As in *The Last Picture Show*, a similar mood of lamentation occurs when the Paradiso is destroyed by fire and later, when the Nuevo Paradiso is demolished in the name of urban renewal. Both houses eventually close due to the encroachment of television and alternative entertainment forms, while audiences move on to other media experiences. Characters remain touched by the images inside the cinema, which are conduits for the spectator's appreciation of reflexivity and the reflexive/reflective stance.

Alfredo (Philippe Noiret), the projectionist, removes scenes from the movies playing at the Paradiso that the local priest found objectionable. Young Toto (Salvatore Cascio) inspects the risqué images in Cinema Paradiso.

Toto Di Vita (Salvatore Cascio) is an eight year-old child in the small Italian village of Giancaldo, fatherless in the period just after World War II. He works under the guidance of Alfredo (Philippe Noiret), the projectionist at the Paradiso where Toto assists in menial duties but mostly sits entranced by the images on the screen. Toto grows up to become a noted film director who returns to his village in the present day to attend the funeral of Alfredo, feel some emotional reconnection with his mother and sister, and witness the demolition of the Nuevo Paradiso. The original theater was destroyed in a fire that blinded Alfredo but deepened the comradeship between the old man and boy. Toto embraces his birth-name, Salvatore, and eventually matures into a young man who experiences love, loss and departure from Giancaldo to seek his own place in the world.

Film acts as a repository of memory, especially in *Cinema Paradiso*, where recollected images and impulses are coded and telegraphed through time. In this case, the conduit is a spectator-turned-filmmaker, the adult Salvatore (played by Marco Leonardi as an adolescent, and by Jacques Perrin as an adult). It is fitting that his position is one of repose at the beginning of *Cinema Paradiso* while he considers, in a near dream-state that is conveyed through flashbacks, his past and the relationship with Alfredo and the movies. Salvatore's relationship to the movies, spanning some forty years, evolves from watcher to presenter to creator. He witnesses changing technologies and shifting audience demands for the movies, but maintains an emotional connection with the father figure of his past.

When the Paradiso is rebuilt after the deadly fire, the theater has changed management. Many other changes have taken place as well. Alfredo has been blinded by the accident, and Toto assumes the job of projectionist. The movies and their audiences are transforming, too. The second act of *Cinema Paradiso* begins with a shot of the new theater's neon sign at its reopening. There will be many changes, however, in the movies, the staffing, and the clientele as Italy and the world enter the 1950s. But for the moment, a ribbon is ceremoniously cut. Father Adelfio (Leopoldo Trieste) leads a procession into the lobby and blesses the surroundings with holy water. Inside, the camera moves toward the screen space that is about to come alive again and follows the crowd to their seats. The new owner, Ciccio, has modernized the theater and the comportment of the crowd is more elegant and reverential in contrast to the boisterous audiences before the fire. Champagne is served as Ciccio implores that the cinema is for everyone! Even the projection booth has been modernized and looks safer. The priest gives his blessing and the films begin. A musical short features exotic Caribbean dancing that is somewhat suggestive, but Father Adelfio merely keeps time with his holy water wand. The absence of the bell that he regularly rang to mark a censorious scene is a harbinger of the changing times. On screen a man slowly pulls away part of a woman's blouse to reveal her bare back and sensuously kisses her skin. The audience gasps. Father Adelfio lurches forward in his seat, sensing a change in the atmosphere. Finally, a passionate kiss that is larger than life occurs, to much applause from the crowd. The priest considers this pornographic but seems helpless in the face of the masses that voice pleasant and amazed reactions to natural, but heretofore, forbidden images. *Cinema Paradiso*, then, celebrates the liberating spirit of the movies that unites an audience in an apparent transgression. It also notes the crumbling authority of the traditional gatekeeper, Father Adelfio.

A family melodrama playing at the theater is particularly evocative for the audience, entailing a couple's separation and ultimate reunion; it forces tearful reactions, such as a man talking back to the screen and new affirmations of fidelity from more than one affected viewer. Roger Vadim's *And God Created Woman* (1956) featuring Brigitte Bardot is shown, and in the front row a few young boys masturbate to the sight of discreet nudity. Back in the powder room, a prostitute is plying her trade. Gangster films unreel for the audience, replete with car chases and Tommy-guns blazing. The soundtrack of gunfire even muffles the firing of a real pistol in the theater, an apparent vendetta murder. Life and death exist side by side on the screen and in the crowd at

Nuevo Cinema Paradiso. Real life mirrors the scenes on the screen and considers how cinema is tutor for more profound or harmful transgressions.

The blind Alfredo still goes to the movies, only now his wife quietly whispers descriptions of the action on the screen. On one occasion, Salvatore sits with Alfredo in the back of the theater alongside some bulky projection equipment unlike anything they have ever used. The seats are filled as before, but the "movie" has become projection television, an experiment several exhibitors tried in the 1950s. On screen, a flatly lit female announcer introduces a game show entitled *Double Your Money* hosted by Mike Bongiorno. Even though he cannot see, Alfredo is unimpressed and confounded at how anyone could see this 'television' without any film. Salvatore explains how you can even watch this at home if you buy a television set, but Alfredo still considers it suspect and indeed the content of this game show is banal. A similar TV programming convention is employed in *The Last Picture Show*, with some of the first grainy, black-and-white images beamed into the homes of west Texas in the form of game shows like *Strike It Rich*. They feature seemingly ordinary people—not unlike the average spectators watching at the Paradiso or in their living rooms—thrust into competitive situations for meager prizes and/or fame. In this variation on reflexivity, it indicates that audiences like to watch versions of themselves on the screen. Perhaps the logical extension of this is the home camcorder and the popularity of reality TV in the decades to

Toto, grown up and now called Salvatore (Marco Leonardi), apprenticed as a projectionist but now discovers love in the shadow of the movies with Elena (Agnese Nano).

follow. Reflexivity, as actively demonstrated, is tied closely to the new technologies of the moving image, right up through today's web cams and cell phone cameras and the ease with which anyone can capture and appropriate moving pictures. Spectators, themselves producers of moving pictures today, create images inspired or influenced by those they have seen.

Near the end of *Cinema Paradiso* Salvatore is a successful film director but an incomplete person, due to an inability to "close" the scenes of his life from the distant past in a way that a filmmaker would conveniently conclude, or fade-out, a movie narrative. His romance with Elena (Agnese Nano/Brigette Fossey), however, is fulfilled when he returns to Giancaldo (in the director's cut of the film). Salvatore's aloofness with his doting mother is overcome as well. Alfredo's funeral gives him an opportunity to seal friendships with those in Giancaldo who still remember him as young Toto. And witnessing the demolition of the Nuevo Cinema Paradiso—because the old movie business is just a memory, according to the theater's last owner—will free the director from his past and enable him to finally "let go" as Alfredo counseled so long ago.

Salvatore becomes a practitioner of cinema without initially understanding its connection to real life. That realization only becomes clear as his life experiences and cinema experiences intertwine, its zenith moment occurring in the projection room of a studio in Rome at the conclusion of the *Cinema Paradiso* where he watches Alfredo's "outtakes"—a collection of romantic images, excised from films shown at the Paradiso at the behest of local church censors. Like most spectators, Salvatore is a "work in progress" who has hopefully approached deeper understanding of himself and his life's journey as a result of his return to home and family. His physical positioning as watcher and creator of cinema is rooted in a reflexive, romantic awareness that ultimately relates life to the movies in both casual and profound ways. The cornucopia of embraces and kisses in the outtakes, concluding with a slow fade out, reflects cinema's ability to enjoin emotion across time and space and brings closure for Salvatore just before the final credits of *Cinema Paradiso*.

In *Cinema Paradiso*, Salvatore has matured from an observer to creator of the moving image, and his transformation has been catalogued through acts of spectatorship. The influence of movies on the people of Giancaldo and, by extension, the mandate that Salvatore has assumed to use the cinema as a vocalizing agent, is an assertion of this dominance and potency.

Salvatore's reflexive awareness grounds him as both a viewer and, later, a filmmaker. Cinema-making, cinema-going and cinematic notions and references guide him toward the renewed purpose of acknowledging Alfredo's importance in his own life: the value of home and family, and the heroic sacrifices that must be made to sanctify those relationships. The movies clearly instruct Toto/Salvatore as he struggles with romantic attraction in his adolescent years, and the cliché of the kiss before a fade-out works to seal the adult Salvatore's relationships with Elena, Alfredo, his past and the meaningful movies of his youth. It also serves the viewer's demand for closure to both *Cinema Paradiso* and Salvatore's journey thus far. While the restorative nature of Salvatore's quest is momentarily secure, he is a working artist who may or may not move forward and incorporate other stances—critical or ironic—mitigating outcomes that can be reconstructive or rejective as he matures with further life experiences. For now, however, it is the movies that bring him back, restored, where he both belongs and is comforted.

THE MAJESTIC (2001)

The Majestic uses reflexivity as it explores the nature of movie-going and movie-making, but complicates matters with the plot contrivance of amnesia. The lead character loses his memory and is unable to appreciate his vital nature as a writer of movies, although he assumes the role of spectator and healer in a community of moviegoers. Whereas *Cinema Paradiso* concludes with romantic images produced mostly by the Hollywood studio factory, *The Majestic* offers an opening title sequence of vintage color postcards of documentary snapshots from that movie capital of the world. They tumble into a pile on a table as a screenwriter's voice on the soundtrack describes how Los Angeles is not like the postcards present it, and that glamour is *not* everywhere you look. The voice—that of Peter Appleton (Jim Carrey)—asserts authority in knowing Hollywood because that is where he lives. This sense of knowing one's place and one's self will soon vanish, however. The narrative of *The Majestic* uses reflexivity to reposition and rehabilitate this screenwriter and the townspeople of Lawson, California, with the renovation and reopening of the city's only cinema as a symbol of restoration.

The awareness known as reflexivity, according to Jay Ruby, can be "individual or collective, private or public, and may appear in any form of human communication." To be *reflective* refers to a manner of thinking about ourselves and showing ourselves to others, he contends. It seems that the movies offer occasion for both practices. We observe the producer (director, writer, projectionist), the process (film production, exhibition, consumption), and the product (movie). As the target of storytellers, audiences are asked to relate to characters and their predicaments, to reflect on choices made and outcomes realized. And other films inform the creative impulses of the producer as well, with a mirroring tendency that can also be understood as reflective.

Viewers of *The Majestic* are provided a window to the process of creation and reception of motion pictures in America of the post-World War II era. While most audiences of the time were unconcerned about behind-the-scenes machinations that politicized Hollywood in the McCarthy Era, that specter is a significant subtext in *The Majestic*. To reflect upon meaning that exists both within and beyond the frame deepens the reflexive posture, and in this case there are personal and political ramifications for the spectator-screenwriter in this film.

In *The Majestic*, screenwriter Peter Appleton is on the way to a success-ful career in 1950s Hollywood. His new film, *Sand Pirates of the Sahara*, is a B-picture and the studio bosses have marked him as a player, shallow but ambitious. Peter is nonpolitical, so he is surprised when called to testify in front of the House Un-American Activities Committee to answer charges of harboring Communist sympathies. Reeling from the possibility of a short-changed career, Peter gets drunk, drives up the coast past the outlying Los Angeles area and crashes his Mercedes convertible into a river. He awakens on the beach with no memory of his past, of who he is, or how he came to this predicament.

Dazed and confused, Peter is brought to the town of Lawson by Stan (James Whitmore) who admits the young man seems an odd bit familiar to him. Lawson embodies a Norman Rockwell-like milieu, with picture-perfect Main Street and window displays, but seems inordinately preoccupied with wartime losses of its young men, even though World War II had been over for more than six years. Stan informs Peter that 62 men from Lawson were killed or missing from the war, and that President Franklin Roosevelt com-missioned a war memorial for the town that the distraught citizens have seen fit to store in the town hall basement. Like *Cinema Paradiso* with its sense of loss and dread resulting from fathers, sons and brothers at war, *The Majestic* also acknowledges the real world outside the movie house. The feature films that play at the town theaters in Giancaldo and Lawson can be escapist or re-alist, but they inform the lives of their spectators and create both community and individuation. In a deeper way, perhaps, *The Majestic* offers a healing narrative that is nationalistic as well as personal.

The amnesiac Peter is mistaken for Luke, the son of Harry Trimble (Martin Landau), who owns the Majestic movie house. Luke had been declared miss-ing in action during the war, and Peter, with no recollection of who he is or how he got to Lawson, accepts the identity projected upon him by the town. He even resumes a romance with Luke's girlfriend Adele (Lauren Holden). Peter-as-Luke in informed by Harry that he has been absent from Lawson for nine and a half years. He is shown old photos to reconstitute memories of his late mother, his high school days, and a life once lived. Harry closed the

Majestic because the townspeople just didn't seem to feel like going to the movies anymore. This is, historically, counter to the immediate post war boom in theater attendance but the severe personal loss of its sons has injected Lawson with a resigned, even morose atmosphere that seems to conflict with the Rockwellian veneer. Dramatically it is believable that the movie house would close, especially if its owner were as devastated as Harry at the loss of his own son, Luke. That afternoon, an exhausted Peter sleeps. Harry unlocks the ticket booth where a dusty portrait of Luke in uniform has sat throughout the years, along with a gold star banner designating the home of a serviceman on duty. The photo indeed bears a resemblance to Peter.

For Peter—a writer of films who has amnesia about his role in life—the space of the cinema will restore his identity and purpose. It will be accomplished through a reintegration with the magic and potency of movies as filtered through the spectators of Lawson who recognize Peter as literal or symbolic representations of lost innocence, an innocence sacrificed to the war and epitomized by the closing of the Majestic. Harry musters the energy to reopen the theater. Lawson becomes a vibrant community once more. And

The amnesiac Hollywood writer Peter Appleton as Luke Trimble (Jim Carrey) with girlfriend Adele (Lauren Holden), help restore a movie theater and the town of Lawson's self-image in The Majestic.

Peter orchestrates the return of the bronze memorial statue to the center of town; what was previously a painful reminder of loss now stands as a signifier of courageous sacrifice. Despite the falsity of Peter's physical nature, his evocation of Luke acts to rehabilitate the town, and this is symbolized by the reclaiming of the statue as much as the restoration of the Majestic.

This is the 'A' storyline of *The Majestic*. The subplot or 'B' storyline is developing in Washington, D.C., and Hollywood. A and B plot lines usually intersect in the concluding act of a film story, providing closure at two levels. In *The Majestic*, a representative from HUAC has been reviewing Peter Appleton's most recent screenplay *Ashes to Ashes* and informs FBI agents that it is Communist propaganda about the West Virginia coal miners' strike of 1920 and the plight of the downtrodden worker. With Peter missing for five days, Congressman Clyde (Bob Balaban) suspects guilt and begins to imagine super-Commie potential in the wily writer, someone with lots of secrets to spill. He even believes that if Peter is located, his trail will lead to a nest of Communists that "will make the Rosenbergs look like Ma and Pa Kettle." The scene is a stereotypical comic representation of the Red-baiters, humorous now only after the decades have passed. The congressman even references a cornpone movie franchise from the 1940s and 1950s—the Ma and Pa Kettle series—where feisty, rural characters are placed in "fish out of water" situations and always come out on top.

This scene—with real-life figures intersecting with movie characters—reminds viewers that movies are not created within a vacuum just as they are not consumed under identical or even ideal circumstances. Spectatorship is conditioned by several factors beyond the reach of filmmaker and viewer, with market forces and political underpinnings also significant influences. A period picture such as *The Majestic* must remind its audience of the context of the times to ensure the dramatic payoff has historic validity. The action of these films within a confined setting such as a theater or small town has a relationship to the outside world to which some characters have a strong connection. Just as viewers retreat to cinemas and engage in escape through narrative before re-emerging and re-entering their real lives, they acknowledge similar tendencies in the characters of *Cinema Paradiso, The Majestic, The Last Picture Show* and *Matinee*.

Although FBI agents are closing in on Peter, the Majestic reopens that night with the musical *An American in Paris* (Minnelli, 1951), a celebration of postwar optimism and the creative spirit. A line of customers stretches down Main Street. At the door, Harry welcomes the people by name. The general atmosphere of well-being continues until some days later when *The Day the Earth Stood Still* is playing. This science fiction classic deals with an interplanetary visitor who appears human-like, befriends inhabitants of

Washington, D.C., speaks out for peaceful coexistence, and yet is misunderstood by some Cold War leaders. Peter is quietly sweeping behind the screen while the movie is being projected. Adele approaches and as the lovers embrace, they are framed against the reverse image of Gort, the robot from the film, who sends deadly laser beams at the tanks and soldiers that wish to destroy him. The couple is oblivious to the way the projected film comments on the present, but audiences of *The Majestic* who are conditioned to the reflexive impulses of movies about movies are not. The contrast of Adele and Peter's elation with the filmic representation of a reaction to Cold War paranoia may signify the lovers' momentary insulation from world events but also hints at what will be a reverse-play in the third act. There, the overconfidence of the HUAC Committee—with similar resolve as seen in the tanks and soldiers—will be met by the tenacity of Adele and Peter in the face of its accusations.

The next feature to play the Majestic is *Sand Pirates of the Sahara*, the film that Peter scripted before his bout with amnesia. Watching it, his memory starts to return. He even begins to repeat lines of dialogue, speaking them in anticipation only seconds before they come from the film itself. He recognizes his own authorship. The realization of his past identity amidst his present predicament fully dawns on Peter as he stumbles into the empty

Peter/Luke sells the first ticket on the night the Majestic reopens.

lobby, approaches the one-sheet poster and goes to the credit at the bottom: "written by Peter Appleton." Upstairs in the projection booth, Harry begins to feel the signs of an impending heart attack. When he misses the reel change, Peter/Luke is able to assist, but the old man has collapsed. He is moved to his home where the young man is summoned to his bedside. They profess their love for one another, and Peter even calls him "Dad." The scene conveys a finality and commission reminiscent of the train station farewell between Salvatore and Alfredo in *Cinema Paradiso*, with the older man having provided guidance and purpose for the younger one's course of future action. Salvatore cannot return to his boyhood village, and Peter must now cast off the mantle of Luke. In these film narratives that invite a reflexive participation, the characters' connection and awareness of the cinematic world of recreated reality is displaced by the demands of lived reality. Some comfort has been experienced, but it is ultimately overwhelmed by the characters' need to move forward with their lives.

Peter confesses to Adele that he is not Luke, a testimony she accepts. Lawson lost its hopes and dreams in the persons of its war dead, and likewise those cinematic representations of hopes and dreams represented by the Majestic that had closed. Peter Appleton appeared and re-represented those hopes and dreams in the flesh and in the space of the cinema. His purpose served a therapeutic function for the town. When federal marshals arrive in Lawson and serve a subpoena to Appleton to appear before the Committee on Un-American Activities in special session in Los Angeles and testify on matters of Communist conspiracy and subversion, Peter's press agent tries comforting him with the news that he is really just a small fish and the committee only wants a few names as a face-saving gesture for both sides. Calling upon the memory of Luke and his simple dedication to notions of duty and honor, Peter resists his agent's advice and stands up to the committee.

With his studio contract renewed and his film career back on track, one would suspect Peter Appleton is feeling better about himself. At a conference with his bosses similar to the one that began *The Majestic*, he listens again to the suggestions on how to "fix" his next screenplay; in actuality, they are suggestions for dumbing it down. Screenwriters and story developers frequently play the "what if" game, prefacing a suggestion with that phrase no matter how cockeyed or compelling it might be. Indeed, this somewhat condescending attitude presumes a strategy of underestimating the intelligence of most audiences. Peter senses it as the language of insulation that keeps minimally creative people afloat in the film production business. After listening to a mind numbing "what if" from his faceless producer, Peter counters that it is the dumbest thing he'd ever heard, finally suggesting his own "what if." And then, without warning, Peter exits the frame, leaving the view through the windows outside the studio in a blur for a full six seconds. It is a hold-shot that infers his world needs to come back into focus, this frame of a window-framed image. But that may be selling this moment short, for Peter is a man now capable of truly restoring a sense of community and familial reintegration to Lawson.

In the finale, Peter returns to the Majestic and is selling tickets in the booth to the current feature *Invasion of the Body Snatchers*. That film was released in 1956, so it can be assumed that the Majestic in Lawson weathered the introduction of television and continued to be a reservoir of dreams, hopes, and fears for the town. Indeed, a pan across framed photographs reveals Peter and Adele getting married, a picnic scene of them with a young child, another on a riverside vacation, and then a joyous portrait of Harry and Peter/Luke taken in front of the Majestic marquee on the night of the grand reopening. The camera zooms in to the pair just as it does at the conclusion of *Cinema Paradiso* on a photo of young Toto and Alfredo on the wall in Mama Di Vita's home in another example of one of the ways narratives about cinema can be self-reflexive and cross-referencing.

Reflexivity in *The Majestic* is a tool for organizing its presentation, and it assists in the process of spectatorship and interpretation. Peter Appleton—like many viewers of *The Majestic* —is well-grounded in the genuine film examples mined for connective effect. An exception is *Sand Pirates of the Sahara*, a mythical title, but representative of the kind of Hollywood factory product that journeyman screenwriter Appleton would deliver. Its success situates Peter on the road to greater things, a road that leads to his accident and memory loss that precede his own rebirth and restoration. By rejoining both the real world (albeit as Luke, at first) and the world of cinema (through work at the Majestic), Peter experiences reintegration and a renewed purpose of life in Lawson. Although a man past the age of 30, these are rites of passage that affect him in ways that are personal, social, and political. Peter's ultimate embrace of what appears to be the status quo of American small-town life in the mid-1950s is a restorative move that—despite the rebel stance he must make against HUAC—reveals *The Majestic* as mostly conservative in its appropriation of traditional values.

At the fade of *The Majestic*, as with *Cinema Paradiso*, we are appreciative of the power of movies, the cinema experience, and of how films can make one feel. While the trajectory of time is some 40 years in *Cinema Paradiso*, it is less than a year in the bulk of *The Majestic* and thus that film lacks the breadth of cinema-going experiences for which it compensates with the cultural significance of events in 1951. Both films utilize the reflexive space of the Paradiso and the Majestic to comment on narrative action that unfolds. As noted, the French New Wave directors in the late 1950s, many of whom were former film critics steeped in film culture, accelerated the use of reflexivity as a film technique. When Jean Luc-Godard, Francois Truffaut and others began to make movies, they offered homage to past film works and directors via manipulations of mise-en-scène and actor iconography, to the outright sampling of excerpts from films via clips or poster art in their scenes. *The Majestic* evokes the work of director Frank Capra and his films that affirm American values such as *Mr. Smith Goes to Washington* (1939), *Meet John Doe* (1941), and *It's a Wonderful Life* (1947). Actor Jim Carrey provides a physical and stylistic reflection of James Stewart and Gary Cooper from those films. He projects an innocence and incorruptibility, champions traditional values with willfulness despite an apparent naiveté about the way things work and, most importantly for a commercial movie, achieves some kind of victory over the oppressive structures as he asserts his individuality and gets the girl in the end.

Films playing at the Paradiso reflect narrative sentiments in the real world in *Cinema Paradiso*, and this holds for the Majestic's programs as well. Some implications have already been acknowledged, but there are a few others. A scene that the theater's doorman, Emmett (Gerry Black), is watching from *The Big Parade* (Vidor, 1925) is of a woman saying goodbye to her lover going off to fight in World War I. She runs after the truck taking him away, and he throws her his watch along with other personal mementos. The pocket watch is a significant prop for Emmett and bears consideration in any film about time and memory. And early in the film, a newsreel Peter watches at Grauman's Theatre gives the context for his eventual subpoena, although he is inattentive to what is on the screen. Other films at the Majestic include *A Streetcar Named Desire* (Kazan, 1951) where the character of Blanche du-Bois prefers a fantasy world, free from the threats of real life and filled with invigorating innocence; this is Peter-as-Luke, although a temporary state. *Invasion of the Body Snatchers* (Siegel, 1956) in which aliens take over the bodies of people in a small California town, is featured with similarities to what Peter has done with Luke's identity. And *The Day the Earth Stood Still* posits aliens trying to limit the hostilities and abuses of a modern world, as Peter attempts to do before the Committee.

The reflexive nature of such moments in *The Majestic* is important be-cause of audience awareness of details that surface later in history and the various correlations to other film texts. This can be deployed for comic or dramatic effect. Drowning his sorrows at the bar just before his fateful detour to Lawson, Peter asks the bartender if he has an opinion of J. Edgar Hoover. The bartender responds while he uses a towel to dry drinking glasses that he wouldn't know Hoover "if he walked in here wearing a dress." The FBI Director's penchant for cross-dressing and his closeted homosexuality were not revealed to most until after his death in 1972, but contemporary audiences may chuckle in recognition of a man considered the keeper of government secrets and lies. And when Peter concludes his testimony in Los Angeles, he delivers a variation on lawyer Joseph Welch's "Have you no sense of decency?" response given to Sen. Joseph McCarthy at the Army-McCarthy hearings in 1954. Welch's honest, emotional indignation contrasted with his normally calm demeanor, much like Jim Carrey's performance as Peter before HUAC. Welch walked away, after defending the reputation of a young lawyer on his staff. This image is part of the early history of television in America. Peter, likewise, does not provide the committee with any new information and exits with dignity.

The emerging presence of television is felt in *The Majestic*, as it is in *Cinema Paradiso*. In fact, by the time of the latter film's release, the Italian film industry had lost much of its domestic and international market. Television took over the function as archivist of the country's historical memory. Tiziana Ferrero-Regis explores this phenomenon and signifies the act of remembering and its filmic representation as similar, manifest in the connection between film images and collective memory. "Films reframe and re-edit images," she says, "thus reframing and re-editing memory, which works as the ultimate channel to the past."[3] In the following chapter, the role of television as represented in cinema will be further investigated as it informs a critical stance, but it is worth mentioning now that the diverse technologies of film and television affect the manner in which each deals with temporality. "Cinema uses temporal distance as a base for historical assessment, especially in the reorganization of events in order to achieve internal final coherence, while television uses archival material which is assembled to fill the uninterrupted flow of programs."[4] In *Cinema Paradiso* and in the 1980s, it was the exponential growth of commercial and cable television—and specifically popular American programs such as *Dallas* and *Dynasty*—that spelled the end for many movie houses in Italy like the Nuevo Paradiso. More specifically in regards to reflexivity, the "internal final coherence" allows the cinema spectator to have a satisfying, conclusive experience of film narrative, while simultaneously illuminating historical or contemporary applications and indications. It must be noted, however, that narrative cinema is not necessarily history nor always an accurate referent to it. These films use historical moments in time to provide backdrop to their narratives. Like memory, these films are selective in what they wish to reveal about the past or the contemporary setting, and the ways in which it is connected to the present moment in the story. The subjective, discursive, and manipulative properties of the moviemaker stand as polar opposites in production style of the objective, static and singularly observant qualities seen in the capturing of images by surveillance/observation cameras—what might be called "pure" documentary—in various public and private spaces. Both styles, however, contribute to an understanding of "history" and events.

Cinema seems equipped, then, to function as a contributor to the archive of a country's historical memory, whether Italy or the United States, in the period prior to the last third of the 20th century or thereabouts. These films provide a view of media presence and proliferation. *The Majestic* furnishes glimpses of the television and newsreel cameras at the HUAC hearings. Harry, a traditional movie exhibitor, meanwhile dismisses "this TV thing" and speaks about the space of cinema as likely Alfredo would, or even Peter Bogdanovich as noted earlier. Harry eschews entertainment consumed alone in a living room and celebrates the magic that an audience creates before a large screen in a darkened envelopment. These sentiments may seem dated now, in the era of home video, DVD, and affordable large screen projection home theater systems. The magic to which he refers is presently diffused and small of scale. Harry is speaking in 1951, long before the funeral of Alfredo that is, in a way, the funeral for a cinema that exists no more. He speaks long before Jean Baudrillard identified the era of simulation as a substitute for history and the infinite possibilities of simulacra and repetition in the digital age. Meanwhile, movie audiences in the 1950s were simultaneously audiences for television, a condition that the movies themselves would soon critically explore as regards the structure and apparatus of the television moving image.[5]

The Majestic reminds us, too, that the infant industry of television was itself also affected by the blacklist in the subpoenaed Peter's naming of a TV producer and colleague as an alleged subversive. Television's presence is observed in the furniture in living rooms of middle class households of Lawson, and as a gathering point among diners in the cafe. There is newsreel footage on TV of the Hollywood Ten, filmmakers who refused to cooperate as friendly witnesses and served jail terms for their contempt of Congress. In the film, Peter successfully invokes the First Amendment and claims freedom of speech as the only defense needed for Americans to express their opinions. He goes free in this rewrite of history and an idealistic representation of dissent not necessarily heralded in this period. Indeed, it was rare for such a strong stand of resistance against HUAC to be rewarded by further employment in the film industry, as is Peter Appleton's case. This blurring of boundaries, through narrative storytelling, between fact and fictional representations, is part of the romanticizing tendencies of nostalgia films that favor the comforting tone of the past and the potential for idealism to triumph over what can be considered more realistic shadings. Other Hollywood films about the blacklist have been more romantic than political, (*The Way We Were*; Pollack, 1973), or earnest but superficial (*Guilty by Suspicion*; Winkler, 1991).

Some even broached the issue of HUAC's investigation of the television industry (*The Front*; Ritt, 1976). The fact that several participants in *The Front*—actors Zero Mostel, Herschel Bernardi, and Joshua Shelley; writer Walter Bernstein; and director Martin Ritt—were blacklisted, a fact made clear to the audience in the credits, lends the film a reflexive authority.

Today, an audience's televisual experiences constitute memory as much as any film's attempt to reconstruct the historical moment utilizing the medium of moving pictures as a canvas. Between the time *The Majestic* was produced (2000-01) and the time it was released (2002), one of the most evocative images on television screens was the attack on the World Trade Center, followed by the news and pictures of terrorist events surrounding September 11, 2001. No doubt, this climate affected the reception of *The Majestic*, which now could be seen both as a valiant and patriotic survival tale, as well as a vehement defense of individual liberties in light of *both* Islamic terrorists *and* the U.S. Patriot Act. Thus, it is that the static nature of a movie is enacted upon by the flow of ever-changing televisual images, granting audiences the opportunity to reevaluate the construction and reception of a film narrative. Narratives or images from cinema and television, then, can intertwine and force reflexive stances otherwise not anticipated. Almost six years after 9/11, a scene from *Transformers* (Bay, 2007) wherein the giant robot Megatron turns into a plane and flies into a high-rise building with office workers incinerated, drew gasps during screenings in New York City and elsewhere

The narrative of *Matinee* is itself affected by a historical event that was widely displayed on television—the Cuban Missile Crisis of October, 1962. In *Matinee*, the surrealistic tendencies of science fiction movies combine with the stark reality of atomic-age holocaust, although the young protagonist is more insulated from the geopolitical world and tuned into the realms of movie fantasy. His reflexive capabilities to process science fiction iconography and narratives would likely prepare him for a future where the possibility of nuclear annihilation requires a sharpened critical posture that is built upon the reflexive/reflective grounding.

MATINEE (1993)

In *Matinee*, a science-fiction film acts as metaphor for world events outside the doors of the theater. Reflexive attributes abound and enrich the characters' lives with motivation and meaning. In the films explored thus far, the space of cinema is continually destroyed and rebuilt, or reconstituted (as emergent TV). It will be likewise here, with the theater resurrected as a multiplex to accommodate the fracturing of the movie landscape that marks the contemporary cinema-going process as it develops in the 1960s. Moreover, we are seeing a televised historical event—the Cuban Missile Crisis—streamed into homes with a density and frequency with which the movies cannot contend, a harbinger of things to come when TV displaces cinema as the dominant purveyor of repetitive narrative or journalistic models, many of which are based on newsworthy events and reality programming, as well as the newscasts and news channels themselves. The evolution of filmmaking and film spectatorship is often marked by a conflict between the traditional and experimental, with realignment the result of tension between market forces (in terms of box office and technological innovations) and critical demands (in terms of film-as-art and narrative innovation). The literal space of cinema, the marketplace, is encountered in a primarily sensual manner; its symbolic space—fashioned from stories on the screen and attendant critical demands from spectators—while contingent on established tangible sensations, is most intensely engaged through intellect and emotion. The interplay among physical, emotional, and intellectual responses to movies assists in enlivening reflexivity. Human beings have been transformed from spectators in 1906 who paid a nickel to watch twelve-minute, black-and-white, silent movies in a converted storefront while sitting on folding chairs or benches, to patrons 100 or more years later viewing IMAX films on a six-story tall, curved screen, relaxing in adjustable seats with headrests and surrounded by multi-track sound design. Over the past century, cinemagoers have consumed and accumulated stories ranging from simple tales told in linear fashion, to ingeniously structured—or convoluted—narratives that can challenge their powers of dissection and understanding.

In the 1950s, the widescreen phenomenon—especially Cinemascope and Cinerama, with their reliance on engaging a viewer's peripheral vision—was a new invitation for audience participation. As the Royal was closing in Anarene, Texas, and the Majestic was moving with the times in Lawson, film spectatorship in the United States was beginning to be redefined with attention to size and sensation. The wider screen entered further into the viewer's space, and advancements in stereo and multi-track sound recording and reproduction altered and enlarged the audio perspective. Some film historians, such as Steven Heath, view spectatorship as mostly ahistorical or at least tied to one place in time.[6] He sees significance in certain constants, such as the codes of Renaissance perspective in painting and how it represented space on the screen, as crucial to the positioning of the spectator. Heath also limits his discourse to the standard film aspect ratio of 1.33:1, which was the dominant canvas of screen size (and television) until the early 1950s. "Aspect ratio" refers to the relationship between height and width of the screen image. Since the 1950s, the standard aspect ratio for most American films has been

1.85:1. Others, namely John Belton in *Widescreen Cinema*, tie its evolution
to historical and technological trends with the most obvious being cinema's
expanding canvas as a reaction to the smaller, limited space of the television
screen. Widescreen motion picture production and exhibition in the 1950s
transformed the previous relationship between audiences and the screen in
a way unprecedented since the coming of sound in the late 1920s and the
introduction of color in the 1930s.

In addition to widescreen, other technological experiments designed to
expand the viewing experience—from 3-D to the carnival-like techniques of
William Castle such as Percepto! Emergo! and Illusion-O!—were unleashed
on audiences in attempts to refine or redefine the traditions of movie-going.
Other historians, such as Thomas Schatz and Christopher Anderson, detail the
struggles faced by the film industry as a result of the sociocultural climate
of the times and its reaction to the changing demands of the marketplace. In
America of the 1950s, this included cinema confronting the challenges of
television siphoning audiences; disruptions to the internal workings of the
studio system resulting from the Paramount Decision (a Supreme Court ruling in 1948 that demanded film companies sell their owned-and-operated theater chains since it constituted a monopoly in some regions); the aforementioned HUAC hearings and its implications (which momentarily diminished
the desire of many filmmakers to deal with certain social problems in their
films); and the growing number of independent producers and foreign films
that emerge as competition for studio-based Hollywood product.

New films embraced the participatory potential of widescreen and incorporated production techniques rooted in prior recreational forms such as the
amusement park and the legitimate theater. Cinerama and 3-D touted the
participation effect with literal representations of roller-coaster rides (*This Is
Cinerama*; Cooper and von Fritch, 1952) or hurling of projectiles at the cam-
era/audience (*Bwana Devil*; Oboler, 1952). Stereoscopy, or 3-D, attempted at
several junctures in film history to enjoin narrative with the visceral appeal
of the technology. The 3-D phenomenon first boomed in the early 1950s,
declined in the 1960s, was resurrected via independents and pornographers
in the 1970s, and again revived in the 1980s and beyond in exploitation films
and theme parks. Even in narrative Cinerama films, plot lines employed action sequences that were amusement ride-influenced such as a river rapids
chase (*How the West Was Won*; Hathaway, Ford and Marshall,1962) and an
escape from a fire-breathing dragon (*The Wonderful World of the Brothers
Grimm*; Levin and Pal, 1962). The legitimate theater was invoked with the
use of dark colored theater curtains filmed as they open to reveal the panoramic spectacle of ancient Rome in the first Cinemascope film (*The Robe*;
Koster, 1953) or when the 20th Century-Fox studio orchestra plays theatri-

cal-style overture music (*How to Marry a Millionaire*; Negulesco, 1953). In the mid-1950s, widescreen processes readily affiliated with a number of Broadway adaptations (*Oklahoma! South Pacific, The King and I*), religious and historical spectacles (*Ben-Hur, Demetrius and the Gladiators, Knights of the Round Table*) and prestige literary adaptations (*Lust for Life, The Bridge on the River Kwai, East of Eden*). Thus, new experiences of spectatorship became associated with spectacle and the use of systems and narratives that literally overwhelmed the viewer. The Ultra-Panavision 70 image, for example, could be projected at an aspect ration of 2.75:1 and was used for *Lawrence of Arabia* (Lean, 1962).

Matinee satirically captures the playful spirit of these types of experiments in filmmaking, showmanship, and spectatorship. Set in Key West, Florida, the narrative covers one week in the lives of several of the town's teenagers and a visit by an exploitation horror film director modeled after real life figure, William Castle. It is an historic and momentous week in October, 1962. The film begins with a bang! A white screen suddenly shows stock footage of the blast of a nuclear bomb test and its destruction of houses, trees, and other things. Then, a credit rolls next to the silhouette of a large man sitting in a director's chair identifying him as the No. 1 shock expert, producer Lawrence Woolsey. Portrayed by John Goodman, he speaks with great solemnity and admits the atomic bomb is something quite terrible. But more terrible still, he suggests, are the effects of atomic radiation. Woolsey then goes on to warn viewers about something that *could* happen, something that *does* happen in his newest motion picture *Mant!* He piques their curiosity by describing the process in which it was shot—Atomo-Vision with Rumble Rama, a new audience participation thrill that promises to makes viewers a part of the show.

An audience of mostly children is watching this movie preview at the Strand Theater. A special one-day test engagement of the film is scheduled on the upcoming Saturday. Gene Loomis (Simon Fenton) is at the picture show with his younger brother Dennis (Jesse Lee). Gene, junior high school age, is the son of a U.S. Navy serviceman. His adolescent feelings of rootlessness prompt him to avoid investing in friendships because of his father's frequent transfers from base to base, so he attends the movies repeatedly. Dad is not present this day, serving on a secretive mission not too far from shore. At their home, Dennis watches Art Linkletter on TV performing an audience participation stunt where a woman reaches into a box and is made queasy by touching an unknown, furry object. Television is once more presented as an inane diversion, but in context this stunt anticipates the overall theme of fear and repulsion that runs throughout *Matinee*. Then, a bulletin from NBC News interrupts with an address by President Kennedy declared officially to be of the highest national urgency—the Cuban Missile Crisis. The boys and their

A master at ballyhoo, film director Lawrence Woolsey (John Goodman) exploits fear and fun at the movies in Matinee.

mother, Anne (Lucinda Jenny), fear for their father/husband who is on one of the U.S. interceptor ships near Cuba.

Within its opening minutes, *Matinee* has generated several layers of dramatic tension with the intertwining of movies and real life. This intertextuality continues through the film. There have already been two sober warnings about atomic weaponry, and a third one is soon to come at school the next day. Meanwhile, at a service station out of town, Lawrence Woolsey and Ruth Corday (Cathy Moriarty) gas up their convertible. Ruth is the star of Woolsey's films as well as his traveling companion and girlfriend. When the station attendant notices the rotund film director and mistakes him for Alfred Hitchcock because they both produced suspenseful, scary films, the joke is a reflexive one, recognized by both the audience and Woolsey. There is no real-life figure of the renowned Hitchcock in *Matinee*; he exists in the world of spectators and filmmakers who are aware of that director and the kind of films he makes.

During a health class at school while the instructor emphasizes the nutritional value of meat at least three times a day, the air raid siren begins to wail. Most students mindfully and methodically "duck and cover" in the hall. One girl, Sandra (Lisa Jakub), refuses to participate, noting that death by the bomb would be a preferred alternative to living amidst nuclear fallout. She proceeds to speak about radiation poisoning while being led away by school officials.

One of the cowering schoolboys calls her a Communist, but Sandra remains defiant. She challenges her teachers to tell the truth about real safety in face of atomic blasts. This brief vignette allows audiences of the 1990s who viewed *Matinee* to acknowledge the absurdity of once-accepted but now outmoded realities, here involving nutrition, safety and politics. It also reminds them that they have seen this sort of thing for nearly a decade, since *The Atomic Cafe* (Rafferty, 1982), and perhaps wonder if there is any end to recycling the 1950s! Indeed, perhaps the viewers of *Matinee* recognize that they are bored to death with these "stock" (footage) events as reminiscent of a fairly complex time in American history. While these realities themselves are nominally disseminated and indoctrinary through other media—such as textbooks, educational films, the popular press—here a Hollywood movie, *Matinee*, exposes them for what they truly are: suspect techniques for managing one's life. Jay Ruby notes that a reflexive attitude assumes that the world as it is being presented is not to be taken at its face value. The reflexive posture ennobles a constant dialogue within the film that builds upon our physical experience and resounds in emotion and intellect:

> "In more protracted reflexive works, we are not allowed to slip back into the everyday attitude that claims we can naively trust our senses. We are brought into a different reality because the interplay between illusion and reality continues. The frame is repeatedly violated, and the two stories, commenting on each other, travel alongside, simultaneously commanding our attention and creating a different world that either represents by itself."[7]

Matinee acknowledges its referential strategies relating fantasy cinema and other media to real life, even as its characters are oblivious to them. At a table in the lunchroom, much discussion takes place about the upcoming *Mant!* The PTA, it seems, is trying to ban the film. When the normally reserved Gene approaches, he eventually befriends the group, who marvel at his knowledge of Woolsey and horror films.

Gene and his friend Stan (Omri Katz) observe the military build up on Highway A1A, now a mobilized thoroughfare with encamped U.S. Army units, radar and weapons on the beaches, sandbagged observation points, and fighter planes overhead. In town, there is panic-buying at the grocery store, but the boys' main concern is to get dates for *Mant!* on Saturday. When Gene runs into Sandra one afternoon as she comes out of the principal's office, he introduces himself. She makes a reference to Mahatma Gandhi and resistance that is well above this shy cinemaniac's head. These young people are from two very different environments. Sandra has a political consciousness about issues like integration and disarmament while Gene is mostly insulated and immersed in monster movie culture. The showing of *Mant!* will bring them together where they encounter situations of fantasy and reality, creating experiences that each will need to mature, to balance their outlooks, and to forge identity. Meanwhile, Stan had planned to take Sherry (Kellie Martin) to *Mant!* but her ex-boyfriend, Harvey (James Villemaire) intimidates Stan into backing off. Harvey, a punk in the Marlon Brando *Wild One* mode, is a delinquent and also a very bad poet. He is a caricature, like most types in this film. Yet, Harvey provides a necessary element for plot propulsion in the later scenes of *Matinee*.

Woolsey gets a few opportunities in the film to explain his intentions, and while this man is a master of ballyhoo, he also has a sincere love of cinema. Like a magician who reveals the key to his tricks, Woolsey enlivens the reflexive inclination of viewers of *Matinee* and that of Gene himself. Gene and Woolsey are returning from a hardware store with supplies to rig some special effects for the show. The boy confesses his devotion to horror genre movies, his lack of real friends, and the pitfalls of always moving around. Woolsey, undaunted, commends Gene on confronting 500 new people every year at school each time his father is transferred. Walking past the shops on the street, he recalls how, as a child, he was petrified of new towns but now gets the revenge of scaring everybody else with his movies. Woolsey explains an antecedent of his work, recalling how prehistoric man had been chased by mammoths and survived the flight. To share the story of that plight, they would draw images on cave walls that likely struck fear in those who never experienced that trauma. Woolsey considers this the first monster movie. He knows that films are journeys, even descents into danger, from which the return marks a kind of resurrection or transformation not only for the character but for the audience as well.

The pair enter the Strand. Framed posters for current films *Lonely are the Brave, Hatari!* and *Whatever Happened to Baby Jane?* hang on the walls. A subjective Steadicam shot glides through the lobby, favors a dark and discolored carpet for a moment, goes up a few stairs to a concession stand, bypasses it and heads for two wooden doors that lead to the viewing space. Woolsey likens the Strand to a cave with a carpet. Inside the auditorium, Ruth is helping affix electric buzzers under selected seats and overseeing the placement of extra speakers and smoke-bomb launchers that will accentuate key moments in *Mant!* The skittish manager, Howard (Robert Picardo), implores Woolsey to consider other priorities at this time because the country is on Red Alert and people are already scared. Woolsey agrees and concludes that it is the perfect time to open a new horror movie. Later in *Matinee*, he will consider how harder it is to scare people with real world dangers so omnipresent.

The day for *Mant!* arrives and two 20-foot models advertising the creature describe it as "half-man, half-ant, all terror." They stand like huge columns on

In a reflexive nod to the exploitation filmmaker William Castle and his film The Tingler, *Lawrence Woolsey wires theater seats with electric buzzers that will startle viewers of his movie* Mant! *Intrepid science fiction and horror film fan Gene (Simon Fenton) observes the root of mayhem to come.*

either side of the Strand's marquee. Patrons, mostly children and teenagers, line up for the Saturday afternoon showing. Inside, Howard is downstairs in a room that has been converted into a bomb shelter/manager's office, listening to Civil Defense bulletins and counting his survival supplies. He watches the news and listens to the radio at the same time, while Nikita Khrushchev's image from a poster for the anti-Communist scare film *We'll Bury You* (Thomas, 1962) scowls from the wall in the background.

In the lobby, Ruth is dressed as a nurse and has all the movie patrons sign release forms relieving the management of any liability should a patron be scared to death. Here, *Matinee* is referencing the work of a P.T. Barnum-like film producer named Kroger Babb who, in the 1940s and 1950s, made a fortune from a heavily promoted sex education film that featured the birth of a baby and clips from sex hygiene and venereal disease prevention films. It was called *Mom and Dad* (Beaudine, 1945).[8] Babb and his promoters would station women in nurse uniforms in the theater to supposedly take care of people who fainted or had heart attacks while witnessing the startling footage. Movies like *Mom and Dad* (and in its own way *Mant!*) operated in the tradition of the nineteenth-century medicine shows—part biology (or science) lesson, part sideshow, part morality play, part medical (or military/scientific) footage. Producer-directors such as William Castle and the fictional Lawrence Woolsey modified the basic elements into other forms of ballyhoo both in the theater, the lobby space, and the community itself. Film spectators, bound by the conventions of the medicine show audiences, would witness the unraveling with some measure of skepticism and disbelief—or else awe and belief—usually culminating in a sense of deliverance and relief. A movie like *Mant!* or *Matinee* uses the reflexive stance to deliver spectators from their worst nightmares to the assurance of survival and transformation.

Gene spots Sandra in the theater lobby. Backstage, Harvey is getting some last-minute pointers from Woolsey on how to run the "special effects" equipment. He doesn't seem to be processing it all that clearly, though. The show begins, and the parting of the curtain quells the noisy crowd. Woolsey himself is in the first scene at an atomic test site location. He explains that the movie will be in AtomoVision, a terrifying new process that puts you, the audience, at ground zero.

Mr. Spector (Jesse White) from Megapolitain Theaters, which owns the Strand, is present to see the preview showing and will consider booking it in his chain if it is successful with this test audience. Spector, Woolsey, and Ruth stand in the back of the theater as the seat buzzers go off, causing several panicked patrons to jump at the same time! Sparks shoot from behind the screen as the Mant touches a high voltage grating! Huge speakers rumble (in anticipation of the 1970s gimmick of Sensurround) as the monster grows to gigantic size. Harvey deploys smoke bombs at a key point, and increases the Rumble Rama decibels to an earthshaking level so that Howard, still below in his bomb shelter, assumes a nuclear attack is afoot. On screen, the Mant is climbing a large building, under fire from the military below. Destruction seems the rule of the day in both the real and the cinematic world. This crosscutting—from the screen story, to the audience watching it, to real life in the bunker that is the theater—is a foundation of film editing called "parallel action" deployed to unite two or more scenes under one thematic thrust. Audiences began to intuitively grasp this as the language of film as early as D.W. Griffith's time, and it is used here as a matter-of-fact, reflexive strategy. So, when action on the movie screen that emerges from the film-with-the-film (*Mant!*) informs action by the characters in the film *Matinee*, spectators of the latter have been conditioned to accept the events as occurring simultaneously. Crosscutting from *Mant!* to *Matinee* (film to film), instead of just within a single movie, creates states of recognition and anticipation between the texts.

The Mant eludes conventional military firepower and escapes to a movie theater in the film, a referent to *The Blob* (Yeaworth, 1958) where a horrifying substance oozes out of the projection booth at a midnight spook show. It also references Castle's *The Tingler* (1958), the film that actually applied use of seat-connected electrical buzzers in selected showings. In *Matinee*, *The Blob,* and *The Tingler*, the audience in the theater on the screen mirrors the audience in the actual theater. Watching an audience view a horror film, in effect, instructs us on the way in which a horror film should be consumed. We scream. We grip the arm of the person next to us. Perhaps we yell warnings to the unresponsive screen. We cover our eyes. As the Mant rips through the screen in the movie *Mant!* it is the cue for a costumed Harvey in *Matinee* to jump among the aisles and seats and scare the spectators in the Strand. He is quite convincing in his Mant outfit, especially when he sees Stan and Sherry, his former girlfriend, kissing with no regard for the movie house action around them. He attacks Stan and it is a real fight, which Woolsey joins and is slugged for his interference. Harvey runs off and the crowd cheers, thinking it is all part of the staged show. So does a pleased Mr. Spector, who applauds what he perceives as old-time showmanship. Real life, at least in this instance, assists and perhaps trumps the fantasy cinema experience.

Gene and Sandra chase Harvey and end up in Howard's fallout shelter, accidentally locking themselves in. They hear sounds that can be interpreted as explosions on the *Mant!* soundtrack, or perhaps bombs dropping in the real world. They are eventually rescued, and upstairs, *Mant!* works towards its finale. But a distraught Harvey deviates from his scripted duties when he abducts Nurse Ruth, demands a ransom, and then forces Sherry out of the theater. A giant burst and explosion behind the screen apparently rips a hole in it and reveals what looks like an atomic fireball. The crowd panics in real terror this time. Popcorn boxes, paper cups, and other debris fly through the air; the smoke gets thicker, people faint, and an apocalyptic moment seems near. While this can be interpreted as real life that again trumps the fantasy cinema experience, it may signify imminent nuclear holocaust for the film's characters!

There is chaos in the balcony, already weakened by cracks in the upstairs structure from the over-amplification of the Rumble Rama speakers. The theater empties into the world outside which, to everyone's relief, is absent of nuclear fallout. But the very foundations of the Strand have been damaged, the floors split, and balcony pillars tumble as what appear to be fires still burn inside. Woolsey calmly goes to the projection booth and shuts down the projector as the final reel of *Mant!* ends. All the chaos and attendant effects—except for the unfortunate collapse of the balcony—was indeed the work of on-screen movie magic and backstage special effects. The screen returns to its solid white, pristine state. There was no atomic fireball, only a filmic representation of it. Howard has to cancel the rest of the shows for the day, but Woolsey seals his deal with Mr. Spector for distribution of *Mant!* Spector assures his manager Howard that the insurance will finance the theater's renovation, and that maybe they should get rid of the balcony anyway and put two more screens up. It is prescient thinking on the eve of the multiplex-theater era.

By violating the frame of reality as well as the frame of cinema for its characters, *Matinee* enables a reflexive stance. There is increased self-awareness of both the threat of atomic fallout and the ability of cinema to dramatize its consequences. While there is relief that the destruction of the world is not real, the possibility of its occurrence certainly remains. *Matinee* concludes with a thought-provoking scene that is especially meaningful for viewers who are historically aware of events that followed in the 1960s, and whose consumption of visual images would be largely influenced by television.

The denouement of the film occurs when a TV newscaster reports that the Soviets have agreed to dismantle their missiles in Cuba and that U.S. Navy ships would be returning to their ports and bases. Of course, this brings great joy to Gene, Dennis, and their mother. But the final shot of this "comedy" is somewhat foreboding. Ruth and Woolsey affirm their hope in the young audiences, especially Gene and Sandra whom they think will survive their adolescent years because "they've seen the coming attractions." This implies an embrace of the reflexive/reflective stance and, perhaps, the stirring of a critical consciousness. While the soundtrack reprises a period song played earlier on the radio in Gene's bedroom—The Tokens' "The Lion Sleeps To-night"—Gene and Sandra are at the shoreline, looking up at helicopters and fighter planes returning home from Cuba. They kick their shoes off and sit at the water's edge, an image of sinnocence about to be overtaken by the future. The song references the quiet jungle where the lion sleeps tonight. And the camera zooms in to the helicopter for its flyby and then cuts to a frontal close-up of the machine—the kind of shot that will become familiar on the evening TV news as the decade advances. It holds for a long fade in what is a hint of the future: the fermenting war in the jungles of Vietnam, overseen by helicopter. The "coming attractions" of assassinations, riots, revolutions, global warming, AIDS, terrorism and preemptive war can also be inferred in that shot.

A reflexive posture organizes *Matinee* and, especially, Gene's dramatic engagement. As a fan—and film-obsessed viewer who earned his status with genuine regard for both the fun and the edification provided by the movie-going experience—Gene is grounded in the referents to science fiction films and cinema culture. His enthusiasm is infectious and provides him with confidence through interactions with Sandra, Woolsey, and onto his ultimate confrontation with Harvey and the burning theater. As a young spectator enamored with the mechanics of moviemaking and able to discern fantasy from reality, he rises to the occasion for heroic endeavor at the film's end. He displays an ability to act in the face of obstacles such as adult authority figures, adolescent girls, bullies and, literally, trial by fire. He is tested and emerges victorious in these rites of passage. While relaxed in a restorative state at the end of *Matinee*, the audience of the film realizes that, perhaps, all will not be quiet much longer.

Matinee, although comic and parodic, displays how our minds surrender voluntarily or involuntarily to larger-than-life fears. The other films discussed—*Cinema Paradiso, The Majestic* and *The Last Picture Show*—present films on the screens within their narratives that spotlight several genres and tap a variety of emotions in the spectator. That surrender of the spectator within the space of the movie house forms the cornerstone of understanding what going to the movies entails, especially for the period covered in these films. These are stories of moviegoers whose existence is shaped by the details of not only films, but other popular media, as well as the tangible experiences of living. The cinema happens to be one of the more vital magnets or intersection points.

THE PURPLE ROSE OF CAIRO (1985)

The Purple Rose of Cairo displays the limits of the reflexive stance as an exclusive posture, situating its narrative, appropriately, during the Golden Age of Hollywood. Audiences watching *The Purple Rose of Cairo* some 50 years after the time-present setting of the film experience a kind of "historical reflexivity" similar to that in the other films discussed. We acknowledge the presence of cinema in both cultural and individual histories, and this is exposed and treated as a kind of nostalgia that infuses the reflexive stance. Arguably, all the films in this chapter can be considered nostalgia narratives in that they look backward from their period of production. But cinema unreels before its viewers in the present, so Woody Allen keeps the "frame" of the present very much alive in *The Purple Rose of Cairo*. The illusion of the film as real is also kept intact. Since the reflexivity is only about the past for the audience of the film, seen in black and white at times—and despite the fantastical transportation of characters—it is a safe and unchallenging way for film to talk about itself. Moreover, the lead character Cecilia, herself reflexively regards the movies of the 1930s she experiences; indeed, it is that propensity that thrusts her into the fantasy world of the interior film.[9] We become aware of both the powers and limits of nostalgia and the cross-collateralization that is inspired by the reflexive stance.

Nostalgia films are constructed and consumed as more than just a look back and contain moments of introspection as well as a forward-thinking, progressive vision. They can create ruptures through calling up strategies of otherness, displacement and fantasy-projection—all capable through the act of spectatorship. This process can illuminate points in the personal and social landscape that are ripe for repair. While it shall be seen that the character of David opts for a reconstruction of the worlds he inhabits in *Pleasantville*, and Truman decides to reject his world in *The Truman Show*, Cecilia in *The Purple Rose of Cairo* selects a restorative strategy that emerges from her experiences. All are able to achieve a closure thanks to their characters' understanding and comfortability with the media forms with which they engage, and this is displayed through cinema's interrogation of those media forms.

The Purple Rose of Cairo is the work of writer-director Woody Allen. Two years earlier, he wrote and directed a pseudo-documentary, *Zelig* (1983), about the ultimate conformist, a man who takes on personality traits of anyone with whom he comes in contact. In that film, Allen signifies the power of the media to reflect and distort reality. He also creates a new environment of mediated reality for character Leonard Zelig. *The Purple Rose of Cairo*, also, particularizes and humanizes a transportation between realms of fantasy and reality and the navigational dangers that involves.

The Interior Film and the Outer Film

The movie-within-the-movie, or the interior film in *The Purple Rose of Cairo*, invites what Stuart Hall calls "the interrogation of the image." The character of Cecilia will probe inside and behind that movie-screen image, but before that the character of Tom Baxter will descend from the interior film story and probe the real world of New Jersey during the Great Depression. In *The Purple Rose of Cairo*, Cecilia deals with the crushing disappointment of the ruptured reality of the movies by surrendering to that world and making a restorative truce with her own world rather than remaking or rejecting it.

Movies create an imagined world, inviting us to live inside that world for a while. In so doing, they intensify some aspects of human experience. This offers film audiences an encounter with "otherness" which can confirm, challenge or transform the world they have constructed. "Humor is Allen's way of confronting, deflecting, and escaping from life's grim realities," notes Gerald Nachman.[10] Allen himself admits, "I'm always fighting against reality. I've always felt that people can't take too much reality."[11] While this notion un-

Cecilia (Mia Farrow) amidst the other spectators at the Jewel Theater in The Purple Rose of Cairo. *She loses herself, literally and figuratively, in the magic of movies.*

derpins most of his work, and for that matter most movies, it is especially prominent in *The Purple Rose of Cairo*.

Cecilia (Mia Farrow) is a waitress in a New Jersey cafe during the Depression, a young woman who looks to movies at the neighborhood Jewel Theater for an escape from her dreary life. Frequently daydreaming about the movies while she works, Cecilia eventually loses her job. She goes to see the current feature film "The Purple Rose of Cairo," a modest programmer about moneyed New York gentry who go hunting artifacts in Egypt, bringing their handsome explorer-guide back to their penthouse in Manhattan, intent on introducing him to the ways of big city life and love. This is surely the saga to raise Cecilia's spirits! Much to her surprise, the dashing young explorer Tom Baxter (Jeff Daniels) walks off the screen and into her life. The problem, however, is that Tom is not real. He is a fictive creation, constructed by a screenwriter, brought to life by an actor playing a part, and ill-equipped to maneuver around the real world of New Jersey. Still, Cecilia will be his guide and mentor.

Meanwhile, the Hollywood studio producer, Raoul Hirsh (Alexander Cohen) is livid when he discovers that other Tom Baxters are trying to leave the screens in other movie houses showing "The Purple Rose of Cairo" throughout the country. The young actor in *The Purple Rose of Cairo* who portrays

Tom, Gil Shepard (Jeff Daniels again), arrives in New Jersey with a studio entourage to help prevent damage to his future career. Cecilia's personal life and her rocky marriage to Monk (Danny Aiello) are upended when both Tom and Gil vie for her affections—Tom because it is written into his filmic character to act heroic and gentlemanly toward the waif Cecilia, and Gil because he wishes to use her gained affection to get his creation of Tom safely back on the screen and himself working again. Before Cecilia is forced to choose between Tom and Gil, she is allowed a "frame-breaking" experience when Tom escorts her into the world of the interior film.[12] Now, Tom becomes *her* guide and mentor.

Cecilia proceeds to both affirm and dismantle several fantasy conventions of the movies during her madcap Manhattan weekend night on the town and its aftermath. The notions that 'true love prevails' and 'the guy gets the girl in the end' are unfulfilled. Hollywood's 'happily ever after' culture where everything works to the protagonists' ultimate satisfaction. Tom's character affirms that where he comes from—i.e., the imagination of 1930s screenwriters--people are reliable, consistent and don't disappoint. Cliché notions are also dissected in several small moments such as when Tom and Cecilia jump into a waiting vehicle and he expects it to begin with no effort, unaware that in the real world a driver needs a key! His use of stage money that befuddles

Actor Gil Shepard (Jeff Daniels) is mistaken for his screen character Tom Baxter by Cecilia (Mia Farrow) in The Purple Rose of Cairo.

a restaurateur and his surprise at the absence of soundtrack music that accompanies a fade out after kissing Cecilia also mirror the larger disappointment of Cecelia's infatuation with this one-dimensional figure. Her misbegotten choice becomes Gil over Tom (real life over fantasy) at the film's conclusion. But, Gil's affection proves ephemeral, while Tom merely disappears/returns into "The Purple Rose of Cairo."

Despite her return to a restored world of both real life and fantasy, Cecilia is a catalyst for change in some secondary characters as she inspires frame-breaking in others. An idealized Copacabana supper club scene during the Manhattan weekend, for example, is reconfigured by Cecilia when she identifies the prop champagne as ginger ale, and by a maitre d' when he breaks from his character because an unscripted encounter with her gives him freedom to reinvent himself as a tap dancer. Other characters in the interior film also begin to question their own scripted motivations when Tom leaves them adrift as he tours the real world.

Hollywood movies' thematic and technical conventions or clichés are also affirmed, especially in the interior film when Tom and Cecilia visit several clubs around Times Square. Several club names appear in lights and logos that are superimposed and dissolve over an image of Tom and Cecilia strolling past lit-up theater marquees on Broadway. The montage continues with a kaleidoscope of stock footage of a champagne bottle being opened, glasses gently colliding in a toast, and then a sophisticated couple dancing cheek to cheek. Romantic music underscores the sequence that finally concludes as Tom and Cecilia return to the penthouse in the back of a taxicab. The Copacabana scene with Kitty Haynes (Sally Kellerman) as a chanteuse is picture-perfect studio staging—a glamorous urban crowd, dancing to the big-band sounds, potted palms lining the walls, a resplendent Kitty with black over-the-elbow gloves and a floor-length dress. Another thematic cliché of old Hollywood is 'the hooker with the heart of gold' and in *The Purple Rose of Cairo* there are a half-dozen of them, led by Emma (Diane Wiest) and her co-workers. Even the match up of Cecilia and Monk is a melodramatic pairing. She is the wistful and sorrowful ingénue, a downtrodden waitress who dreams of better things, while he is an overbearing, unemployed lout of a husband, content to wallow in the malaise of the status quo and keep his wife there as well. Through reflexive/reflective interplay with both real world and fictive recreations, *The Purple Rose of Cairo* asks its viewers to either challenge or embrace the tension in their marriage as Cecilia moves toward her restorative conclusion.

When Cecilia eventually chooses the flesh-and-blood Gil over Tom, she is first elated and then dismayed. Gil, a Hollywood star, has only been playing another part—that of the nervous actor who wants to salvage his career. Cecilia, however, fails to recognize this deceit. Finally removed from the interior film and left standing under the Jewel marquee and not in the arms of Gil-as-Tom when *The Purple Rose of Cairo* concludes, Cecilia cannot reinvent and reconstruct herself in the movies. Perhaps this can be inspired *at* the movies on another visit. She looks forward to seeing the Astaire-Rogers musical that soon replaces "The Purple Rose of Cairo" at the Jewel. Cecilia is victimized to some extent, and unable to reject her situation as a woman, a wife, and a struggling unskilled worker in the Depression years. But she has also demonstrated an intelligence and charm that begin to distance her from the brutish Monk, and point to possible new breakthroughs for her future. Still, that may be an all too hopeful conjecture.

The Closed Film and The Open Film

A filmmaker selectively isolates and excludes images when constructing a work, resulting in two kinds of films or film experiences—the closed and the open film. Leo Braudy (*The World in a Frame*, 1976) positions closed and open films as part of a historical and aesthetic continuity, collaborators not antagonists in affording different ways of sense-making with cinema. Braudy's consideration of what constitutes closed and open films illuminates the possibilities for understanding and enjoyment of these texts.

A closed film is totally self-sufficient in that the world of the film is the only thing that exists. The frame of the screen fully defines the world inside the film as a picture frame does a painting or photograph. The story in an open film, on the other hand, does not exhaust the meaning of what it contains in effect and affect; the world of the film is a momentary frame around an ongoing reality. The frame of the film is "more like a window, opening a privileged view on a world of which other views are possible."[13] Braudy contends that the closed film is perhaps "purer" and a more schematic form than the open, since the open film is porous and not only opens outward, but also allows other elements into it. "In closed films the audience is a victim, imposed on by the perfect coherence of the world on the screen. In open films the audience is a guest, invited to collaborate on a vision of reality only nominally that of the director alone."[14] A closed film is characterized by the "false summary" or happy ending. Here the form itself, which is usually Classical Hollywood or its descendants, supplies an answer or resolution. Closed films enable hierarchies with their complete message and assert that all details are the expression of an invisible order. Open films are more challenging for the spectator and give an incomplete message, asserting that there are more details to be discovered and considered.

The New Jersey neighborhood theater where Cecilia's world is transformed for the price of admission, at least for a little while.

The Purple Rose of Cairo is ultimately a conservative, restorative, closed film that affirms the value of movies as a momentary escape from the real world. Despite the yearning for a state of "otherness" and a temporary, tactile experience of that state—in this case, Cecilia as a character in a Hollywood movie—the worlds of fantasy and real life remain separate and restored to their original state. Nostalgia depends, in large part, on the irrecoverable nature of the past. An "open" reading would anticipate change on the parts of Cecilia and Gil, and perhaps the pensive look on Gil's face as he flies back to California at the end of the movie is a small signifier to substantiate that hope. But Cecilia is truly, madly and deeply mired in screen reality, a fiction-fantasy. An open reading of the film as it stands, would allow that her earlier experience of frame-breaking has conditioned her for more of the same when future opportunities arise. But with the long, lingering take on Cecilia at the end of *The Purple Rose of Cairo* we are situated back in our seats, restored, and not imperiled, to change. She watches Fred Astaire and Ginger Rogers in *Top Hat* (Sandrich, 1935) float on a spectacular dance floor in a graceful duet. Cecilia is totally engrossed and immersed in the movie. Peaceful and contented, she starts to smile.

Reflexive and Restorative Impulses in Nostalgia Fantasy Film

The kind of return or recession at the conclusion of *The Purple Rose of Cairo* represents an overall hierarchical mandate that narrative art often exploits— that is, the masses may be allowed to vicariously rebel during the course of the play or film, as long as in the end they return to a place of control and con- tentment. A restorative order results. Under Napoleon, for instance, French theater was little different from that of the late 1780s, specializing in neoclas- sical drama. Popular drama, as performed by what was known as "boulevard theatres," then introduced melodrama, a form that would dominate theater in the 19th century and influence film in the 20th century. Melodrama is episodic, and takes place in a simplified moral universe where good and evil are embodied in stock characters. The villain poses a threat, and the hero or heroine defeats or escapes from that threat. The world is made right, whole and content again, often at some cost or sacrifice.

Melodrama emerged as the middle-class began to attend the theater in in- creasing numbers. Northrop Frye in *Anatomy of Criticism* describes a central theme in melodrama as "the triumph of moral virtue over villainy, and the consequent idealizing of the moral views assumed to be held by the audi- ence."[15] Since melodrama exists in a mass cultural framework, it could easily become "advance propaganda for the police state." Hal Himmelstein affirms the desire of the hero in melodrama to assimilate: "In tragedy, the hero is isolated from society so that he or she may better understand his or her own and the society's moral weakness; but once enlightened, the hero cannot stave off the disaster embedded in the social structure beyond the hero's con- trol."[16] Were *The Purple Rose of Cairo* Tom's story—that is, there would be a central and stronger identification with Tom—it very well may have been framed as tragedy. But the normative characters representing incorporation into society are Gil and Cecilia, the protagonists with whom the audience chiefly identifies. They are agents who act to restore order to their worlds of hierarchy—the movie business and the marriage. Both those worlds are af- firmed and made whole again.

Cecilia has an affective investment in the movies that works similarly to the attraction of nostalgia fantasy films, where audiences create a strong sense of investment in an earlier time such as the 1930s or 1950s. Frederic Jameson names *American Graffiti* (Lucas, 1973) as an inaugural nostalgia film with its use of period cars and dress styles to signify a return to the past. Nostalgia films approach the past through other stylistic conventions—such as period music or black-and-white cinematography—and the time-present of the nar- rative can be inconsequential. *Body Heat* (Kasdan, 1981) and *Blood Simple* (Coen, 1983) are set in the present but connote the past through an evocation of the film noir genre (most prolific from the late-1940s through the mid-1950s) and the recycling of old movie plot lines, the type of actors cast, the title designs, and the choice of locations. Jameson considers the allusive and elusive referencing and concludes that the nostalgia film "tells us stories that are no longer our own." They invite a kind of "schizophrenia" in postmodern practice. Nostalgia films are not "a matter of some old fashioned 'representation' of historical content, but instead approached the 'past' through stylistic connotation conveying 'pastness' by the glossy qualities of the image, and '1930s-ness' or '1950s-ness' by the attributes of fashion."[17]

The "privileged lost object of desire" by which Jameson views the 1950s through the prism of *American Graffiti*, infects the environment of nostalgia fantasy films with frame-breaking characters who try to fill the void in their contemporary setting with the reproduction of a past era or distant environment—such as 1950s sit-com America in *Pleasantville*, or 1930s Hollywood escapist films in *The Purple Rose of Cairo*. Jameson links nostalgia films to a moment of lost desire in the 1950s through the rhetoric of capitalism—the past is commodified, repackaged, and sold back to us through the text of the film as well as through the many synergistic strategies that market the music, fashion styles, attitudes, and other iconography that accompany the film. The schizophrenia of which Jameson writes, according to Vera Dika, is "a barrier to the real and to history erected by such an instant pastiche."[18] That schizophrenia or dislocation, enabled by the reflexive/reflective stance, can mire a character or spectator in the lockstep of their present state. Their release comes with incorporating additional stances of a critical or ironic awareness

So, Cecilia represents a reflexively grounded moviegoer of the 1930s, habitually attending the same films and genres so that she is comfortable in literally penetrating their frame and interacting with the on-screen ensemble. She moves from observer to participant in the drama, and approaches a chance to change her life by scripting her future and rejecting her lamentable real life of the present. Cecilia is poised for a new purpose in her life with either Tom or Gil. Because she is so invested in the reflexive notions of cinema as they might inform real life—but is cognizant of Gil as a real person—she chooses him over the movie character Tom, thinking that happiness will follow just as it does in the movies. Reflexivity has led her to a rite of passage that results in bittersweet romantic disappointment, but she perseveres through envelopment in the space of the cinema and its further reflexive incarnations. In the chapters that follow, the focus will be on films using television as a setting, and those that have media-saturated social and political reality as a backdrop. These movies further enlarge the reflexive posture to encompass and accentuate critical and ironic perspectives.

NOTES

1. Indeed, by 1973, 40 percent of the U.S. population ranged from ages 12-29, but that group comprised 73 percent of spectators at the movies. (Thomson, 338).

2. Gabler, Neal. (1998). *Life the Movie: How Entertainment Conquered Reality*. New York: Knopf. 18.

3. Ferrero-Regis, Tiziana. (2002). "Cinema On Cinema: Self-Reflexive Memories in Recent Italian History Films" from *Transformations*, No. 3, May, 2002. 2. http://www.cqu.edu.au/transformations

4. Ibid. 4.

5. By 1956-57, 85 percent of U.S. homes had at least one television set, and those sets were being watched for five hours each day. Thus, with the country's population of about 170 million this translates to about 135 million people seeing the equivalent of at least two films a day. Yet, in cinemas, the audience was less than a quarter of that number attending one movie a week. (Thomson, 295).

6. Heath's essay in *Screen* (1976) entitled "Narrative Space" envisions film narrative's codes and figurations inherited from the Quattrocento perspective—the visual techniques developed in the fifteenth century Italian painting for creating the illusion of three-dimensional reality. Heath argues that the camera has followed this tradition in positing a view from a central perspective and that spectatorship has been trained to understand representation in these terms.

7. Myerhoff, Barbara and Ruby, Jay. (1992). "A Crack in the Mirror: Reflexive Perspectives in Anthropology" from *Remembered Lives*. ed. by Myerhoff and Kaminsky, Marc. Ann Arbor: University of Michigan Press. 310.

8. For a detailed study of *Mom and Dad* and the practices of Kroeger Babb—who billed himself as "America's Fearless Young Showman"— see *Profoundly Disturbing: Shocking Movies That Changed History* by Joe Bob Briggs, Universe Publishing, 2003.

9. As with *Pleasantville* and *The Truman Show*, the title of a movie is also the name of a TV show. There will be a distinction in typography when dealing with texts of the same name. *The Purple Rose of Cairo* as italicized refers to Allen's film; "The Purple Rose of Cairo" is the interior film-within-the-film.

10. Nachman, Gerald. (2003). *Seriously Funny: The Rebel Comedians of the 1950s and 1960s*. New York: Pantheon Books. 535.

11. Ibid.

12. The condition of "frame-breaking" is present in several films explored. It infers that a character has penetrated the boundaries of a media text through some narrative ploy or creative license of the filmmaker, and has entered a world different from the one from which he or she has lived. Frame-breaking asserts both the artificiality of media-made worlds as well as demonstrating the human need to understand them.

13. Braudy, Leo. (1976). *The World in a Frame: What We See in Films*. Chicago: University of Chicago Press. 48.

14. Ibid. 49.

15. Frye, Northrop. (1957). *Anatomy of Criticism: Four Essays by Northrop Frye*. New Jersey: Princeton University Press. 47.

16. Himmelstein, Hal. "Melodrama." www.museum.tv/archives/etv/M/htmlM/ melodrama/melodrama.htm

17. Jameson, Frederic. (1984). "Postmodernism or, the Culture of Late Capital- ism." *New Left Review*. No. 146. July/August.

18. Dika, Vera. (2003). *Recycled Culture in Contemporary Art and Film: The Uses of Nostalgia*. New York: Cambridge Press. 11.

Chapter Three

Movies About Television:
The Critical Stance

Reflexivity can encourage a critical, and often ironic, perspective. By illustrating that *this* exists (the subject) because of *that* (the referent), or in light of that referent, the reflexive impulse suggests comparison. That comparison invites an implication of judgment or value, accompanied by a sense that things may not be what they appear to be.

With the proliferation of television as a mass medium of communication, especially after the 1950s, the movies begin to more critically focus on it, resituating cinema's own posture towards enlightening and entertaining a mass public. Although images generate meaning, it is not merely the image itself and the producer who are responsible. Additionally, the audience's manner of interpreting or experiencing the image and the context in which the image is seen must be considered. This approach assumes the viewer has a history of interaction with the moving image, and with other mass mediated and cultural experiences.

Until recently and for most of its existence, television endured a competitive relationship with cinema. From its early proliferation in the late 1940s, TV began to lure audiences away from the movies even though its production values offered less spectacle and sensation than film. As color television was refined and additional broadcast stations arose in the 1960s, cinema attendance further declined. The film industry counterattacked with a new candor on its screens that TV at that time was unable to match. When television eventually reached a parallel position regarding its program content—via the widespread access of subscription cable programming with its absence of network censors—movies had already claimed the high ground by telling stories postured with serious moralizing about significant subjects. The initial burst of films between the late 1960s and late 1970s explored the role of important contemporary social structures and events in the lives of audiences. The films included subjects such as the Vietnam War (*Coming Home, The Deer Hunter, Apocalypse Now*), the military (*M*A*S*H, Catch-22*), women's rights (*Klute, An Unmarried Woman*), the generation gap (*Easy Rider, The Graduate*), political campaigns (*The Candidate*), political conspiracies *(All the President's Men, Executive Action, The Parallax View)*, dangers of nuclear power plants (*The China Syndrome*), and several other issues involving race, sexuality, and ideology. Not surprisingly, the industry, practices, and programming of television became targets of this criticism as well.

In the films explored in this chapter—*Medium Cool* (Wexler, 1969), *Network* (Lumet, 1976), *Bamboozled* (Lee, 2000), *Natural Born Killers* (Stone, 1994), and *Pleasantville* (Ross, 1998)—the movies investigate the space of television as central to the narrative. The plots seem more complex than those in the previous chapter. They employ techniques of documentary film, satire, surrealism, and time travel and are distinctively engaging at both emotional and intellectual levels. While the narratives in the previous chapter extended from the mid-1940s to the early 1960s, these continue from the late 1960s through today. Appropriately, this coincides with the increase in television use by producers and spectators. Cinema, then, acts as a prosecutor of television culture, its structures, and its influences. This critique positions the movies as truth-seeker and art-maker, casting the medium of TV with its relentless flow of sounds and images as something more ephemeral, even vulgar, as it serves powerful forces that seek to profit despite accepted notions of truth. In the previous chapter, cinema enabled and supported character struggles and offered some hope or channel for survival. Here, it shall be seen, television usually enables and ensures their defeat.

Television encroaches upon its spectator's life unlike any other medium. Cinema interrogates this encroachment in a way that encourages a critical stance. To avoid a critical reaction could allow the incorporation of TV—that is, the manner in which it operates on and for us—into the psyche and physical being of the spectator, so that it becomes a benign or malignant force. These films show that an uncritical spectator is not only a complacent observer, but also a willing (or unwilling) participant in what is likely a dystopian and Orwellian world.

The films that follow share some similarities with those already discussed. The relationship of a father or father figure to the protagonist, evidenced in the films on reflexive development, has not wholly disappeared in these narratives. The grounding of characters to some filial needs and notions—a condition shared by spectators—creates fertile opportunities for reflexive/reflective moments as we ponder our own relationship to a parent or parent-figure. *Bamboozled, Natural Born Killers,* and *Pleasantville* have that relationship as central to the identity-formation of their lead characters and a reference point for their own self-critique. Once more, the films include an essential element of romance, although the survival and transcendence of the romantic couple is assured only in *Natural Born Killers*, perhaps the most subversive and critical of the lot. The traditional Hollywood narration pattern of Normality-Crisis-Normality also adheres in these films, although the state of normality becomes a crucial consideration when the demise of protagonists with whom we have identified affirms, in some cases, the oppressive nature of media structures and systems and the indifference of their audiences.

Cinema employs its fade-out—the image or sensation that is left near the conclusion for the audience to ponder as it leaves the theater space—as a trump card in evoking critical thought in the spectator. The act of watching television eschews this moment in favor of sustained program flow and viewer loyalty as it immediately moves on to the next program installment. A movie, on the other hand, sanctifies this period of decompression for an audience as spectators communally or individually comes to grips with the message of the film, without the distraction of other competing narratives. Stories in cinema are generally conclusive, in that they do not promise further development (unless they are franchise films or sequels). That is not usually the case with series television. It exists, primarily, to deliver its audiences to a sponsor or a subscription service provider on a consistent basis. Even notions of nonconformity or subversion on television (*NYPD Blue, Sex in the City, Big Love, Deadwood*) are delivered with a promise of consistency from week to week for the discerning viewer. Thus, the need to take a stand with some surprise and conclusiveness is more opportune and evident in film than in TV, since TV demands return engagement with the narrative at a later date. The result is a collection of incomplete or near-complete narratives, at least until the series finale.

The experience of television viewing or the production of television programming centers the critical tendencies encouraged by the films in this chapter. In addition, the viewer's identification with audiences and key players within these films intensifies those tendencies. The signifying image in each of these films serves to combine that association between spectator—which can be considered both the audiences *in* the film and those *watching* the film itself—and performer/producer. In *Medium Cool*, it is the final shot of the director himself, Haskell Wexler, photographing a graphic car accident; he pans his camera until its lens is centered in the frame we are watching and the spectator peers into the circle of glass. In *Network*, the image is Howard Beale, the distraught news anchor, who is advising his viewers to open their windows and vent their frustrations by yelling out at the world; a young girl watches Beale on the TV at home and does just that. In *Bamboozled*, it is a studio audience of white people who don blackface makeup in imitation and celebration of the performers at the taping of a hit TV minstrel show; their outlook affirms and consolidates a racist representation that is the unfortunate result of complicity of producer and spectator. In *Natural Born Killers*, a TV journalist interviews young fans throughout the world about Mickey and Mallory Knox. One star-struck young man admits to the camera and microphone that he does not believe in mass murder, but if he was a mass murderer, he would want to be like be Mickey and Mallory. And in *Pleasantville* the signifying image is David, the ultimate fan who is transported into the world of his favorite TV show only to be transformed—and act to transform that world—by enlivened passion. The red color of a rose, lipstick, and blood, along with the other sensations they invite will force David and others to reconstruct their world after undertaking a critical exploration.

Medium Cool is offered as an example of how cinema gives resonance to a television-made event, in this case the 1968 Democratic Convention in Chicago and the ensuing street riots. *Network* considers TV as a tool of multinational corporations that has abused its role of public servant and treats the audience like sheep to be herded for ratings and profit. *Bamboozled* contains some similar attitudes toward its TV audience but allows means by which the personal and cultural identity can be forged despite the oppressive structures. By the 1990s, movies about politicians who use television to further connect with its viewers unveiled duplicitous strategies employed by both candidates and media professionals in their attempts to gain the attention and allegiance of spectator-voters. While *Bob Roberts* (Robbins, 1992) and *Wag the Dog* (Levinson, 1997) display rank-and-file mainstream politicians in the spotlight, *Natural Born Killers* thrusts outlaw heroes to the forefront of society and manages to also question the mass media's complicit role in obfuscation of truth.

In exploring these films, we keep in mind a dual focus—the role of the audience within the text, and the role of the audience watching each film. This seems appropriate enough, since they are movies *about* television and we are audiences watching audiences watch and make meaning, even as we are charged with that likewise. *Pleasantville* resorts to a dual vacuum—the closed, scripted world of a TV situation comedy, and the seemingly closed, oppressive world of present day suburbia. By critiquing the idyllic, nuclear family of the 1950s that is pictorialized by mass media, characters in that film and spectators in the audience are afforded manners in which to renegotiate their own identity by unveiling the myopia of TV's construction of it. In all these cases, cinema reveals and prosecutes the medium of television for the manner in which it has shaped perceptions of reality, providing the viewer with a critical focus that can evoke alternative notions and strategies for change.

Television's omnipresence can be an obstacle as well as an enhancement to developing a critical perspective were it not for this interrogation by cinema. Because TV and the visual moving picture culture are so much a part of our everyday lives and, arguably, accessible at will and in various permutations (computer screen, video game, kiosk monitor advertisements, iPods, etc.), we may tend to be uncritical of their nature. Indeed, cinema exists as part of this overall visual landscape. Many of these films presuppose a self-designated purity and primacy in that medium but cinema, too, is guilty of lies and brainwashing through relentless stereotyping and propaganda techniques.

These films exist as gentle or acerbic satires on the structures in television. But they are not the only illustrations nor is satire the only methodology through which cinema has attempted to understand TV and its audience. The world of television is a frequent backdrop for cinematic drama about the personalities that manufacture contemporary television—*The China Syndrome* (Bridges, 1979), *To Die For* (Van Sant, 1995), *Up Close and Personal* (Avnet, 1996) *Mad City* (Costa-Gavras, 1997), *The Insider* (Mann, 1999). Comedies, too, are given a chance to reflect the world of TV—*The*

A Face in the Crowd *(1957) was one of the earliest and more scathing indictments of television and celebrity culture. Lonesome Rhodes (Andy Griffith) projected an affable and genial manner to the cameras, but revealed to be duplicitous and mean-spirited in his personal life.*

Groove Tube (Shapiro, 1972), *Broadcast News* (Brooks, 1987), *Wayne's World* (Spheeris, 1992) *Groundhog Day* (Ramis, 1993). Television has been treated with nostalgia and innocence in *My Favorite Year* (Benjamin, 1982), *Avalon* (Levinson, 1990), and *Pleasantville*. It has been a harbinger of evil, an alien invader of heart and home in *Poltergeist* (Hooper, 1982) and *Video-drome* (Cronenberg, 1983). A few films have dared to critique TV's history and structures such as *The Front* (Ritt, 1976), which looks into the blacklisting of television writers in the 1950s, and their strategies of survival. *Good Night and Good Luck* (Clooney, 2005) recounts the struggle of Edward R. Murrow to broadcast a counterattack on Sen. Joseph McCarthy during that same period. *Quiz Show* (Redford, 1994) explores the game show scandals of the late 1950s. One of the earliest films to offer a critique of television, its sponsors, and its viewers is *A Face in the Crowd* (Kazan, 1956). Produced at a time when TV was mostly considered a benign, if not beneficial and welcome presence in the home, it is an intellectual and spiritual precursor to both *Network* and *Bamboozled*.

A Face in the Crowd is the story of a homespun, guitar-playing philosopher (portrayed by homespun, guitar-playing Andy Griffith) who is launched on a career in radio, then television, by a smart producer. She renames him Lonesome Rhodes, and he soon becomes a powerful network performer who uses the media to bolster his fame and manipulate his audiences. Eventually, he is drawn into circles of political power that intend to use his fame and connections to advance their social agenda. The author of the script, Budd Schulberg, expresses the fear that television will become a political tool, that there are those in power who take advantage of the medium, that through its use you *can* fool all of the people all of the time, and that the spectators of TV have a responsibility of vigilance that they usually avoid. As a movie *about* television, *A Face in the Crowd* is a bold and early attempt to critique the new electronic medium, released at a time when television was accelerating its presence in American homes. The film's dramatic climax comes when a proud and boastful Lonesome Rhodes, assuming his microphone has been cut off, verbally insults and ridicules his core audience during the transmission of a live TV show. Cinema manipulates through the careful construction and reconstruction (editing) of sound and image, and not the constant uninterrupted flow of televised transmissions, which were mostly live and continual in the early days of the medium. *A Face in the Crowd* employs a technical demand and limitation of television to undermine its character that thinks so disparagingly of his audience.

It can be said that discussions of films about TV blend easily into discussions of films that are about American culture, politics, and the systems through which we view and constitute ourselves, because television is the most ubiquitous representation of those systems. Indeed, the very connection of the film medium with television goes back to some of the first televised programming in America on General Electric's experimental station WGY in Schenectady, New York. Barely five months after its initiation, WGY presented, in February 1929, a brief talk by director D.W. Griffith who called the new invention the last miracle of miracles. It was a gracious acknowledgment, but the relationship between Hollywood and television was soon marked by ambivalence and distrust, before settling into a mutually beneficial companionship. A brief overview of some interweaving of TV in films, as the two mediums wrestle with 20th century events, seems in order.

An early incorporation of television in Orwellian terms occurs in the film *Modern Times* (Chaplin, 1936). This satire on depersonalization in the workplace opens with a factory boss setting aside the funny papers, flipping a switch and announcing his orders on a huge screen to the workers on an assembly line in an effort to speed up their productivity. Later, when Charlie Chaplin's Tramp is sneaking a smoke during a bathroom break, the boss' larger than life image appears on the wall, and demands that he get back to work. This is television as 'Big Brother,' "not only invading the workers' privacy but also buttressing and sustaining the authoritarian and hierarchical structures of the workplace."[1] Some later films spoofed the early TV genres, such as *It's Always Fair Weather* (Donen, 1955) and its send up of "This is Your Life." Others might take a moment to ridicule the quality of sound, picture and content on TV, such as *Will Success Spoil Rock Hunter?* (Tashlin, 1957). Others still merely used the TV set as a prop signaling disenfranchisement of some sort—a broadcasting executive comes home to find his small boy mesmerized in front of the TV and unable to communicate with him in *The Man in the Gray Flannel Suit* (Johnson, 1956); a widow with an eye for a younger man is presented with a TV set by her adult children that will provide her a more matronly distraction in *All That Heaven Allows* (Sirk, 1955). Of course, television as a prop became a convenient way to connect several characters/observers in a film narrative, especially if the unifying event was of national or global concern such as the HUAC hearings in *The Majestic* or the encounter between earthlings and the alien robot Gort in *The Day the Earth Stood Still*. So, even if consumers of the 1950s had not yet purchased TV sets, they were being given models of TV spectatorship at the movies. Cinema in the 1950s was more apt to show us how to use or "consume" television than to ponder the manner in which we could be used *by* television.

Among the many stirring images in *The Manchurian Candidate* (Frankenheimer, 1962) are the shots of television sets in kitchens and living rooms, rows of monitors in studios and at points of observation removed from the actual broadcast event site. The film is a political thriller about a brainwashed

Korean War veteran who is programmed to assassinate on command by a Communist agent. Several plot twists, including one that has the right-wing operatives turn out to be subversives, invite complex readings of a film that toys with perceptions of reality. Albert Auster notes that in *The Manchurian Candidate*, "Television is merely the most technologically advanced and omnipresent illusion-making element in a system permeated by illusion."[2] As the political "event" became a focus in the contemporary film drama—of confirming a controversial candidate for Secretary of State in *Advise and Consent* (Preminger, 1962), of the battle for a party's presidential nomination in *The Best Man* (Schaffner, 1964), and of a military general's attempt to wrest control of the government from a pacifist-minded President in *Seven Days in May* (Frankenheimer, 1964)—the incorporation of television became a necessary plot device by which characters communicated with the national audience. TV becomes part of the reality and is efficiently inserted into films that recreate the political tensions of a particular era, as we have seen in *Matinee*. Cinema in the early 1960s, then, offers television as a character or a conduit that explores traditional characters in its narratives. It is a sense-making tool, shaping the perceived reality and in service to political, corporate, and social forces of control. Its manipulative implications are less obvious than by decade's end when world events begin to irrefutably transform the landscape of both media and culture.

With the publication of *The Selling of the President* (1969) by Joe McGinnis, a book that details the role of media and public relations specialists in manufacturing both political events and candidates, more spectators became aware of the inner mechanics of creating a 'face' for political campaigns. Narrative films such as *The Candidate* (Ritchie, 1972) soon appeared, which anticipated the career of California governor and presidential candidate Jerry Brown. Like *Medium Cool, The Candidate* uses actual footage of real personalities such as Hubert Humphrey, George McGovern and John Tunney at a banquet scene. More than any other film before it, *The Candidate* addressed the power of the media, and asserted it at the expense of the voice of the candidate. It also marked a change in the way movies saw politics and insured that television's role in any future film narratives about contemporary politics and its perception by voter-spectators would be crucial.

Gary Trudeau, creator of the syndicated *Doonesbury* comic strip, developed a storyline about a politician running for the 1988 Democratic Presidential nomination that became an HBO series, *Tanner '88* (Altman, 1988). Michael Murphy portrays Jack Tanner and actually interacts with real politicians such as Bob Dole, Jesse Jackson and Pat Robertson. The film is shot in pseudo-documentary style, and thus, the uninitiated viewer could well construe Murphy as a genuine candidate. Similarly, *Bob Roberts* employs this style for its effect. Appearance-vs.-reality continues with television as a mediating presence in *Dave* (Reitman, 1993) where a dead ringer for the President of the United States has to playact the role, convincing TV pundits and the public, as well as those personally close to him. Two films about the 1992 presidential race situate TV and its image-consciousness front-and-center: the documentary *The War Room* (Hedges, Pennebaker, 1993) and *Primary Colors* (Nichols, 1998). And finally, *Bulworth* (Beatty, 1998) offers a candidate who voices a challenge to prevailing modes of ownership in the media itself. Some of these films will be examined further in the following section of this text. They are evidence that cinema after the 1980s, in its prosecution of TV, was more apt to deliver narratives involving the techniques and conceits of television—most of which were revealed or already known by audiences—to unmask both the medium's pretensions and those of its subjects, significantly in the triad of Political, Corporate and Media (PCM) elites.

Natural Born Killers is a multifaceted look at media sensationalism and tabloid-TV mentality. It shares with other films the contrived usurpation of the media spotlight by those not traditionally trained or formerly qualified, and the willful cooperation of the entrenched media operatives who benefit from such maneuvers. In *NBK*, the crime-spree perpetuated by its main characters is not covered by a seasoned journalist who may have been tested by real life-and-death situations (as would a war correspondent, print reporter, or experienced newscaster), but rather a handsome personality who creates, and then delivers, the news. Here, cinema explores how spectacle and sensation can numb an audience into accepting just about anything. *The Truman Show* (Weir, 1998) and *EDtv* (Howard, 1999), meanwhile, are concerned with the TV medium's ability to engage spectators with the most ordinary sounds and images. Here, cinema explores how the repetitive and mundane can transfix an audience, anticipating the plethora of reality-based television shows of the next decade.

Cinema showcases a triumph in *The Truman Show*, with the elevation of the hero, who is at first ordinary and is made extraordinary because s/he successfully functions in extraordinary circumstances. This narrative trope is really at the heart of much of what passes for dramatic construction. It is evidenced when we witness a struggling, white-collar everyman (or everywoman) strive to please Donald Trump in *The Apprentice* reality show, which is in fact, merely a variation on *Wall Street* (Stone, 1987) minus the critique of capitalism and produced for TV in the name of sanctifying competition. The preponderance of reality television shows since premieres of *The Real World* (1992) and *Survivor* (2000) confirms that viewers are interested in the dual-state of participant-viewer which has itself grounded popular genres in the past such as game shows and talk shows.

Cinema invites us to use the structures of television as a means of re-constructing society; this entails a turning outward and a focus upon what surrounds us. It also provides a means of reconstructing self; this requires a turning inward and taking inventory of what inhabits us.

Many characters in the films discussed in this text display a great love of freedom and creativity, and they face obstacles rife with rule and order that are negatively manifest in structures of power prompted by the expansion of mass media. These films and their representations of a televisual world that inspires a critical stance by cinema move us from the community of the theater space explored in the previous section to the cocoon of home, bedroom or desktop. Given the satiric impulses of many of them in comparison to the homage to cinema detailed earlier, we would do well to closely observe the fissures and gaps that these films-about-television expose. Apart from cinema, we know that television at times aspires to convey real life as it is lived, especially in the areas of news, personality and politics. It does so, however, often without inviting the critique that the mechanism of cinema does in these examples that follow.

MEDIUM COOL (1969)

An organizing pretense of *Medium Cool* is the notion of shooting—shooting film and shooting guns, the cultural preoccupation of capturing violence as well as creating or containing it. Along the way it questions the ideological power of images and reveals reality as something that can be artificially con-structed just as any other fiction. The interpretation of the images, meanwhile, depends on who is wielding the camera, who controls the larger institutions of power that disseminate those images, and finally, the willingness of the spec-tator to confront those images and understand them for what they really are.

The title of the film adapts and questions Marshall McLuhan's definition of television as a "cool medium" that one merely receives, with little thought of what is being conveyed; TV supplies all the information one needs.[3] In so doing, *Medium Cool* blurs the line between illusion and reality. The director, Haskell Wexler, has called this film a "fusion of fact and fiction."[4]

Like the other films about television in this chapter, *Medium Cool* can be discussed at three levels of interpretation: the personal trauma and transforma-tion of character, the professional role of the media practitioner and its ethical imperatives, and the wider political implications of the deeds performed and stances taken by them. The focal character and guide through this narrative is John Cassellis (Robert Forster), a television cameraman who is apolitical at the outset as he and his soundman Gus (Peter Bonerz), pursue stories for a Chicago station in the summer of 1968.

The film begins with the wail of a stuck automobile horn that sounds like an air raid siren, or maybe the audio tone of a TV test pattern. Indeed, an automobile accident is a framing device of *Medium Cool*; that is, its opening and closing scenes are those of car wrecks. Wexler shoots the two journalists who come upon the initial accident through a cracked glass of the wrecked car, as if it were a broken lens through which perceived reality can be distorted. Gus unplugs the horn cable and it becomes silent. It is their only gesture to interrupt and affect reality at this single-car accident where a woman dangles to the ground out of the open, passenger side. John and Gus film for a few moments, as they circle around the damage and then head back to their car. John advises that they'd better call an ambulance, but only after they get their shots and plan to drive away. They appear nonplussed, even passive. The violent car wreck that will also end the film, accompanied by an equally dispassionate group of observers, invites a critical stance in the spectator who, at the film's conclusion, now disdains a passive response. The 105 minutes of film between the accidents speaks to both the sensation and the threat of

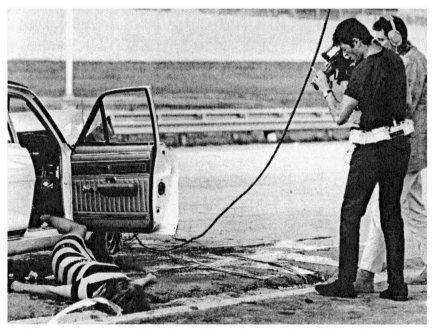

Traffic accidents begin and conclude Medium Cool. *In the opening scene, TV news photographer John Cassellis (Robert Forster) and his sound man Gus (Peter Bonerz) are first on the scene of a fatal highway wreck, recording its aftermath and rendering no aid.*

overwhelming spectacle, and it is Wexler's intent to charge us with complicity and to challenge us to do more than merely watch. He uses the cinematic representation of television's role in a volatile historical event to this end.

Later that day, journalists, cameramen and others gather at a cocktail party and discuss the moral implications of their work. Some dismiss it as just a job, and there is little critical engagement about what they do. Still, most can agree before the last drink is downed that all good people deplore problems at a distance. The reference is to the distance that television and mass media provide. That is to say, people do not want to get any nearer and close that distance, which serves to desensitize individuals to real feeling and real emotion. In the first few scenes, *Medium Cool* shows the practice of, and the rationalization for, the news gathering profession. According to Valentin Katz, we are witnessing:

> . . . a media that views itself as performing a civic and intellectual duty by disseminating information to the masses, however, the media never helps any of their subjects, no matter how gruesome or disturbing the scenes they are capturing may be. The media's, and thereby man's, fascination with disturbing images is a motif that appears often in *Medium Cool*. By showing disturbing images to in turn condemn those who do, Wexler is exhibiting a form of reflexivity that further interrogates the medium of filmmaking.[5]

A reflexive stance, then, assists to further encourage and inform the critical one. The unfolding narrative engages through performances that have been, thus far, improvised and only slightly scripted. *Medium Cool* mixes fictional characters in nonfictional settings as well as inserting real life characters and events in the background of key scenes to add context and authenticity to its storylines. Intermixed as backdrop to the 'A' storyline (John's growing politicization and humanization as he leaves the television station to work as a freelance reporter; falling in love with a subject of one of his stories, Eileen, in the process) and the 'B' storyline (Eileen and her son Harold's adjustment to Chicago life, his coming to terms with John as a father-figure, and his eventual flight from home and the search for him) is the impending 1968 Democratic National Convention and the chaos it brings a nation, a political party, a city and its diverse groups and individuals. That chaotic state is captured by television. Wexler will place his actors in the thick of real riots and demonstrations in the hope of shaking viewers from states of complacency. At many points henceforth, *Medium Cool* will flip between staged action and real life.

The spring and summer of 1968 was a time of great turmoil in America. In *1968: The Year That Rocked the World* (2003), Mark Kurlansky qualifies the ruptures that were a spontaneous combustion of rebellious spirits around the world. It began with the Tet offensive in Vietnam and the drowning out of President Lyndon Johnson at several speaking engagements around the country by hecklers and protesters. It was the year of the Martin Luther King Jr. and Robert Kennedy assassinations; the riots at the Democratic National Convention in Chicago with seventeen minutes of police clubbing demonstrators shown on national television; the rise of Yasir Arafat's guerilla organization; Prague Spring; the antiwar movement and the height of the Vietnam War; Black Power; the generation gap; avant-garde theater; the birth of the women's movement at the Miss America pageant, stormed by feminists carrying banners that introduced the phrase "women's liberation" to the television-watching public; a war in Biafra; and the beginning of the end for the Soviet Union as live broadcasts beamed pictures of unarmed students facing Russian tanks in Czechoslovakia. This pivotal year for television carried the sounds and images of these events into the homes and consciousness of Americans at this dawn of Marshall McLuhan's "global village."

> Four of the most world-changing events in the history of television were in 1968: the coverage of the Vietnam War's Tet Offensive, bringing filmed battle into homes the same evening; the police brutality at the Chicago Convention being filmed and aired that night; smuggled film proving that the Soviets were invading Czechoslovakia without any local support and completely against the will of the Czech people; and the dazzling trick of broadcasting astronauts from outer space. In 1968 the world tumbled into a media age that only a few people understood. It was the awkward beginning of the world we live in today. But that is only one of the consequences of that pivotal year, a year of such grave seed changes that 35 years later we are only beginning to understand them.[6]

Events both unexpected and planned took place in late November 1963, that prominently positioned television as an apparatus that could reveal history in the making. Jack Ruby's assassination of accused presidential assailant Lee Harvey Oswald was transmitted live to the nation, as was the funeral of President John Kennedy the following day. Shock and grief unified the American viewing public in an unprecedented fashion. In 1968 it was clear that one now needed television to make things happen, a cultural revelation with enormous consequences for all. Kulansky addresses the role of mass media then, from the standpoint of its position now, when select reporters are often "embedded" in political or military situations:

> Media was so effective in 1968 because its power was not fully understood. Today it is, and the news is packaged with an eye toward public opinion in a sophisticated manner that was only in its early stages then. And government has become far more skilled at controlling news, especially war news. Journalists are not free to roam Iraq and Afghanistan the way they were in Vietnam but are

generally kept in controlled situations. The journalists themselves could learn
much from 1968 by studying the way the press corps at the time came to understand that they were being lied to and found a new independence that allowed
the public to learn the truth about the war.[7]

Medium Cool moves its action to Washington D.C., momentarily, where
John and Gus cover the funeral of Robert Kennedy. The journalists walk be-
side a pool at their hotel in search of interviewees with whom they can talk
about the state of the country. The music recalls the underscoring first heard
at the beginning of the film, a jaunty gunslinger theme of sorts. Looking like
outlaws or lawmen in *The Wild Bunch* (Peckinpah, 1969), the two reporters
amble around the pool, as John holds his camera like a large weapon, pointed
downward, at his side. Gus has a microphone that is even called a "shotgun"
mic, as befits a modern seeker of truth and justice. Wexler is able to contrast
the two Americas of 1968 when the reporters conclude a poolside interview
with a wealthy woman who giddily anticipates a move to her family's summer home in Ontario to get away from the city, the crowds and the heat. Then
there is an abrupt cut to the run-down tenement in Chicago where a social
worker pays a visit to Eileen (Verna Bloom) and Harold (Harold Blanken-
ship). The juxtaposition of these images is an example of invoking critical
awareness of poverty and class distinction through the editorial applications
of film, specifically the use of a straight cut.

For John, the personal, professional, and political begin to entwine with
two significant events. These events in the narrative prompt a critique of the
social systems in which John operates, and thus are important junctures in
the development of the critical stance in *Medium Cool*. John is sent to cover
a story about an African-American cab driver who has turned in an envelope
of $10,000 found in his vehicle.[8] Arriving at the taxi terminal, John finds the
police second-guessing the driver and inferring that it is unusual he would
hand in the money. They suspect other motives or a cover-up and, implic-
itly, find it hard to believe that a black man would be so honest. The cabbie,
Frank Baker (Sid McCoy), even receives criticism from his neighbors when
he goes back home. One man asks is he is acting as a Negro or a black man,
reasoning a black man in a white-dominated society would not have given
back the money. Frank is a little distraught about doing the right thing. John
lobbies his editor to do a follow-up "human interest" story on Frank but is
told to move on to other things. Still, John and Gus go to Frank's neighborhood where they are the only white faces to be seen. Stories had been circu-
lating—both at the TV station and on the streets—that the FBI and the police
were using the news media to infiltrate ghetto and black communities, and
asking them to share footage and information they had gathered.[9]

John and Gus are taunted as they make their way to Frank's flat. They represent the mass media in which the African-American community has no apparent voice. Meanwhile, the reality that media conveys is foreign, even disrespectful, to the voiceless. Gus is very uncomfortable and leaves to wait for John in the car. Frank has been easy-going and cooperative, but his friends are confrontational. As John is about to leave, one of the activists stops him and accuses John of spending 15 minutes to try and cover a story—the deepening of a racial divide—that has taken 300 years to develop. Wexler then gives us a head-on angle and another man speaks with passion and controlled rage about the arrogance of the media that readily distorts, ridicules and emasculates its African-American human subjects. The containment of this outrage, captured by TV/film, contrasts sharply with the riotous scenes that soon follow in the streets. There, cameras and microphones will make little attempt to understand or dialogue with the forces of intimidation.

Medium Cool powerfully mixes a variety of photographic choices in camera angles and positions—moving and fixed, close-ups and establishing shots, subjective point-of-view and third person observations—and this leads to an enveloping sensation of intimacy and intimidation. Because it plays on the viewer's twin acknowledgments of cinema and television techniques, the mixture is effective.[10] Additionally, because the subject matter is highly contemporary there is a feeling that the possibility of dialogue with characters is attainable. Both the audience, and John, are willfully confronted in direct address by the activists and have no choice but to critically engage. When *Medium Cool* was released in 1969, the role of media as conduit for dialogue was highly stratified and limited. Wexler is using cinema as an alarm and a call to arms, asking spectators to open their eyes to the reality of the surrounding world before it swallows us up. One more challenge is given to John by another activist (Felton Perry) as he leaves Frank's flat. He informs John that the "former invisible man lives" when he gets a gun, shoots up whitey and gets a reputation thanks to the media, because the tube makes him the TV star of the hour. This chilling indictment of the system and its inclinations towards violence as the result of misunderstanding ends with the last head-on shot of a black man, and it match-cuts to a similarly composed shot of a white, middle-aged woman at a firing range, shooting her pistol squarely at the camera. Here, then, is another way to critically engage—with violence, not understanding. John and Gus interview the manager of the range, and he proudly notes that gun registrations have increased 46% in the past year. The data and images in *Medium Cool* come quickly, as historical tidbits and statistics congeal with scripted narrative play.

The second significant event in his professional life that shakes John is the knowledge that the TV station where he works is indeed sharing his footage with authorities. Incensed, John objects and is ultimately fired for disobeying orders and going into the black neighborhood to explore Frank's "human interest" story.

John gets some pick-up work on a documentary crew that will cover the upcoming Democratic National Convention. As he walks across the International Amphitheater floor that is undergoing preparation for the event, a tape machine plays the opening strains of "The Star Spangled Banner." It is a prerecorded version that never quite sounds right—too slow, then too fast, distorted and off-key at places—so the tape gets rewound and replayed a few times in a moment on the soundtrack that engages both reflexive and critical sensibilities. We have knowledge of this patriotic song from past experiences at pageants, baseball games and ceremonies, and know that it should not sound this way. John surveys the stands being built for media crews and dignitaries, and viewers of *Medium Cool* recall how the ruptures within the Democratic Party at the 1968 Convention worked against party leaders' hopes of a scripted play. The film inserts these notes of premonition. Events

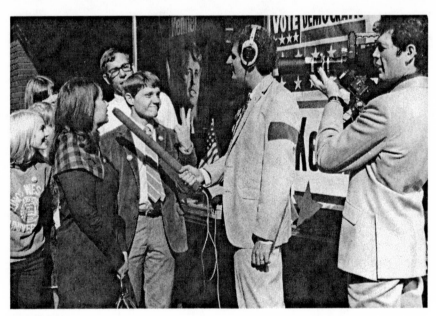

Spring, 1968, and the calm before the storms of riot and protest, as young Chicago voters speak their minds to the camera. Millions on television would see the turmoil at the National Democratic Convention as depicted in Medium Cool, *later that summer.*

would not follow their preferred plotline, much as the National Anthem could not find a proper pitch and tempo.

Eileen and John enjoy some nightlife at what passed for counterculture hangouts in a late 1960s studio-distributed film.[11] They dance amidst strobe and psychedelia to the music of Frank Zappa and The Mothers of Invention. Harold flees from home and Eileen gets on the CTA bus, searches for him and ends up near the perimeter of some evening vigils and protests. She asks for police help in finding Harold, but they cannot spare a man.

Meanwhile, John is working in a hall full of delegates, as Eileen searches for Harold who has become lost in Lincoln Park among the mostly peaceful, small crowds. But then, police vans suddenly appear and use loudspeakers to order people to leave at once. Eileen walks past protesters flashing peace signs, shaking their fists in power salutes and carrying posters that read "Sanity Please" and "Bring the GIs Home Now." Lines of men in blue uniform are seen with helmets fixed and holding billy clubs. It is the calm before the storm as Eileen soon comes upon a crowd chanting "Hell no, we won't go, " a reference to both the request to leave the park and a battle cry for draft-age men protesting enlistment to fight in Southeast Asia. Sloganeering provides and signifies an immediate critical stance in these riot scenes, and the apparatus of film and television captures this for their viewers to ponder. Audiences in 1968 would be especially familiar with this kind of rhetoric from watching TV news coverage of recent riots and demonstrations.

The protesters encourage one another to head for State Street, to stay together and avoid panic. An ABC network truck is allowed to pass, and its camera atop films the chanting masses: "The whole world is watching! The whole world is watching!" Eileen is among this real world of mayhem and Wexler has carefully ascribed her a yellow dress that stands out amidst the protesters so she can be located more easily in the frame. Yellow is the color associated with neutrality—a state Eileen certainly maintains towards the conflict in the streets, as she is preoccupied with her son's whereabouts. Had we not been following her story through the fictional narrative, she would likely be merely one of many "protesters" at this moment in history. *Medium Cool* employs a trustworthy narrative trope (the longing of parent and child to reconnect) to open access for a critical inquiry (what/why is this happening on the streets of Chicago?).

Wexler continues mixing newsreel footage with his actors in the fray. "Get those cameras outta here!" roars someone with the police, and an NBC crew drives its truck away from the coverage despite the pleas of the protesters, "Come back, NBC. Stay with us!" Now, U.S. Army tank-like armored personnel carriers roll in and approach protesters who have lain down in the middle of the street. We empathize with Eileen in search of her son, and also with those in imminent danger as both the tangible tools (riot shields, barbed-wire jeep bumpers, tear gas) and the verbal, intangible ones ("Fuck you, pigs!" "Seig, Heil!") escalate the drama. When a tear gas canister explodes in front of the camera, a loud coughing sound is followed by a voice saying, "Look out, Haskell. It's real." At this point, the makers of *Medium Cool* are real participants, not merely recorders of an historical moment. Indeed, cinema and television are shaping that moment as a kind of street performance.

In the years since the events of *Medium Cool*, the media has learned how to manage the filming and dissemination of riot footage. Wexler says, "The authorities—the military, the police—have learned how to handle public display. What you see are the action sequences. What the media wants out of civil disturbance is something that will get the people to the TV set so they're there when the commercials are on . . . You don't realize that 98% of the people are probably nonviolent and a group that they call 'anarchists' represent the fringe." More recently, serious issues like globalization are met with protests at a WTO gathering in Seattle and gain media attention by showing images of people breaking windows or illegally gathering in places outside their "free-speech" zones (such as at the Republican National Convention in New York City in 2004), and not with discussion and deliberations on real issues at hand. Both film and television are reliant on gatekeepers who determine what sounds and images are captured and made available, and a critical awareness is sharpened—or made dull—by the manner in which those are compiled and disseminated.

Inside the Convention Hall, Mayor Richard Daley of Chicago is introduced to more boos than cheers from the crowd, which is eventually drowned out by the old Democratic anthem of, simultaneously, hope and denial: "Happy Days Are Here Again." Wexler uses a 1930s rendition of the song by Casa Loma Orchestra, as he cuts to images of pain and confusion outside the hall, in another layering of the critical upon the reflexive. Eileen weaves among the bloodied faces, the battered and fatigued protesters, and the stern and sometimes stunned police officers. She is just a few feet away from the police lines, moving with the flow as the confrontation intensifies in the park. Benches are overturned and baton charges push bodies where they don't want to go. From the floor, a delegate from Colorado asks the Chair if there is any rule under which Mayor Daley can be compelled to suspend the police-state terror perpetrated this minute on kids in front of the Conrad Hilton? The Chairman refuses to answer and reminds the delegates that their only need is to respond to a roll call vote at this time. Daley had given his police explicit orders. According to Wexler, they were to "clear those fuckers out of the city!"

Small protest rallies still convene outside in the park. Eileen works her way through a line of National Guardsmen, a group that has now greatly increased its size. When a marching unit passes, there is a reprise of Mike Bloomfield's music that was underscore earlier in the Washington poolside scene when Gus carries his shotgun mic and seems suitable enough in a western gunslinger movie, but this time real guns are in the scene. It is another appropriation of the reflexive that underpins the critical. Here, a musical motif associated with one context/experience informs appreciation of another and provides editorial comment. Eileen walks against the momentum of the jeeps and marching soldiers past the Field Museum and the Art Institute in a striking image of culture wars—an Army against its own people. She locates John and together they drive away to try and find Harold.

In John's car, the radio issues reports of the riots. Wexler provides shots of the passing scenery and trees overhead as the car makes its way down a nearly deserted suburban road. On the soundtrack, another radio news broadcast dissolves over the current one with mayhem in the streets, and a studio newscaster describes the victim of the accident as former Channel 8 news cameraman, John Cassellis, who is now in critical condition at Michael Reese Hospital. His unidentified felmale companion, the report continues, was dead on arrival at that hospital.

This broadcast of the aftermath of the impending crash is, of course, the ultimate news scoop—constructing an event *before* it happens and reporting the preordained facts that play as scripted. Spin-doctors have since become comfortable in calling this "managing the news" if not "manufacturing" it. The apparatus of film, television, and radio combine to create this heightening of the critical stance in *Medium Cool*. The scene concludes with a blatant reminder of reflexivity as an invitation to critical engagement.

The sound of a blowout is heard, and John's vehicle spins out of control. Eileen screams and the car crashes into a tree with a horrible thud. A passing station wagon slows down so its riders can get a better look at the wreckage. From the back window, a little boy snaps a picture of the carnage with his Instamatic flash-camera. The boy is not a journalist, more a tourist or just a curious watcher and part of the mesmerized mass audience for spectacle. The station wagon moves on, and its riders do not render aid to John and Eileen. Does Haskell Wexler indict passive onlookers with this shot? Yes, but he then presents its alternative of involvement and activism. The movie camera composing *Medium Cool* zooms back and cranes upward to reveal the fire at the back of John's car on this quiet suburban, tree-lined road. In a purely self-reflexive moment, the camera then pans to the right—as the soundtrack reprises the protesters chant of "The whole world is watching! The whole world is watching!"—and there is a scaffold on which is perched a camera operator and his equipment. It is Haskell Wexler himself. He pans his 35mm movie camera so that its Panavision lens points directly at us and becomes the image being captured in *Medium Cool*. There is a zoom in to the shade over the lens and into the darkness it contains. The soundtrack of live radio reportage from the scene of the riots continues. The director, then, is himself filming the sensational car crash that just occurred. Wexler defends the shot thusly: "I as a filmmaker am guilty of the same insensitivity, but I know that I'm guilty and am throwing the challenge back." *Medium Cool* uses reflexive/reflective and critical stances to demonstrate how the mass media can rise to a sense of moral obligation and how the spectator-public can transcend its tendencies of gullibility and complacency.

It can be seen how the personal, professional and political levels have operated to resonate the themes of *Medium Cool*. John transforms from a detached and unconcerned person, keen on the mechanics of professionalism but not its ethical imperatives. The political machinations of his supervisors at the station force him from a role of chronicler to one becoming more astutely observant; the context and events of the time only reinforce his trajectory. He is now willing to sacrifice personal and professional gain to help Eileen find Harold. The tragedy of their failure, captured as cinema in *Medium Cool*, is a reminder of the perilous state of the journey but also the capability, and the culpability, of the media in making sense of it.

The tagline in advertisements for *Medium Cool* at the time of its release was, "Beyond the age of innocence, into the age of awareness." Several films released in the next 30 years would explore that destruction of innocence, provoking an awareness of the mass media's willingness to entertain and inform in stories about the systems and structures of television. Cinema, admittedly, mostly takes a critical rather than a celebratory view of its sister media.

Any discussion of films-about-television should include some examination of the authorial voice in these movies, that is the writer and/or director who is the filmmaker, and the degree of expertise in the subject matter he or she brings to the production. Just as Peter Bogdanovich and Frank Darabont brought measures of their own reflexive consciousness to *The Last Picture Show* and *The Majestic* in an effort to inform the spectator's own reflexive tendencies, writer-directors of films noted for their critical stances often have backgrounds that influence their media-making strategies. Born in Chicago, Haskell Wexler had been an amateur filmmaker since his teenage years. He began his career by making educational and instructional films before breaking into feature work as a cameraman on documentary and narrative films. He won Academy Awards for his cinematography in *Who's Afraid of Virginia Woolf?* (Nichols, 1966) and *Bound for Glory* (Ashby, 1976). His political activism informs his nonfiction work such as *The Bus* (1966), *Brazil: A Report* on *Torture* (1971), *The Trial of the Catonsville Nine* (1972), *Underground* (1976), and *Target Nicaragua: Inside a Covert War* (1983). As cinematographer, Wexler's more commercial narrative pictures also contain critiques of social structures: race relations in *In the Heat of the Night* (Jewison, 1967); rebellion against institutional fascism in *One Flew Over the Cuckoo's Nest* (Forman, 1975); the Great Depression as witnessed through the experiences and songs of Woody Guthrie in *Bound for Glory*; the quagmire of Vietnam in *Coming Home* (Ashby, 1978); and coal miner union-organizing in *Matewan* (Sayles, 1987). Wexler's personal connections within the antiwar movement of the 1960s alerted him that "it would all go down" in Chicago, and he seized the opportunity to turn a routine shooting schedule on a film with the working title *Concrete Wilderness* into the visceral and timely work that would become *Medium Cool*. As part of an emerging school of American cinema vérité filmmakers that included Albert and David Maysles, D.A. Pennebaker, Frederick Wiseman and others, Wexler, along with direct cinema counterparts such as Robert Drew and Richard Leacock, had an immediate influence on TV news gathering style in the late 1960s. Narrative filmmakers such as John Cassavetes were also influenced by the cinema vérité manner; in fact, Wexler had originally cast actor-director Cassavetes as the cameraman John in *Medium Cool*.

Paddy Chayefsky is the screenwriter of *Network*, the next film to be explored. A novelist and playwright, Chayefsky wrote for television in the mid-1950s, creating dramas such as *Marty*, about ordinary people in realistic, humble settings. Twenty years later he was ready to satirize the medium in a way that was daring and prophetic. The director of *Network*, Sidney Lumet, also had a television background. He joined CBS in 1950 and worked most of the decade directing live television drama on *You Are There, Omnibus, Best of Broadway, Alcoa Theater*, and *Goodyear Playhouse*. Moving to Hollywood he made films that addressed issues such as the fragility of justice (*Twelve Angry Men*, 1957; *The Verdict*, 1983; *Daniel*, 1984), the perils of a nuclear stand-off (*Fail-Safe*, 1964), the everlasting memory of the Holocaust (*The Pawnbroker*, 1966), police and corrupting influences (*Serpico*, 1973; *Prince of the City*, 1982; *Q & A*, 1992; *Night Falls on Manhattan*, 1999), and the radical left (*Running on Empty*, 1989). Lumet has directed over 40 films, and many, like *Network*, take place in New York City. Both Lumet and Chayefsky are wont to bite the hand that once fed them in their films. They also strike out against TV news, the ratings system, and multinational corporations. *Network*, unlike *Medium Cool*, is a satire. It is also more heavy-handed and provocative in its portrayal of the radical left and accuses it as more likely part of the problem than the solution.

NETWORK (1976)

The functions of television as a source of entertainment and information, the audience's role in shaping it and, in turn, the industry's fiat that emerges from interpreting that response, are issues addressed in *Network*. Its relevancy has not diminished with the passing of time. Several other films from the years surrounding its release offer protagonists who attempt to penetrate structures of authority while they are on their own journey toward understanding the world and themselves. They are, often, professionals in their field of work, coming to terms in a critical fashion with their roles. Cinema illuminates the terrain and explores the dilemmas that arise. While *Network* deals directly with the world of television, *The Conversation* (Coppola, 1974) focuses on a master at wiretapping and eavesdropping and *Shampoo* (Ashby, 1975) on a professional hairdresser. At the conclusion of these films, a central character is often more confused and less in control than at the outset. This cinema of frustration, while somewhat depressing relative to narrative closure, can be enlightening and empowering when looked upon as a critique of systems, and thus indicative of the critical stance. Yet open-ended films that ask provocative questions do not, as a rule, perform as successfully at the box office as those that provide simple answers just before the final credits roll. William J. Palmer puts *Network* in a context with its contemporaries:

> Francis Coppola's *The Conversation* (1974), Hal Ashby's *Shampoo* (1975) and Sidney Lumet's *Network* (1976) are perhaps the best examples of this frustration. . . . The heroes of non-genre films are more often anti-heroes. Instead of being perceptive, persistent and strong in their individuality, they are often timid, tentative, confused, and sometimes, as in the case of George Roundby, the hairdresser in *Shampoo*, not even very bright. Almost universally in non-genre films conflict simultaneously moves in two directions from the central character—outward and inward. Harry Caul (Gene Hackman) in *The Conversation*, Max Schumacher (William Holden) in *Network* and George (Warren Beatty) in *Shampoo* are individuals who find themselves questioning the operation of society. However, simultaneously, they are also constantly questioning their own motives, exploring their own interior landscapes as they move through the exterior worlds of their respective films. At the end of both *The Conversation* and *Shampoo*, the anti-hero is left alone, defeated, puzzled, and frustrated. *Network* ends apocalyptically, but shares the same sense of non-resolution for the individual which is so strongly underlined in the final sequences of *The Conversation* and *Shampoo*.[12]

A critical stance, then, is provoked in these films. Palmer justly defines these characters as "anti-heroes," and with that comes the possibility that they are not representative of the mainstream spectators and thus unable to fully integrate with the systems that these films critique, systems that might even give comfort to several spectators. With *Network*, especially, the seductive nature of television is essential to its stranglehold. Television news has become more explicitly "entertainment" in this film. The seven years since the release of *Medium Cool* had exposed viewers to extraordinary real world events while at the same time granting an increased sophistication to the technological aspects of broadcasting. Thus, the ability to acknowledge referents (a trait of the reflexive/reflective stance) continues to provide grounding for critique (an attribute of the critical stance).

From the twilight months of 1969 through the year of America's Bicentennial— roughly the years between the release of *Medium Cool* and *Network*—television networks covered specific stories which set the backdrop for the frustration of the anti-heroes in the previously mentioned films: the My Lai massacre; Altamont; Kent State; the Pentagon Papers; Attica; Watergate; Wounded Knee; an attempted assassination of George Wallace; Spiro Agnew's resignation as vice-president and Nixon's as president, followed with his pardon by successor Gerald Ford; Saigon's fall; the seizure of the Mayaguez; Jimmy's Carter election. World and national events became overwhelming forces that spectators needed thoughtful guidance to comprehend. They often looked toward the mass media. By the mid-point of the 1970s, a period that Tom Wolfe termed the "Me Decade," the potential for broadcast television to be a genuinely unifying national force was still manifest. But challenges to that hegemony were evident in two upstart, but eventually compatible consumer products that would also channel information and entertainment: in 1975 Sony VCRs invaded the U.S., and in 1976 Apple Computer began accepting orders for PCs (personal computers). As early as 1972, additionally, several innovations forecast the kinds of competitive communications systems that would soon co-exist with broadcast television and create "new media" spectator-participants. That year brought the first home video game to appear on the market (Magnavox's "Odyssey"), the first prerecorded videocassettes available for rental and sale to the public, MCA and Phillips Corp. demonstrations of a videodisc product using laser-beam scanning technology, and the first pay-cable channels offered for public subscription (achieving satellite distribution by 1975). *Network*, then, arrives at a flashpoint in American history where both media consumerism and the sociopolitical landscape are undergoing rapid transformation.

In *Network*, Howard Beale (Peter Finch) senses the emergent cocooning of spectators in their homes and bedrooms, speaks out in alarm, and then is co-opted to proselytize for holistic, global capitalism that presages the one-world, new economy of the millennial Internet era. Diana Christensen (Faye Dunaway) is a programming executive whose decisions are guided by audience polls and ratings. She pioneers an early form of reality television that features the radical Ecumenical Liberation Army and a Patty Hearst-like character, filming their outlaw exploits that are then incorporated into a mainstream network program. Diana also has her sights set on the news division, and in a further blurring of news and entertainment, she will be given control of the network's evening news show. At one point, she castigates her staff and demands counter-cultural, anti-establishment programming that includes personalities who can articulate their rage for them.

Diana's working methods celebrate a kind of "controlled nonconformity" which media uses to signify and even glorify traditionally unorthodox, abhorrent or marginalized behavior and transform it into a product or attitude that can serve the prevailing ideology.[13] Co-opting and even sanitizing revolutionary impulses makes them safe and neutralized. Revolutionary integrity is replaced by calculated pragmatism, and not wholly without the cooperation of the revolutionaries themselves! *Network* smartly exposes tactics of control through this assimilation. Diana knows, meanwhile, that there are three characteristics of television viewers that need to be exploited: a love of scandal, a taste for the lurid and shocking, and a short attention span. Watching Diana construct her strategies for television network and audience manipulation from the perspective of the critical stance provides a model for recognizing similar tactics and traits in the real world outside the film

In the movie, the fictional UBS-TV sits in last place among the major networks. Its evening news veteran, Howard Beale, is fired to make room for a younger, fresher face. Upon learning of his dismissal, a despondent Beale goes on the air and informs the public he is retiring and, realizing that his show is the only thing he had going in his life, decides to kill myself on the air in exactly one week. Director Sidney Lumet provides shots of Beale in the studio and intercuts with scenes from the control room, where the technicians are not even listening to Beale's diatribe; they are most concerned with time remaining until the next commercial. When the magnanimity of his announcement finally sinks in, panic ensues. Television and its spectators thrive on the potential, or the tease, of provocative ruptures of live broadcast events. Yet when such things really happen, both media practitioners and spectators often meet the occasion with shock and concern.[14]

Beale confers with a trusted colleague, newsman Max Schumacher (William Holden), and decides to call off the suicide watch, but the veteran anchor wants an opportunity to publicly depart with some dignity and he is allowed to return to the air. Max, meanwhile, is told that his news division, nominally an independent entity, will become accountable to the network corporate office, which is fast becoming embroiled in buyouts and mergers. The reorganization dismays Max, a traditionalist, but in the post-*Network* world of mass media this manner of realignment and reorganization has become a common occurrence. Howard is given his chance to atone and he speaks to the UBS viewers, admitting that public suicide would be an act of madness. Still, he confesses that he "just ran out of bullshit" and goes on to castigate everything including the institution of corporate-controlled television, family values, the nobility of man, and God.

Beale's "performance" is electrifying to Diana, and she first ingratiates herself with Max through an adulterous affair with him before moving on to overtake supervision of *The Howard Beale Show*. Diana temporarily rescues Howard's career and puts him back on TV advertised as "the mad prophet of the airwaves." Much like many contemporary radio and TV talk show personalities, Howard Beale is articulating the rage of the audience as he offers a vent for critique. Screaming that he is mad as hell, and not going to take it anymore, he instructs his viewers to open their windows and yell likewise. Soon, his nightly audience has increased by thirty million people and UBS has a hit show.

Howard tells his viewers that, like other prophets, he has experienced visions.   Beale's tendencies are sincere at this juncture. But the network executives will eventually exploit the high concept of a prophet-character in a TV news show as just another way to turn monetary profit. Howard is conferred this prophet status of a chosen one, his voices and visions tell him, because he is on television. Access to audiences, in a mass mediated world, is itself a symptom of validation. David MacDonald addresses the nature of the prophet as both a receptacle and conduit for the critical consciousness, the system that supports him, and potential believer-followers who are the television spectators:

> It is quite clear that Howard Beale is a prophet in more ways than one. Insane he may be, but, as with Moses, Joan of Arc, Jesus Christ and many others, he is not a phony; he is, instead, a person who sees the world in a wholly new and, to his mind, elevated light. And the incredible irony of his success is that his speeches are brilliantly delivered and wickedly composed attacks on the culture of television. The most powerful speech in the film is when the show has taken on its new form, and Beale rants on the passing of the old network president (i.e., the old-school media) and the new order of the major conglomerates. He makes the case that such large companies will use the propaganda machine that is television for ends which are more evil than before. He states generally that television is an utter lie, yet everybody gets all his or her 'information' from the tube. The only way to save ourselves is to look for truth—in religion, in books, in ourselves—and to turn off the TV. These are words, and behavior, of a true messiah. . . The audience may scream out windows with him, they may send the White House telegrams when Beale pleas them to, but they are not true

followers. If they were, they would turn off the TV, and do something else. Like all prophets, Beale is used, abused, exploited and misunderstood by the evil society. And as with many others, Beale will be silenced somehow.[15]

While Howard Beale is the oratorical center of the film, other characters engage in activities that work to advance or retard their individual development in those three areas of the personal, professional, and political that solidify *Network*'s embodiment of the critical stance. Max's affair with the younger Diana has broken his marriage and family life. Despite a level of sexual satisfaction, Max doubts, she is incapable of any real feelings as part of the television generation whose known reality largely comes to her over the TV set. Diana has stoked her critical tendencies in a way unlike that of Max; she is driven by the bottom-line and the rules of corporate ladder climbing. Meanwhile, Max and Howard were part of "Murrow's Boys" during World War II and have a tradition of journalistic integrity and quest for truth they wish to uphold, but times have changed. When UBS executives demean his job performance, Max leaves the network to write his memoirs. Diana has usurped control of *The Howard Beale Show* which eventually features a cast that includes a psychic (Sybil the Soothsayer), a televangelist, and carnivalesque aspects of a three-ring circus which are presently very much a part of the infotainment television culture—hyped-up announcers, moving podiums, jumbo screens, kaleidoscopic graphics and stages, and pulse-pounding bumper music. In many ways, the show taps into evangelical religious fervor.

William Palmer explores several aspects of religion in *Network*. Although organized religion had a media presence dating back to the early days of radio, arguably its explosion on the TV airwaves would come shortly after this film with the proliferation of cable networks in general, and the establishment of national religious programming (The PTL Club, Eternal Word Network, Trinity Broadcasting). Palmer notes how *Network* elevates the corporate villain to the level of God in society; Beale's speeches are peppered with deity references and counter-references; there are set designs that factor religious iconography such as stained glass, altar-laden boardrooms and pulpit-podiums. Regarding even Diana, he says she:

. . . graduates to corporate evangelist in another scene where she stands in a white dress before hundreds of network affiliates, extends her hands in priestly blessing and exhorts them to follow the prophecy of the Nielsen numbers. She is the Anti-Virgin who turns bank robberies, politics, even the weather, into a prime-time Black Mass and man's most fundamental expression of shared humanity and love, the sexual act, into a mechanical matrix of corporate emotions.

The Anti-Christ kills a man for getting bad ratings; the Anti-Virgin gets off on corporate success.[16]

Frank Hackett (Robert Duvall) is the Executive Senior Vice President of UBS-TV, responsible for coordination of the main profit centers of the operation, but Max pins him as CCA's hatchet man, a reference to the mega-conglomerate (the Communications Corporation of America) that, Max knows, is planning a takeover of UBS Systems and the network. This is symbolic of the collapse of news standards as Max sees it. Frank's supervisor is Arthur Jensen (Ned Beatty), president and CEO of CCA. He compliments Frank on his exemplary work in bringing the network a positive cash flow. Jensen, an ex-salesman and now the consummate corporate pitchman, becomes another "voice" for Howard Beale. The newsman had advised viewers to turn off their TV in a compelling monologue that bemoans the death of reading, edification and the culture of inquiry in favor of television's penchant for escape, amusement and propaganda

Howard Beale (Peter Finch), the "mad prophet of the airwaves" in Network. *His articulation of rage is respected when viewer ratings are high, and undermined by the network when they are low.*

Earlier, Howard had reiterated that his life, as well as those lives in his audience, has value. Now, he goes a step further and advises spectators to disengage from the false succor of the tube and reclaim those values, including that of free will. It will prove Beale's undoing, though, even as it underscores the presence of a critical stance speaking truth to power.

Howard Beale begins to reveal specific names, business and political partnerships, including interlocking directorates that force a spotlight on CCA's international dealings. One reference is to an impending takeover of CCA by Arab interests, and this especially raises the ire of Jensen. The newscaster even goes so far as to encourage his viewers to flood the White House with letters and telegrams that demonstrate anger and concern over the identities of those who are, essentially, buying and selling America. The CEO summons Beale to his dark, imposing conference room, which he calls "Valhalla" and delivers a hypnotic lecture that explains the global corporate mentality, the omnipotence of currency, and the insignificance of the individual. His performance invokes parallels with the combined spirits of Ted Turner, Donald Trump and Billy Graham. Beale had been able to generate a public outcry to stop the Arab buyout, but now, mesmerized by Jensen and with his critical capabilities neutralized, he seems to understand the futility of his past exhortations once Jensen has explained that what exists is one vast and ecumenical holding system for which everyone will stand in service. In the place of America or Russia now stands an international system of currency that determines the totality of life. The new nations of the world are IBM, AT&T, DuPont, Dow, Union Carbide and Exxon. Although the word 'globalization' had been used by social scientists in the 1960s, it was not until the 1980s—well after the release of *Network*—that the term defined this integration of national economies into the international economy through trade, foreign direct investment, capital flows, migration, and the spread of technology.

Globalization is affected by a combination of economic, technological, sociocultural and political forces. Jensen convinces Beale that he has been selected to preach this evangel.

Jensen intimates an inclusiveness that speaks to all men, with all necessities provided. This, of course, is not forthcoming. A stratified society results from global corporate hegemony, as local and community interests are jettisoned in favor of larger, more profitable endeavors. But Jensen's mixture of realism and idealism is compelling to Howard, whose critical perspective has been blurred; in a reversal, he then goes on to preach the corporate cosmology of Arthur Jensen. Combined with Howard's rants on dehumanization and the death of democracy, however, it makes for depressing television. Now, the network's viewers become alienated with talk about their meaningless existence. It is sad and, more significantly, unsuccessful television. Upon his return to the air after the encounter with Jensen, Howard is solemn and forthright with his audience. He reveals dehumanization as the future, with the whole world's people becoming mass-produced, programmed, numbered and insensate things. Obviously, audiences did not care to hear their lives were utterly valueless and the ratings for Beale's telecasts plummet.

The ratings continue a downward spiral as executives point to Beale as a destructive force that causes the network financial losses. Diana conspires with her reality-show stars and presents a possible solution to Frank Hackett: she will get participants from *The Mao Tse Tung Hour* to kill Beale on the air. It is a chilling scene—American business executives planning a capital crime—the assassination of one of their own employees. As they discuss its machinations, Lumet shows us the lobby of the UBS studio a few days later as the planned events are unfolding. The voice-overs of Diana and her conspirators continue to strategize as we see the audience parade into the studio and take their seats. Among them are a few suspicious-looking, familiar faces from *The Mao Tse Tung Hour*. A UBS executive is heard discussing Beale's insurance policy from the planning session, his buyout clauses and syndication potential. In a clear reference to Watergate, he chuckles and voices the hope that there aren't any hidden tape machines in the office.

The warm-up is over in the studio and the audience sits expectantly. After an introduction of the various acts on *The Network News Show*, host Howard Beale is announced. He strides from the wings in his black suit and tie, and stands basking in the spotlight as the applause heightens. When it subsides, the hush is shattered by an enfilade of gunfire from members of the Mao troupe who were stationed in the studio audience. Red bullet holes perforate Howard's shirt and jacket as he falls to the floor. A bank of four color television monitors, representing the network news programs on CBS, ABC, NBC and UBS are shown with real life newscasters Walter Cronkite, John Chancellor and Howard K. Smith joining the character Jack Snowden who substitutes for Howard Beale on UBS. They speak over one another while horrific images of the shooting flicker across the four screens. Relentlessly, television continues as the movie *Network* concludes.

The mad prophet is alone, defeated, frustrated and . . . dead. All but the last condition—death—also describe Harry Caul at the end of *The Conversation* (he destroys his apartment piece by piece in a paranoid delusion that someone has been recording *his* actions) and George at the conclusion of *Shampoo* (he is left alone in the Hollywood hills, distraught, unemployable and looking down upon the woman he loves as she rides away with another man). While audiences in the 1970s may have not been comprised of many wiretappers and hairdressers, the systems that are critiqued in these two films—the corporate world that views human life as just another commodity to manipulate in

The Conversation, and the personal relationships that are marked by shallowness and selfishness in *Shampoo*—are worthy and accessible areas of concern to most audiences.

Viewers of *Network* approach the film as spectators of television as well. They are aware of the apparatus of each medium. Howard Beale has the capacity to activate and animate his audiences, both in the film narrative and in *Network*'s audience, and we see instances where viewers are going to their windows and screaming out as Howard had asked. We know that his audience sent the telegrams and made phone calls that blocked the perhaps illegal transfer of UBS assets to an Arab company. His ratings are lofty, however, only when he is the angry prophet supported by other purveyors of sensation and spectacle. By making his audience an active part of the communication process, able to generate response and feedback, he gives them purpose. When that purpose is finally identified as inconsequential and Beale forces his viewers to reconcile the reality of their abject worth with the bread and circus of media distraction, the newsman is deserted by his followers and terminated, literally, by his employer. While this can be read as a devastating defeat for engaging the critical stance as engendered by viewers of UBS Television programs, it illustrates cinema's power to critique the structures of broadcasting for *Network*'s viewers. UBS-TV viewers, on the other hand, pass on an opportunity to turn off the TV and a chance to begin to think for themselves. When Howard is assassinated, it is merely one more installment in their program flow, and the cancellation of a prophet who had overplayed his welcome.

Television persists and continues relentlessly. There is, admittedly, an extremist view to a satire such as this: We are told we must either disconnect from the tube, or find a place within its seductive net to work, watch, and consume. Most of us opt for the latter. But the warning of *Network*, especially coming in the mid-70s, fell upon a nation not yet media-saturated. The explosion of cable carriers and niche-channels, reality shows and pundit news-interview programs, and corporate mergers and media consolidations, would mark the following decades. The prescient commentary of *Network* anticipated many of the transformations brought about and multiplied by the emerging electronic media technologies and their production strategies.

BAMBOOZLED (2000)

It would be almost a quarter-century before another mainstream film would so consistently lacerate the landscape of American television as did *Network*. The mega-deals and corporate media consolidations critiqued and anticipated in *Network* had become the rule instead of the exception in the 1990s, as the broadcasting and cable industry restructured itself in an era of deregulation. In 1999, the top 25 television group owners controlled 471 of the 1200 commercial TV stations on the air, and monopolies and mergers increased as the century turned. Looking back to 1983, there were fifty dominant media corporations; today there are five.[17] Non-traditional distribution systems such as the Internet would soon utilize cyberspace, and the hope, as always, burned eternal that more—and more accessible/affordable media outlets—would give space and time to those viewers not always able to use the airwaves for truly interactive, empowering, and culture-changing endeavors.

By the time Spike Lee's *Bamboozled* was released, the viewer had indeed become the star in many aspects of television culture. Both radio and television programming often presented studio audiences as part of the program recording process. When the live audience was not present or interactive enough, a "sweetened" soundtrack enriched laughter and other reactions at desired points, thus cueing the home spectator how to respond. Early television adapted audience-participation tactics from radio whereby ordinary people (i.e., not media personalities) engaged in the programming. These took the form of game show contestants, "man-on-the-street" interviews and commercial testimonials. Stereotypes emerged, including the "everyday housewife," "career girl," "businessman/shopkeeper," and "newlyweds" just to name a few. Some shows were merely conversational, such as Groucho Marx's *You Bet Your Life* (1950-61) or Art Linkletter's *House Party* (1952-69) where the laughs came from the host's gift of stimulating dialogue that exposed some authentic, and frequently humorous or disarming notions of his guests. A person's ordinariness was highlighted in shows such as *Queen for a Day* (1956-64) where women whose stories evoked the most sympathy were awarded home appliances and timesaving devices that would supposedly ease their homemaking burdens. *Candid Camera* (1948-present) spotlighted the antics of "people caught in the act of being themselves" according to creator Allen Funt; hidden cameras and microphones were employed in setups meant to create surprising or startling responses. The conscious ploy for recognition in *Queen for a Day* and the undercover revelations of *Candid Camera* and its many descendants such as *America's Funniest Home Videos* (1989-present) have developed into the reality shows of recent times (*An American Family, Survivor, The Real World, The Apprentice, COPs, Average Joe, Blind Date, The Osbornes, Who Wants to Marry a Millionaire?*) and even extend into variations on carnival freak shows such as *The Littlest Groom, Fear Factor,* and *Newlyweds*. Talent search programs from *Ted Mack Amateur Hour* (1948-70) to *American Idol* (2002-present) likewise operate "in the now" pursuant to Andy Warhol's dictum that everyone would be capable of fifteen

minutes of fame in the mass media age. These programs often reflect upon
other cultural and media activities with less regard for historical and critical
sensibilities than for a marketing strategy to enthrall and hold viewers. Although it examines African-American programming at a modern TV network,
Bamboozled invites an excursion into the past 200 years of representation and
encourages a critical stance to build upon its reflexive/reflective evocations.

In the years since *Network*, developments in the consumer camcorder market had put affordable, portable, lightweight video cameras into the hands of
hobbyists and amateur filmmakers, as well as others who merely wanted to
record aspects of their life and times. This technology effectively replaced
the home-movie practitioners who used 8mm, Super 8mm and 16mm celluloid for their image making and preservation. Video, of course, offered
instantaneous playback and the ability to reuse tape stock, two attributes that
made it attractive and affordable for many. Beginning in the early 1970s with
consumer portapack recording decks that were cable-connected to a shoulder-
mounted camera, the next analog recording wave was facilitated with VHS,
Beta, 8mm, and VHS-C cameras that were self-contained as one unit. More
recently, broadcast quality digital video is captured on camcorders less than
the size of a thick, mass-market paperback book with tape cartridges only
slightly larger than a matchbox. With consumers now technically able to create and edit their own video images, they were more poised than ever to "do"
television. The boom in local cable access and in video production courses as
early as elementary and high school also facilitated a culture that encouraged
the mirroring of mediaplay seen on the increasing number of national cable
and digital video channels in most households. Less prevalent, however, were
critiques of the new televisual culture, critiques that could often be at odds
with TV's mandate of celebrating consumerism. With the increase of technology and opportunities for expression, the question "Who speaks for whom?"
became more relevant. *Bamboozled* reveals itself in this atmosphere.

Pierre Delacroix (Damon Wayans) is an Ivy League-educated writer and
the only African-American executive at CNS, a struggling television network. Their New York offices stand amidst several other media outlets in
an intensely competitive industry that has grown considerably in consumer
choices since the mid-1970s. Those outlets, out of necessity, have begun to
cater to minority programming demands, and are scrutinizing how they represent those faces and voices. Thus, Delacroix is both token and beacon in these
times. Like Sidney Lumet, director-writer Spike Lee satirizes the structures
of television, its owners, decision-makers, performers, advertisers and, to a
greater extent than *Network*, the TV audiences who are either complacent or
resistant to its programming.

Delacroix's boss Dunwitty (Michael Rapaport), like any TV executive, craves higher ratings and instructs Pierre to create a hit show or be fired. Dunwitty presumes his own awareness of black culture. He fills his office with African-American sports memorabilia, overcompensates for his whiteness by feebly attempting ghetto street slang, and gives Black Power salutes. The white media establishment and its public relations spin-doctors are further caricatured by network consultant and publicist Myrna Goldfarb (Dina Pearlman) who claims she has a Ph.D. in African-American Studies and even lived with a black man! She makes offensive programming seem relatively benign in an illustration of how the power elite can rationalize that which is reprehensible and marginalized so that racial affronts are willfully accepted by the public. Here, the strategy of controlled nonconformity is applied, at first, to accent racial distinctions, and then to diffuse and trivialize them through distortion and hyperbole when they are featured as television entertainment.

In *Network*, Diana's breakthrough series—*The Mao Tse Tung Hour*—diffuses and trivializes radical politics by placing it in the context and service of television entertainment. In *Bamboozled*, Pierre's attempt at creating the most offensive and racist TV production—*Mantan: The New Millennium Minstrel Show*—backfires when it fails as an example of racism and becomes an entertainment success.

Pierre offers *Mantan: The New Millennium Minstrel Show* as an example of bald racism, hoping both the public and the network executives will recognize the folly of its extremity. The program features a Stepin' Fetchit-inspired character called Sleep 'n Eat (Womack, played by Tommy Davidson) along with Mantan (Manray, played by Savion Glover) and the Alabama Porch Monkeys in a series of vaudeville sketches reminiscent of nineteenth century minstrel shows.

To Pierre's surprise, however, the show becomes a hit. Black audiences seem to perceive it as an ironic appropriation of their past, and multiracial audiences see it as a form of resistance to mainstream politically-correct postures. As the ratings and critical reviews validate the show's success, Pierre accepts his creation, despite warnings from his assistant Sloan (Jada Pinkett-Smith) and her activist brother Big Blak Afrika (Mos Def). It is not until the stars of *Mantan* ultimately defect and Big Blak's gang usurps some control of the programming that Pierre begins to question his display of "entertainment." The revelations are meant to operate on the three levels of the personal, professional, and political.

As the characters, and by extension the spectators of this film engage in the potential for transformation, *Bamboozled* questions the notion of authenticity. In a general sense, it asks, Who can speak for whom? But other

*Womack and Mantan (Tommy
Davidson and Savion Glover) in
their roles as Sleep 'n Eat—"two
real coons"—before the television
cameras on* Mantan: The New
Millennium Minstrel Show *in*
Bamboozled.

thought-provoking inquiries are made by the critical stance, some of which
are answered more satisfactorily than others: What are our responsibilities for
fully understanding the past? Is the ease with which it can be distorted or even
sublimated a coping strategy to accommodate the difficulty of the present?
Are there ways that we can, perhaps unknowingly but with the complicity of
the mass media, engineer our own ruin? The answers to these questions are
that we have a total responsibility, often sublimate the need to confront it, and
indeed can be undermined by forces in the mass media.

The title of the film is inspired by Malcolm X, who warned against being
"hoodwinked" by false teachings. While *Network* never broaches the subject
of institutionalized racism, one of its signature lines about anger and refus-
ing to take it anymore is spoken by Manray on the air in *Bamboozled* and
powerfully resonates against that crime. He asks his "cousins" to go to their
windows and yell likewise to all who will listen. The shell game of television, according to *Bamboozled*, is to hoodwink or bamboozle spectators out
of their time, energy, talent, money, and identity.

Spike Lee is America's best-known African-American filmmaker and provokes black viewers, especially in this film and in many of his others, to "wake up!" Interpreting Lee's films requires spectators to consider both contextual and textual factors. Gerald R. Butters notes:

> The filmmaker is asking black audiences to seriously consider the entertainment they view on a daily basis and question how this medium impacts the navigation of their everyday lives. These contextual factors are critical in the social formation of the black community. Unfortunately, some critics are so far removed from this community that they would not understand the majority of intertextual knowledge which Lee transmits into film or the social dynamics presently at work in the African-American community. Simply put, how can you interpret Lee's films if you haven't watched hours of misogynistic and homophobic rap videos on BET or unbelievably insulting black characterizations on television comedies on the UPN, WB or Fox networks.[18]

Indeed, that reflexivity is evident with the casting of Wayans as Pierre Delacroix. Dunwitty tells him at one point that he knows you Pierre is familiar with minstrel shows and variety shows like *In Living Color*. That is the Fox TV sketch-program that Wayans and his siblings (Keenan Ivory, Marlon, Kim, Shawn) used as a springboard to Hollywood success. But Lee makes Delacroix self-conscious about his background and not a little ashamed of his own father, a character named Junebug portrayed by standup comic Paul Mooney. Their attempt at mutual understanding falls short of reconciliation, as Pierre professionally distances himself from the working-class, chitlin' circuit world of his father. *Bamboozled* addresses network politics, urban discontent, family dysfunction, racial and cultural stereotyping, art and egoism, gang violence and even inserts a romantic subplot.

Bamboozled begins in the penthouse apartment of Pierre Delacroix, prominently featuring a large picture window that is also a clock. Spike Lee's films often are described as "wake up calls" and their imagery telegraphs that view. Delacroix is getting up for the day and preparing to go to work. As a narrator's voice-over in the film, he defines "satire" for the audience as a literary work in which human vice or folly is ridiculed or attacked scornfully, and as a branch of literature that composes such work. He continues with a definition of "irony" as derision or caustic wit used to attack or expose folly, vice or stupidity. Indeed, an academic and slightly haughty tone of the film is announced in this voice-over. Pierre's words are clearly enunciated, sounding crisp and eloquent. Pierre talks this way because he is unsure of his identity and has an issue with his blackness. He had, in fact, changed his name from Peter Dothan to its current, more effete incarnation. Sloan's brother, meanwhile, elects to call himself Big Blak African instead of Julius, his given name. He points to other African Americans who made the decision to rename themselves, such as Muhammad Ali and Malcolm X. The ability to name, or rename, certain things imbues the designator with some power or control. It implies the right and the desire to change perceptions of observers as well as a self-perception. Lee pokes fun at designer Tommy Hilfiger with a commercial parody in *Bamboozled* using a character named 'Timmi Hillnigger', lampooning both the white merchants who benefit from ghetto garb and commodities-as-attitudes, the black consumers who willingly wear the Hilfiger logo as a walking billboard, and also the white consumers who buy into the product and think they have gained authentic access to black culture.

Pierre passes two street performers—Womack and Manray—dancing for a crowd gathered outside the CNS network offices. He has obviously witnessed their act before and gives them some money as they offer their talent services to the network man. Here, two worlds intersect—that of a self-satisfied, affluent, professional African-American and that of itinerant performers who know not from where their next meal will come.

When Delacroix is commissioned by Dunwitty to write an edgy show with black credibility, he is listening to a man who is unaware of the difference between liking a culture, appreciating a culture, and bogarting it (trying to take it over). Yet, Dunwitty—with a picture of "Number 24" on his office wall whom Pierre is unable to identify as Willie Mays—continues to berate his worker for not being black enough. At home that night while eating Chinese food (another white signifier), Delacroix stares at his flat-screen TV that is not turned on. He recites a mantra that is printed on a placard atop his set: "Feed the idiot box. Idiot, feed the idiot box." With Sloan's help, he hires Womack and Manray who have just been evicted from their building. Delacroix perceives that Dunwitty wants a "coon show" so that's what he intends to give him. The show will be so negative, so offensive and racist that he will prove a point. The point being that the network does not want to see African-Americans on television unless they are buffoons. Pierre is confident the show will fail and he will be fired and/or released from his contract.[19]

Delacroix begins researching his program-to-be with viewings of old *Amos 'n' Andy* TV shows. He meets with Womack and Manray and tells them the pilot show may be all that is accomplished, depending upon audience response. They become willing pawns, seduced by the lure of television stardom whatever the face, and eventually are introduced as "Mantan and Sleep 'n' Eat. Two real coons . . . The Dusty Duo." Dunwitty nearly salivates when Pierre clicks off their traits: ignorant, dull-witted, lazy, and unlucky! He admits there will be other characters as well--Honeycutt, Rastus, Topsy and Little Nigger Jim, Sambo and Aunt Jemima. With Pierre's goading, Dunwitty become giddy with the hope of high ratings. Sloan, Manray, and Womack, meanwhile, are somewhat skeptical of this charade that seems to be coming into a life of its own. Even Pierre appears carried off by thoughts of his own Frankenstein-like creation at this point. When Dunwitty suggests a plantation setting for the ensemble he calls "Alabama Porch Monkeys," Sloan objects, but then Pierre ups the ante and suggests a watermelon patch environment because he knows there'll be nothing else like it on television! Add to this the demand that the stars wear blackface, to which Manray agrees because, he argues, they are black anyway and the dancing is genuine, too. Then Manray is asked to dance on Dunwitty's desk. His artistry is most assured as he taps away, agreeable but not a little submissive.

Meanwhile in the 'B' storyline, Big Blak has affiliated with a group that calls itself the Mau Maus. Sloan thinks they are flag-waving pseudo-revolutionaries but he wants her to get them an opportunity for TV exposure for their political songs and poetry. Lee perceives much of gangsta rap as "a 21st century version of the minstrel shows" and he says, "What's sad is these brothers don't even know about it." [20] *Bamboozled* makes the connection between these performance styles and the ease with which they reinforce stereotypes through institutionalized, mediated, repeated play. This is accomplished in television, music, film, fashion and politics.

When Lee shows the Mau Mau Crew at their recording session, smoking weed and drinking Hennessy, he presents them as sloppy and inarticulate, not profound spokespersons for race and cause. He cast real life rappers and MCs for the group. Crosscutting with the minstrel show of the present is minstrelsy from the recent past. Sloan and Delacroix show Manray and Womack scenes from a movie from the 1940s starring Mantan Moreland, a round-faced comic whose specialties included bulging eyes, nervous twitches, and perfectly-timed double-takes that were especially effective when he spotted ghostly figures and found himself running in place but getting nowhere. Sloan and Delacroix explain how their show will break apart such stereotypes by exposing and satirizing them. But Delacroix will become, like Howard Beale, a deluded prophet; his intentions to illuminate and educate will be consumed by audiences of *Mantan* as just another diversion of entertainment. To persuade Sloan, he tells her that Martin Luther King did not enjoy seeing his people beaten on the 6:00 news. However, white America needed to see that in order to move this country to change, and that they need to see this show for that exact same reason. While the real era of minstrelsy back in the 1800s, like the fight for civil rights in the 1950s and 1960s, might well have been another rite of passage in racial politics, its repackaging in *Mantan* will serve to celebrate, not condemn, its display. The stream or flow of television is often absent of context. Programs come forth somewhat indiscriminately and are plucked for consumption by passing (or passive) markets. And since

TV reaches a collection of audiences often simultaneously, it is rarely framed for deep understanding that accommodates an integration of several identities and publics. Viewers of *Mantan* are more likely content with their state as reflexive spectators and unable to fully incorporate a critical stance, which viewers of *Bamboozled* can embrace.

Spike Lee's films contain healthy measures of social history, so they serve a comic-dramatic purpose of entertainment but also enlighten spectators as well. This is especially true regarding identity politics. Sometimes he provides lengthy recreations in docudramatic fashion of the recent past: the Million Man March in *Get on the Bus* (1996); straight out biography in *Malcolm X* (1992); a serial killer's rampage and its consequences to those living in neighborhoods affected in *Summer of Sam* (1999); the travails of U.S. Buffalo Soldiers during the Italian campaign of World War II in *Miracle at St. Anna* (2008). His documentaries are direct investigations of racial implications in historical moments such as the 1963 Birmingham church bombing (*4 Little Girls*, 1997) or the U.S. government's response to the devastation of New Orleans by Hurricane Katrina (*When the Levees Broke*, 2006). Significantly, many films deal with racial tension and cultural identity (*She's Gotta Have It*, 1986; *School Daze*, 1988; *Jungle Fever*, 1991; *Crooklyn*, 1994; *25ᵗʰ Hour*, 2002). In most Lee films, cultural commentary is inspired by the manner in which his characters decorate their lives—their ways of dress, the music they listen to, their means of recreation, and what kind of photos hang on the wall of their pizzeria (*Do the Right Thing*, 1989). With *Bamboozled*, the director has several opportunities to display examples from the pop cultural past but acknowledges how media practitioners and audiences have constructed that past. At a meeting with his all-Caucasian writing staff, Delacroix lets them revel in their own recollections and illustrations of black America, and they are all images and sensations filtered through television. When the writers mention a classic TV show that features African-Americans it is usually via a catch phrase ("Here Comes Da Judge!" or "Dyn-O-Mite!") or a buffoonish character (George Jefferson, "Weezie") and often with the admission that this is the extent of their encounter with black culture. Lee continually intercuts the actual video footage from these references to simultaneously jolt the viewer into reflection or remembrance and to mock the writers who must construct storylines about people they really do not understand. Of course, that is Lee's point, and he underscores its persistence in media making with a snippet from *Babes on Broadway* (Berkeley, 1941) that features white actors Mickey Rooney and Judy Garland in blackface for a vintage MGM production number. All along, mostly white media-meisters have been allowed to represent the black experience. Who, indeed, is speaking for whom? While this scene is key in advancing the 'A' storyline, it also allows viewers to acquaint themselves with and acknowledge the reference points in past film or TV examples, keeping the reflexive consciousness energized in order to fortify the critical stance.

Delacroix feels he is in control, and yet, like Howard Beale, his creation of a stylized TV program will eventually overwhelm him. At the audition for supporting players in *Mantan*, Delacroix observes some real life performers—such as musicians The Roots, and actor-comic Thomas Jefferson Byrd as the character Honeycutt. Even the Mau Maus try out, but their radical brand of performance insures that they do not make the cut. They represent a threateningly dangerous, unapologetic, and non-docile performative style unsuited for television.

Dunwitty and the show's director, a very white fellow from Finland named Jukka, have made revisions and suggestions that take *Mantan* even further into minstrelsy. At the first show's taping, Honeycutt welcomes the studio audience with a call and response of "Oooooooweeeeee!" that is borrowed from Kazan's *A Face in the Crowd* where it was Lonesome Rhodes' signature shout-out. An additional history lesson follows as we see the actual recreation of blackening-up that was part of minstrel tradition. While watching Womack and Manray in backstage preparation, Sloan describes the process. They pour alcohol over corks in a small bowl and light it. The corks burn to a crisp, and when burnt out are mashed into a powder. Water is added and mixed to a thick paste. The duo applies cocoa butter on their face and hands to protect the skin from the paste. Then, fire-truck red lipstick highlights the mouth in the midst of deep, black face and white eyes. It becomes a recurring ritual in *Bamboozled*, which eventually takes its toll on Manray, but for now the pair is excited to face the footlights. "Show time!" they exclaim and freeze a pose with palms upraised, fingers flexed and pointed outward. This self-induced psych-up for a performance is a dressing-room tradition, used in several films about show business including *All That Jazz* (Fosse, 1979), *Raging Bull* (Scorsese, 1980), and with a provocative variant in *Boogie Nights* (Anderson, 1997).

The studio audience sits stunned as Sleep 'n' Eat enters in his bellhop uniform and cap, coaching the loosely tuxedoed Mantan to speechify in a perversion of the tent-revival "altar call." Mantan raves about drugs, about crack babies born out of wedlock to crackhead, AIDS-infested parents. He shouts about inflated welfare rolls and whore-mongering professional athletes. Sleep 'n' Eat echoes his concerns and eggs him on until Mantan, on a roll now, admonishes his listeners to go to their windows and yell how sick and tired they are of "niggers." He has the audience where he wants them, transfixed.

Mantan collapses backward, just like Beale in *Network* had, only he is to be revived when Sleep 'n Eat brings a huge watermelon—called a "nigger apple" much to the comic delight of the audience—to tempt him back to consciousness. The stereotype supporting cast, all in blackface as well, dance their way to Mantan's climactic freeze of white-gloved hands crossing his black face that reveals his smile and his pearly-white teeth. Dunwitty informs Pierre later that night that CNS executives loved the pilot and have commissioned twelve installments of *Mantan: The New Millenium Minstrel Show* as a midseason replacement airing in three weeks.

Delacroix gets the news at home where he seems to be distraught about the unexpected hit program he has created. A call from his mother interrupts Delacroix's reverie, and she informs Pierre that his father wants to see him. With the introduction of a new character at this point deep in the film narrative, Lee manages to contribute an important back-story to Delacroix's character, as well as some insights on the politics of performance, through the presence of his father, Junebug. A father figure is a significant type that imposes universal reflexive/reflective tendencies in the spectator since most viewers have experienced its presence and impact. Furthermore, it enhances the critical stance of the narrative as it explores the degree with which father (or mother or mentor figure) and son (or daughter) relate, react and critique one another, usually in light of their past and present lives or personal/professional potential. This dynamic has been seen at play in several of the films explored thus far, and it is also present in others to follow. At Mama's Sugar Shack, Pierre watches his father perform for a small but responsive crowd. When he tells bawdy "street jokes" Lee is exposing the professional schism between father and son. Pierre is in the comedy business because of Junebug, but views him as a failure because he works the chitlin' circuit and has not sought the fame his talent deserves. Yet Junebug is quite content with his life. Meanwhile, Junebug sees Pierre—or Peter Dothan, as he had been originally named—as a man with no knowledge of self and one living a false life. Junebug is an authentic whose act cannot and will not transfer to television because it is too candid, too black, and too real.

Mantan: The New Millennium Minstrel Show is finally broadcast and it is framed—that is, surrounded—in ways that Manray, Womack and Sloan do not expect. There is a computer-generated opening sequence, reminiscent of one used for the real TV show *The PJs* that further exaggerates the lips and noses of the leading characters. A commercial advertisement celebrates a 64-oz. bottle of "125% pure pleasure malt liquor" called Da Bomb that "makes you get your freak on." Another commercial features hip hop dancers testifying to the colors and styles of "Timmi Hillnigger" fashion; it is a satiric and devastating put-down, and exemplary of white usurpation of black culture and the management of controlled nonconformity with both white and black performers striking poses of the new minstrelsy. Lee lets the real message come through when he has his Tommy Hilfiger stand-in promise that if his customers want to never get out of the 'gheeto', stay broke, and continue to add to his multibillion dollar corporation, they should keep buying all his gear!

In anticipation of negative audience response, network publicist Myrna Goldfarb proposes The Mantan Manifesto as a series of defensive moves and postures calculated to stave off criticism. When she finally gets to her trump card she identifies Pierre Delacroix as the biggest asset because the show is created and conceived by him, a non-threatening African-American male. She concludes that the show can't be racist because Delacroix is black. Sloan admonishes her and informs the white woman that Pierre is not black, but rather, in Sloan's eyes, a Negro. We are reminded of the challenge of difference, even within a racial group, and how color and culture can affect knowledge, authorship, and authenticity. Similar sentiments were expressed by Frank's activist friend in *Medium Cool*.

With the show a hit, however, Delacroix continues to oversee its production, although he appears to be in a denial over what it truly represents. Sloan is responsible for trying to "wake up" Pierre, and she gives him the gift of a 'Jolly Nigger Bank' that rapidly slides coins into the head of an open-mouthed caricature. This racist artifact is meant to remind them of a time in history when, Sloan contends, African-Americans were considered subhuman, and this should never be forgotten. Ironically, the success of *Mantan* allows Pierre to feed that bank.

Lee situates the Mantan phenomenon alongside other cultural fads as he displays footage of the hula-hoop craze, the Pet Rock, Beanie Babies, and Pokemon. The revived minstrel fad has become equally as popular, with "Blackface" the new phenomenon evoked on magazine covers, city bus advertisements, T-shirts, and even Halloween masks. From a dissenting side, WLIB radio talk show host Gary Byrd grills Delacroix as "the Clarence Thomas of television." Pierre defends his work as "art" despite community voices—such as the Mau Maus—calling for the cancellation of the show. Lee even gets Rev. Al Sharpton and attorney Johnnie Cochran to appear as themselves in a rally protesting the show outside the CNS offices. Their chants of "Painted face, disgrace to the race!" conclude a montage that has, as in *Medium Cool*, positioned real life personalities within the ongoing film narrative. Viewers accustomed to consuming more video images than those of film would likely accept the blurring of real life with a movie about TV, especially when considering how Spike Lee composes *Bamboozled*. The film itself is shot almost entirely on digital video, not celluloid. The insertion of real characters and actions assists in blurring or dissolving the boundaries between real life and the recomposing of it in narrative films. Boundaries that are porous, ruptured, or dissolved become more arbitrary, as will be seen in the following section that explores the ironic stance. Here, a critical stance prompts a redrawing or reconstruction of those boundaries.

The office of Pierre Delacroix becomes crowded with African-American collectibles that represent the racist past. He rewards Manray with a very special one, however, in another cultural history lesson. Pierre gives his star the last pair of tap shoes worn by Bill "Bojangles" Robinson, a real-life vaudeville and film performer. Historian Donald Bogle remembers Robinson in this way: "Robinson's greatest gift as a dancer in the movies was that his sense of rhythm, his physical dexterity, and his easy-going naturalness all combined to covey an optimistic—a copacetic—air. . . The Robinson figure was obviously the familiar contented slave, distinguished however, because he was congenial, confident, and very, very cool." The character of Robinson, as a reflexive and critical device then, speaks to both Manray and to Pierre. When Manray is told that Robinson died with these shoes on his feet there is a sense of connection in those words, filled with foreshadowing. Meanwhile, at a meeting of the Mau Maus, they complain about *Mantan* and conspire to disrupt it. All the gang members point their fingers at the TV screen where the show is playing, and a series of clicks is heard on the soundtrack, the noise of guns being cocked for firing. Lee contends the group is misdirected, but capable, nevertheless, of performing a symbolic intrusive act that gains global attention. *Bamboozled* notes the Mau Maus' action as disruptive and corrective, and merely one of several ways to deal with the issues raised in the film.

The studio audience starts to show up for tapings in blackface. It mirrors and mimics Mantan and Sleep 'n Eat in a most pedestrian example that manifests the reflexive stance—sheer imitation. Womack, who has had an epiphany, confronts Manray during a rehearsal. Fatigued with performing the disgraceful routines, upset at his partner castigating the back-up performers and bristling from charges that he is not carrying his weight in the duo, Womack explodes and calls out the new minstrelsy as the same "bullshit," just remade for modern times. Womack leaves the act, the scene, and the film. This character has experienced a personal transformation and enacted a critically informed change of heart.

As Sloan's concern over the direction of *Mantan* grows, she becomes romantically involved with Manray and begins to pull further away from Delacroix. With Womack gone, the show will need to regain its balance and the high-flying Delacroix is worried. They argue, but Sloan has reached her limit. Before leaving Delacroix, she drops a 3/4-inch videocassette box on Pierre's desk. It will later be revealed that the videotape is a collection of racist film images and TV representations from the past, which could have informed Delacroix's personal and professional life with a greater understanding of his

Television producer Pierre Delacroix (Damon Wayans) with one of the numerous racist artfacts that inspired his deliberately offensive social satire, a minstrel show for the millennium.

identity and responsibility. Like *Cinema Paradiso,* past film images return at the movie's end to signify buried emotions and passions.

Despite the show's success, Delacroix is unable to gain the respect of his father or mother. His mother voices disappointment, concluding "a coon is a coon." In his office, surrounded by an ever-increasing number of racist artifacts, statues, and toys, Pierre's 'Jolly Nigger Bank' begins to take on a life of its own, shoveling nonexistent coins into its mouth over and over again without any human activation. The bank character becomes a mirror image of Pierre, a body in perpetual motion of demeaning activity but unable to nourish itself. This is the reflexive stance at its most static and dispirited, able to animate postures from the past and activate deep-seated attitudes in the present yet unable to engage critical tendencies.

T.J. Byrd's character of Honest Abe Honeycutt warms up the studio audi-ence for another taping. He is being groomed as Womack's replacement. We see the audience, all in blackface waving their white-gloved hands and wearing Mantan-logo blue sweatshirts, responding as one. It is eerily milita-ristic. "It was very important to include the audience," says Lee, "because the audience is America, the America that is watching this show, an America that has embraced this show and made it the Number One show in television."

As Honeycutt goes into the stands for audience participation and conversation, the word "nigger" is freely used with several variations and testimonies until it reaches a preposterously nauseating level. The spectacle seems part religious revival, part Klan rally, part nightclub show, and part sporting event. Backstage, Manray contemplates his makeup kit on the dressing room table. This night, even Dunwitty has donned blackface.

Eventually, Manray decides not to go on wearing the blackface makeup. When the curtain is lifted, his appearance without it silences the cheering crowd. He reprises the *Network*-influenced speech to the "cousins" and collapses again. Then Manray jumps up and dances with the most expressive energy he can muster in a natural, "non-coon" display of performance craft. Dunwitty interrupts and has security guards usher Manray out of the building. Content with himself and the stand he has taken, Manray walks away but runs into the Mau Maus, who have not been privy to the dancer's transformation *away* from blackface. This, unfortunately, allows them to only perceive Manray as a reflexive rather than a critical representation. They abduct Manray, strap him to a chair, and point a video camera at him. The Mau Maus had sent anonymous e-mails to the web sites of CNN, ABC, NBC, and CBS, inviting them to witness what would be called the Dance of Death. The networks sought a court order to carry the feed, live at 10:00 p.m. It was granted.

The Mau Maus call Manray a Tom, a disgrace, a head-scratchin' foot-shufflin' Negro. Lee shows us most of the significant characters from *Bamboozled* watching the live execution from the comfort of their living rooms. The Mau Maus fire away at the feet of a now unbound Manray, forcing him to leap and pivot the best he can. Their camera captures it all for live transmission.[21] They cease fire. Manray continues without missing a beat. Then they raise their weapons a few inches and unload them into his body. He falls and a few more rounds are discharged into it.

In his office, Delacroix destroys many of the collectibles in a scene reminiscent of the end of *Citizen Kane*, as a dispassionate Kane surrounded by the treasures and mementos of his past life demolished them. The police encircle the Mau Maus and all are killed, except for one named 1/16 Blak, its only visibly white member. He asks to be killed by the SWAT team that carries him away, using the one-drop defense wherein only one drop of black blood constitutes racial identity. On the soundtrack is Public Enemy's 2000 version of the song "Burn, Hollywood, Burn" with lyrics that implicate violence as a viable means of institutional reform and restitution in modern media and in the modern world. Embracing both reflexive and critical tendencies, the music references and recontextualizes a song first released in 1990.

Amidst the debris in his office, Sloan confronts Delacroix. At gunpoint, she forces him to watch the tape she had given him earlier. The montage of racist imagery plays on the TV, as Delacroix implores Sloan to put down the gun. She fires as he tries to take it away, her action part accidental and part purposeful. Delacroix is gutshot. As he bleeds to death, Delocroix recalls a quote by author James Baldwin (1961): "People pay for what they do, and still more for what they have allowed themselves to become, and they pay for it very simply: by the lives they lead."

Delocroix dies, and the last images he sees are those flickering racist ones on his television set—Stepin' Fetchit, Mickey and Judy in blackface, Al Jolson singing "Mammy," Willie Best at the chicken house, animated cartoons with Black Sambo characters, a 'watermelon derby' newsreel, Mantan Moreland, *The Birth of a Nation*, lots of maids and butlers saying "Yes, sir" and "Yes, ma'am," Aunt Jemima-like servants, Stymie and Farina from the Our Gang comedies, Disney's *Song of the South*, African natives as cannibals in crude, exaggerated animated drawings, and others.

While these images are part of the historical past, they are often unseen in the present, which lends credence to the notion that those who cannot remember the past are apt to repeat it. This certainly is the case with some who laughed and applauded *Mantan: The New Millenium Minstrel Show*. Yet the tendency to disallow or deny these images is still quite strong and even affected the promotion of *Bamboozled* itself when it was theatrically released. The original artwork in advertisements for the movie prominently featured a small black child eating a large slice of watermelon. The red of the child's lips complements the red of the melon, and both contrast with the ebony of skin. To call the image politically incorrect—a phrase that usually requires an explanatory context—is an understatement. And yet it powerfully communicates an expository notion of *Bamboozled*: that media representation can be misguided and misleading. *The New York Times* refused to accept advertising for the movie that featured African-Americans in blackface, deeming that pictorialization too demeaning. So the ad campaigned was revamped and toned down. The point made here seems to belabor itself, but it informs the critical stance of the film: Unless provocative images are presented in a way that mass media structures package and permit, they will have difficulty getting disseminated. In *Bamboozled, Mantan: The New Millennium Minstrel Show* is allowed to thrive and be a ratings success under the auspices and control of CHS despite its promotion of racial stereotypes; and Manray's sensational Dance of Death is allowed broadcast due to its newsworthiness. The critical stance of *Bamboozled* considers the reflexive nature of both the banned advertising and the issues raised by the film. Those spectators portrayed in the film itself are unlikely to do so. Institutions and their hierarchies, then, are singled out as needful of rehabilitation as much as the media-makers and consumers.

Lee simultaneously exhibits reflexive and critical strategies. From *A Face in the Crowd* he borrows the elevation the authentic performer and perverting him/them through the auspices of mass media falsehoods and demands. From *Network*, he has taken the ploys of sensational programming that seem abhorrent (on-air suicide, televangelical ravings, sheep-like audience interactivity, intrusion of real world violence) and "spiked" them for the millennium! Another cinematic influence on Lee is *Sunset Boulevard* (Wilder, 1950). Here, a screenwriter who is first glimpsed face down in a swimming pool—the victim, we learn, of a shooting—narrates this film about the movies. Stories told from the grave rarely reveal the full authority or perspective of their source until near the end, which is the case with *Bamboozled*. Only at the end and in retrospect, do we see that Delacroix has, in Lee's words, "bought the farm."

Between the release of *Network* and that of *Bamboozled*, the role of the television spectator had shifted from that of a generally passive but occasionally motivated viewer-consumer to one capable of more active participation in the progression of narrative play. This includes a greater interactive response to the programming impulses, but more importantly, the ability to insert themselves into the narrative and even redirect its trajectory. When the national networks pick up the Mau Maus' transmission of the killing of Manray, it is not an example of hacking or hijacking the media forum. It is a critical and creative, albeit transgressive, act that the structures of the industry allow. When Sloan redirects our attention to the media forces and representations that promulgated this rupture, it is with the hope that the repository of images brings transcendence and liberation, and not other forms of subjugation. A critical stance, then, strives to re-envision and remake both film spectators and their world.

The extremism in *Bamboozled* was anticipated six years earlier in *Natural Born Killers,* and exploited by director Oliver Stone with rampant free-association and cross-collateralizing of images and sounds from the media landscape. Besides their shared background of studies at NYU Film School, Lee and Stone are both known to construct intense and relentless filmic critiques of American social structures and relationships within them. *NBK* explores the infatuation with outlaws and social miscreants as filtered through the lens of TV celebrity, the addictive nature of TV watching and program production, and the critical stance that emerges.

NATURAL BORN KILLERS (1994)

Natural Born Killers dissects dysfunctional aspects of modern society using its characters simultaneously as audience, featured players, and purveyors of their own media myths. The film situates the viewer alongside Mickey and Mallory Knox (Woody Harrelson, Juliette Lewis) as they generate a murder/crime spree, spend time incarcerated for their deeds, and finally escape into America's heartland. Strategies of exaggeration and distortion inform *NBK*'s deconstructionist strain, lending it a surreal or hyperreal aura, and the spectator is more aware of watching a movie than in the average viewing situation. Three stylistic applications continue to stoke that awareness: the use of various recording media, an intentionally subversive manner of editing, and a heightened sense of shifting points-of-view (p.o.v.). Although these applications work together, they are best identified separately. As indicators of media making and media watching, they feed both the reflexive and critical stances in this film about celebrity, television and spectatorship.

Eighteen different formats were used to record images in the movie, including film (color and black-and-white 35mm, 16mm, 8mm), videotape (VHS, 8mm, Beta cam, digital), animation, rear-screen projection formats, distressed and filtered stock, and others. This creates a unique psychological landscape for characters in the film, something quite literally and expressively evoked when rear projection is shown in picture windows or through the windshields of traveling automobiles. Director Oliver Stone occasionally makes the soundtrack more dense than normal, overlapping sounds and layering up to three different, even discordant audio tracks. The onslaught and combinations of these images and sounds force the viewer to deepen the reflexive involvement and move forward critically. For example, the TV show-within-the film entitled "I Love Mallory" is shot on videotape (which evokes a reflexive/reflective connection to the television medium and the traditional family values celebrated by the sitcom), but the material and the framing of the shots are exaggerated through filmic techniques to foster critical awareness (a violent and abusive father figure who likely molests his children, filmed using hand-held camera and distorted close-ups with a fish-eye lens).

Within the movie there are nearly 3,000 cuts, approximately 38 for every minute of film.[22] Two types of rhythms associated with film cutting, internal and external, are used. Internal rhythm is linked to the action happening within the frame. Traditionally, a slow, internal rhythm might be evident when a character is at rest, quietly eating lunch or sitting on a park bench, or perhaps in the initial stages of a romantic interlude. A quick internal rhythm would likely be inherent in a bank robbery after an alarm has been sounded, during the closing moments of a particularly close chess match, or in an argument or chase scene. Internal rhythm is controlled by manipulation of mise-en-scène (literally, what is occurring within the frame), primarily in the composing and capturing of the image. External rhythm, on the other hand, is linked to the length of each shot and can be measured in terms of frames or seconds. Its manipulation occurs chiefly in the post-production, or editing, stage of the film. The two rhythms work together to create a poetic essence in cinema, singularly qualifying a recorded sequence with the imprint of its makers.

The editing in *NBK* leans toward an acceleration of both external and internal rhythm. Much action occurs within shots of short duration. Stone increases the external rhythm to an extraordinary pace, especially when one considers the average length of a shot in mainstream contemporary Hollywood films is about 4-7 seconds. He is not averse, for instance, to cutting dialogue within a line or even a word, sometimes to a closer shot of the speaker's face or lips. Whether Stone and his editors, Hank Corwin and Brian Berdan, use this strategy to lend emphasis or simply keep a viewer on edge and visually stimulated, the effect is ultimately fatiguing. By the end of *Natural Born Killers*, the audience has the heightened sensation of having experienced a three-week killing spree with the duo who took the lives of 52 persons, witnessed the media circus surrounding their capture and trial, and then embarked on a prison breakout with them. The last two scenes in the film may be pastoral—one in the woods with birds chirping and leaves rustling on the soundtrack, the other in the motor home with the Knox family tooling toward what the Leonard Cohen song on the soundtrack calls "The Future"—but we have arrived at both locations quite world-weary.

Along with the rapid-fire editing pace, the state of fatigue is also achieved by the shifting point-of-view shots in the film. Not only Mickey and Mallory, but also detective Jack Scagnetti (Tom Sizemore), investigative reporter Wayne Gale (Robert Downey, Jr.) and prison warden Dwight McClusky (Tommy Lee Jones) are over-the-top characterizations that force the audience to consider these players' grounding in reality. We experience their perspectives through subjective camera placement that apes their points of viewing the action. Moreover, since sympathies are shattered in any realistic way for all these characters, we seek some moral center that may exist at the very place where we would traditionally least expect it—with Mickey and Mallory themselves. If the viewer is in the position of stand-in for the duo through the use of first-person or subjective p.o.v. shots, it makes us complicit in their actions. When the opening crimes are committed at a roadside diner and Stone uses a special effects shot to place the camera directly behind the bullet Mickey has just fired or the knife he has just thrown, we piggyback on the weapon as it makes its way to its target. In the same scene, the camera straddles the killer's arm that holds a pistol as it moves from one potential victim to the other, finally settling on one and firing. Later after a vengeful Mallory has viciously attacked Scagnetti in her cell, she is filmed head-on as she asks him (and the audience) if he still likes her. This implicates the spectator as both potential and punished rapist. It alternatively forces the audience to experience the brunt of action and emotion flowing from character to character. This is a position invested with an authority of perspective and participation not normally gained from more passively filmed texts.

Slanted, or dutch, angles are employed often in the movie. Occasionally, Stone will also use vertical cutting—a slightly skewed framing that cuts to a shot that is more or less deviant from the normal horizontal axis. This provides the character/spectator with an outer and an inner moment in the narrative, with the inner being imagined and internalized, or an alternate reading of the outer reality. The inner moments are also distinguishable since they are shot in black-and-white and are also slightly mismatched with the outer action. These techniques, normally associated with avant-garde or experimental films, enliven the critical stance.

Natural Born Killers has leading characters who not only enlist the support of the mass media—television in particular—to advance their notoriety, but then go on to fight and destroy that media to gain their freedom. They ensure that the TV's craving to provide vivid stories of sex and violence will even facilitate their escape from the penitentiary. Warden McClusky is powerless during the prison riots as Wayne Gale and his TV crew provide live coverage of the melee. Television, with a hunger for spectacle, trumps the needs of the real world, which include facing its shortcomings—in this case, the justice/prison system—and restoring order through some reconstruction of it. In the end, when Mickey and Mallory tell Wayne they will be "killing you and what you represent," they leave the camera and its videotaped record to tell the tale. Gayle's murder is a purely amoral act committed by two people desensitized to their environment and conditioned by their upbringing, their parents and the mass media that distorted their value systems. Most narratives about homicidal rebellion in America end in the deaths of the main characters. In *Natural Born Killers*, they survive as a family on the run down an endless highway. Stone invites his audience to ponder the violence and the crimescape that has invaded modern life, television's compliant role, and the potential for suffocation or escape under these circumstances.

The images from television are among the first seen in *Natural Born Killers*. After some shots of barren landscape, a coyote, a hissing snake, and a Santa Fe Railroad train, a waitress is shown switching channels on a TV in the diner where she works. In quick succession there are four images. Three are emblematic of the time past: the 1950s (*Leave It to Beaver*), the 1960s (*77 Sunset Strip*), and the 1970s (news footage of Nixon resigning). Then, Stone provides a brief flash of a demon character on the screen, which will soon be recognized as a recurring motif in the film. The ghosts of TV past have morphed into the demons of TV present. It is as simple and clear as changing channels.

Mabel, the waitress, flirts with Mickey at the counter. He orders a slice of key lime pie, which is a luminescent-green just like the lights on the diner's jukebox that Mallory approaches. She makes a selection and does a seductive bump-and-grind. This entices one of three deer hunters, who have just arrived as customers, to dance alongside her. Mickey's becomes both aroused and jealous, and he soon joins Mallory in killing the hunters as well as the workers in the diner. It is a ferocious and surrealistic scene and sets the standard for the expectations of further violence in *Natural Born Killers*. These are seemingly demented characters that have moved beyond the bounds of reasonable behavior. When Mickey and Mallory leave one customer surviving to "tell their tale," the lighting dramatically shifts to low-key as the couple affirm their love for one another and pirouette in a dance to a vintage recording of "La Vie en Rose." If the ersatz romanticism of the scene's closing was not enough, Stone deploys the first of many rear-screen projections with a shot of fireworks over Paris skies on the back wall of the diner. Viewers of *Natural Born Killers* must balance being drawn to characters that truly love one another along with being repelled by their abject behavior. Stone is, however, careful to align us with the depth of their feelings for one another and the proficiency of their criminal aim before fingering the real villains in this film.

During the opening credit sequence, Mickey and Mallory drive through the landscape of southwest America. Stone mixes stock footage and images of deserts, roadways, wolves, telephone poles, horses running, newspaper headlines of the pair's exploits, the neon signage of Las Vegas, scenes from monster movies, tunnels, roadblocks, and shots of dangerous roadways that make Mickey and Mallory seem to be in a driver's education simulator car. Mallory effusively confesses that she's loved Mickey since the day they met, and then relieves herself when the pair stops on a deserted road at night. This de-romanticized moment of professed love is also a cue for the 'show within the show' called *I Love Mallory*, a vicious send-up of television sitcoms. With its ever-present laugh track directing the audience's emotional responses, *I Love Mallory* offers a dysfunctional, incestuous, violent, and vulgar representation of family values, undeterred by a TV network's guidelines for standards and practices.

Mickey and Mallory are revealed as television personalities playing themselves, comfortable with the artifice of a sitcom framework and yet ready to subvert it, which is exactly what they will later do to the larger TV structures in this film. The *I Love Mallory* episode is shot in Beta SP, a format that allows for rich saturation of colors, making the environment seem hyperreal.

It is especially shocking to witness the interior moments that are inserted in black and white during this section, such as when Mallory is groped by her sitcom father (Rodney Dangerfield) and we sense the real abuse and violence enacted in monochrome just beneath the colorful facade. Mickey enters the sitcom as a butcher boy, a meat-delivery person who sweeps Mallory off her feet, and takes her away from her home in the television show.

At select points in *Natural Born Killers*, especially after a scene of uneasiness like the aforementioned, Stone inserts parts of television commercials. On some occasions he uses Coca-Cola advertisements featuring docile polar bears enjoying the popular soft drink. From the critical perspective of cinema, this represents the soothing, narcotizing tendencies of commercial television that can frame the most horrendous sounds and images from reality within the comforting choices of consumerism. While the television viewer is lulled, Stone proposes that the film spectator of *NBK* can critique with reference and reflexivity, a tactic utilized through much of the movie. He appropriates the traditional Marxist view of editing here, as the clash of opposites (thesis and antithesis) extrapolates a new perspective (synthesis).

Mickey had spent time in prison for grand theft auto and when Mallory visits him there, it is clear that she truly longs to get away from the life with

Mickey and Mallory Knox (Woody Harrelson, Juliette Lewis) are lovers on the run in Natural Born Killers *who both use, and triumph over, the dictates of celebrity and media.*

her father. Mickey escapes from prison in a scene filtered with the ethos of western movies and that of *The Wizard of Oz* (Fleming, 1939). While working in a prison rodeo-ranch setting, a twister brews on the horizon. Other inmates are herded into a transport bus, but Mickey upends a guard on horseback and using the dust storm for cover, gallops away. A rattlesnake attacks the horse of another guard, topples it, and ensures Mickey's escape. When Mickey comes to rescue Mallory from her father, the old man is watching institutionalized violence on TV in the form of a World Wrestling Federation match. Mickey enters and strikes the old man, and Stone utilizes sound effects and music associated with animation such as Tom and Jerry cartoons to punctuate their fight. With both father and mother killed, Mallory tells her brother, Kevin that he is now free. The modus operandi of Mickey and Mallory, later revealed by reporter Wayne Gale, is that the killers always leave one person alive to tell the tale.

With the institution of television pilloried, *Natural Born Killers* moves Mickey and Mallory on to the institution of matrimony as they conduct a self-styled ritual service on a roadside bridge overlooking a picturesque ravine. She wears a makeshift veil and he uses a knife to cut their palms to make a blood oath, which Stone vivifies in an animation segment as their blood drips into the river below. The wedding is documented with a stylized balance of home movies in Super 8mm alongside amateur snapshots and 35mm still professional photography, which is how most conventional ceremonies of that sort are recorded and remembered as well.

Just over 20 minutes into *Natural Born Killers*, Stone introduces the electronic news media representative who will become an important part of the story. Wayne Gayle (Robert Downey, Jr.), a somewhat spineless character, is seen introducing the current installment of *American Maniacs*, a TV show patterned after the likes of *America's Most Wanted* and *Hard Copy*. These programs and their imitators often take unsolved, real life criminal cases and apply sensational tabloid journalism and TV techniques: an ego-driven, ostentatious 'host' (Gayle has four separate credits at the opening of *American Maniacs*—host, writer, producer, director); a jigsaw montage of words, sounds and images; flashy, theatrical and histrionic opening graphics that signify the self-importance of the show; quick-bites of reportage; melodramatic interviews with victims and witnesses; and docudramatic recreations of crimes. Gayle affects an Australian accent that connects him to video tabloidists such as Robin Leech (*Lifestyles of the Rich and Famous*), Steve Dunleavy (*A Current Affair*), and even media mogul Rupert Murdoch whose Fox Network was a groundbreaker in reality television programming in the 1990s. Later in the film when Gayle is allowed to interview Mickey in prison, a major referent is the jail cell interview conducted by video muckraker-journalist Geraldo Rivera with Charles Manson. *NBK* taps these reflexive totems, revealing the context of Mickey and Mallory's crime spree when *American Maniacs* situates them among such notorious real-life notables as Manson, Charles Whitman, and Richard Ramierez. These, and others such as John Wayne Gacy who is invoked by Mickey in his later jail-cell interview, continually remind viewers that actions like those performed by Mickey and Mallory are a part of our living discourse, made even more strident by the media's representation of them.

Stone exposes the sentimentality of television tabloid shows. The story of Mickey and Mallory's killing of a young police officer—only three weeks out of the Academy—is recounted by his partner. Officer Dale Wrigley (Dale Dye) recalls how the shooting of his partner occurred just outside of a donut shop. The victim was just bringing him a bear claw, notes the older cop, breaking down with an exaggeration of glycerin tears on his cheeks. Idealized TV stand-ins portray Mickey and Mallory during the recreation of the crime in *American Maniacs*; the real killers do not look as handsome. Stone films the re-enactment and the duo's getaway like low-budget, Roger Corman-produced films such as *Big Bad Mama* (Carver, 1974), or *Grand Theft Auto* (Howard, 1977)—lots of close-ups and quick cuts of screeching tires with lovers on the run in wild embraces, honking and swerving down the highway as they elude the police.

This sequence is part of an installment of *American Maniacs* that Gayle is currently editing, and he is trying to milk the story for utmost gain. He ponders the editing monitors with his post-production crew including David, the editor. They have pillaged earlier shows for sounds and images, cannibalizing themselves. Gayle believes that repetition is in order because the "nitwits" in "zombie-land" (his spectator-audience) just want junk-food for the brain. He asks that the piece be edited foremost to create anticipation for the upcoming live interview with his maniac subjects.

Self-referential assurances and redundancy resound in Gayle's working method. His character, however, will soon transform and eventually sustain a critical stance in the film. *American Maniacs* proceeds to provide more back-story and explores how Mickey and Mallory have become international celebrities, with their faces on the covers of countless magazines including *Newsweek, Time,* and *Esquire.* Teenagers interviewed on the street describe them as "totally hot!" One carries a sign that reads, "Murder Me, Mickey!" Another admits that if he were a mass murdered, he would want to be Mickey. An still another insists that the duo is the best thing to happen to mass murder since Manson, but much "cooler." Simultaneously, the killers reduced to a commodity fetish and elevated to the status of pop heroes.

While on the run, Mallory leaves Mickey at a motel and goes to a gas station that is bathed in green fluorescent glow. There she seduces and kills a young attendant. This serves to introduce Jack Scagnetti into the plotline. As a detective after the pair, he is expected to represent authoritative, civilized instincts but instead is simply tough and sleazy, preferring to peddle his book *Scagnetti on Scagnetti* to any lawman he sees. *Natural Born Killers* acknowledges the would-be authority figures as bankrupt and self-serving. Later at the prison, it will be revealed that Warden McClusky has arranged for Scagnetti to transport Mickey and Mallory from the grounds to an asylum and to "write any script you want" that insures their deaths and increases his own prowess and renown. Scagnetti fancies himself a modern day Jack Ruby, and is, in fact, a killer himself. He strangles a prostitute in one scene. The most venerable institutions representing family, media, and especially law enforcement are not free from critical examination in *Natural Born Killers*.

Life on the lam has indeed become more complex for Mickey and Mallory who have killed 50 people by now. So they drive into the desert. They ingest mushrooms, get lost, and run out of gas, ending up at the hogan of a Navajo Indian (Russell Means). This encounter displays how too much TV and other things ingested by Mickey and Mallory have wrought a world of ghosts and how even traditional, tribal medicine is ineffective in restoring order to a world that needs reconstructing. Inside his hogan, the Indian sits among rattlesnakes, an outcast from his tribe and a renegade shaman. The Indian, whose grandson lives with him, sees through these two white people who have come to buy or steal gasoline. Stone literalizes this power by projecting words on Mickey's shirt ("demon") that the Indian and viewers of *NBK* can see them. Then, "Too much TV" stretches across both Mallory and Mickey's chests on their T-shirts. The Navajo shows them a letter from President Lyndon Johnson consoling the Indian—now revealed as Warren Red Cloud—on the loss of his son in Vietnam. The four sit in the hut and eat around a fire. Red Cloud speaks about Mallory in Navajo to his grandson. He concludes that she has "sad sickness" and is "lost in a world of ghosts," and perhaps does not want to be helped. But as Mickey and Mallory sleep, Red Cloud goes to work exorcising the demons from them. Mickey has been dreaming and hallucinating, recalling his own abusive father and the ghosts of his past. He awakes while still under the mushrooms' influence, mistakes Red Cloud for one of those very demons, and shoots him dead.

Red Cloud's death is a turning point in the film, and the only killing for which Mickey will later express remorse. Mallory is distraught and the two leave the hogan separately, only to find themselves in the middle of a rattlesnake field. She speaks directly to the camera, asking why Red Cloud had to be killed. The fourth wall that exists between actor and audience is now

nonexistent in this film. Here, viewers are most fully participant with this un-
answered question posed to them (and Mickey) by Mallory. The snakes surround and bite the duo, striking again and again. Escaping to The Drug Zone,
a large retail outlet with an all-night pharmacy, Mickey and Mallory search
for an antidote to the venom. They nearly collapse in the aisles of the deserted
store. One lone clerk is behind the glass pharmacy office. The pharmacist
is, in fact, watching the television on which the aforementioned *American
Maniacs* episode plays starring the very characters in his building! He alerts
the police with an alarm button near his counter. So, in effect, the media has
brought about the capture of Mickey and Mallory and set the stage for the
next act. Ironically, in this super-sized drug store the pharmacist is unable to
locate the snakebite antidote, and the pair is forced to return to the outside
world. Mallory has run into the gathering storm of policemen. A Japanese
camera crew is also on the scene. Its female reporter notes with perkiness how
Mickey is quite virile and has a very large gun. And then, once he is subdued,
she describes his as "rendered impotent." Considering the language, framing,
and media coverage of this saga, sex and violence intertwine with universal
alacrity. Jack Scagnetti strangleholds Mallory, cuts her chest to draw blood,
and convinces Mickey to come out and surrender. Mickey taunts Jack as he
points to the meager coverage of the event by a one-camera Japanese crew,
noting his lowly status as a crime-fighter. Mickey continues fighting, but is

*Mickey Knox (Woody Harrelson) is the center of a media frenzy as celebrity and killer
in* Natural Born Killers.

finally taken down by taser gunfire. Scagnetti becomes drunk with power
and demands his backup troops pummel Mickey. In a scene that engages both
the reflexive and critical stances, Stone closes with a pullback shot that shows
the police beating Mickey in front of The Drug Zone, an image that recalls of
the Rodney King beating video.

One year later, after a trial that is the center of media attention, Mickey and
Mallory are incarcerated at Batongaville Penitentiary.[23] Ostensibly a men's
prison, Mallory seems to be the only woman there. Warden Dwight Mc-
Clusky welcomes Jack Scagnetti to the prison for his purpose of transporting
(but really eliminating) Mickey and Mallory. Wayne Gayle is at the compound as well, explaining his show *American Maniacs* to a neck-manacled
and handcuffed Mickey Knox, who sits listening. The success of Gayle's
episodes about the pair on the lam have led him to this point—setting up a
penultimate live interview with the notorious serial killer. Mickey questions
the newsman about the other killers he has showcased—John Wayne Gacy,
Ted Bundy, Charles Manson--and how the Mickey and Mallory segments
compared. Gayle shares the Nielsen ratings for the other programs and regretfully admits that his Manson show topped the ones on Mickey and Mallory.
Resigned, Mickey concludes that it is "pretty hard to beat the king."

Here, cinema presents television culture as a competitive one, subject to
realignment through comparisons that are understood primarily by ratings
and audience shares. Thus, Mickey has a bar to which he can aspire—a bigger
audience for his interview than Charles Manson accrued. Just as with advertising, the medium largely responsible for the growth of television, placement
and position are important in the quest for high ratings and viewer response.
In this pre-interview Gayle is pitching Mickey's interview for a time-slot immediately after the Super Bowl so as to reach the largest possible audience.
The critical stance allows one to interpret this interview as an extension of the
post-game shows that are largely discussions about the violence that trans-
pired earlier on the football field and feed the competitive nature of players,
fans, owners, cities, and leagues.

In order to seal the agreement for a live interview, Gayle appeals not only
to Mickey's vanity but also to his sense of survival. He reveals McClusky's
plan to later neutralize the pair at a mental hospital. Going even further,
Gayle posits that McClusky could well do the same thing to him because of
what he can reveal to his audience as a dangerous tabloid journalist. Their
conversation hints at a shaky alliance that will eventually betray itself. His
pitch is disingenuous, of course, because Gayle is really just interested in
creating a media event that will further his own career. He is almost hysterical
as he pleads his case, referencing those interviews that made media history:
Wallace and Noriega. Elton John confessing his bisexuality to *Rolling Stone*.

The Maysles brothers at Altamont. The Nixon-Frost interviews. Convinced, Mickey becomes a willing subject, coerced and/or complicit as well as knowledgeable and aware of TV's programming demands.

In their production studio, Gayle and his crew compose the lead-in to the live interview show, using clips from the past programs on Mickey and Mallory. Stone gives a window to the false hysteria of many media practitioners in this sequence, focusing on Gayle's private life and habits (chain-smoking, phone always to the ear, shirtsleeves rolled up, arguing over minor things with his staff, negotiating calls to both his wife and mistress) as TV monitors play a variety of sounds and images. He seems to be simultaneously exercising and exorcising his ego, and this will be especially clear when later, as a more critically nuanced participant during the prison riot, he puts down his media equipment, picks up a gun and starts firing along with Mickey.

Natural Born Killers has divided itself into three clear-cut acts. The first act, nominally about 20-30 minutes in most feature films, extends for almost a full hour. It concludes with Mickey and Mallory's apprehension at The Drug Zone. The title card "One Year Later" introduces Act Two, which ends with a recapitulation of the duo's exploits, via Gayle's program reviews. That second act layered the complications that must be addressed in Act Three, now beginning with the title "Super Bowl Sunday." Traditionally, a second act is the most lengthy but Stone elects to front-load the film with kinetic momentum that steamrolls into the middle act which is itself mostly devoid of overt violence even as it plants the seeds for more to follow.

As McClusky inspects the room where the interview is to be held, he removes potentially violent tools—a pencil, a small stake in a potted plant, the cord attached to eyeglasses. Meanwhile, Mickey is undergoing a purification rite of sorts as he shaves his head bald. In parallel action, Gayle trims his nose hairs with a small electric clipper. Finally, the newsman is poised to announce to himself in the mirror: "Showtime."

The interview is framed in TV teaser ads as a mano a mano between Mickey and Wayne, but it might as well be one of the WWF stagings that Mallory's father was watching. Hype and glory punctuate the ads for the interview show, which finally gets underway. Despite Gayle's showboating, he gets a solid interview out of Mickey. When Gayle presses Mickey to talk about his father, the inmate turns violent and Warden McClusky reacts to help subdue him. They go on to something else and Gayle wonders How Mickey could kill an ordinary person who is innocent of any wrongdoing. Mickey justifies his actions by claiming no one is innocent and that everyone is guilty of some transgression; many, he notes, are already dead and just need to be put out of their misery.

With this cue, Stone drops in a stock footage shot of a 1950s era nuclear family watching a TV console in their comfortable middle-class living room; on the television screen is a keyed-in image of Mickey being interviewed. Here is the collective, anonymous, and malleable audience from both past and present, neither shaken nor stirred. *Natural Born Killers* asks its viewers to examine their consciences *critically* and consider their own position in the continuum of perpetrator-victim. As their exchange continues, Gayle presents the theory that victims meet a serial killer halfway, but Mickey is cagey in a Manson-like manner. Still, Gayle gets him to admit regret about killing one of his last victims, Red Cloud. It is the closest Mickey has come to remorse and confession. Stone applies a digital effect that morphs and distorts Mickey's face somewhat at this moment, giving a visual evocation of demonic possession. This is the point at which Mickey begins to take the reins of the media apparatus that hang on his every word. Wayne feels he is getting his prime-time moment and allows Mickey to speak at length. Television, live or otherwise, prefers brief, pithy sound bites to lengthy expiation. That preferred mode of performance does not occur here. And, it is a potentially volatile rendering because Mickey's broadcast is going to the inmates at Batongaville as well. They watch the TV monitors around the prison with much intensity. He begins to entrance the truly captive viewers, speaking more slowly and with a kind of apostolic succession. He confesses to having demons experienced by all, and how the Indian was trying to help by exorcising them but was unsuccessful. Mickey is trancing out here, going into a shamanistic trick and although it relaxes those who attend to him (McClusky, guards, Gayle, his crew), his words seem to energize the inmates viewing the show on TV. This is a drifting moment not often allowed on national television. Stone calls it an anti-media moment. Mickey is even allowed to rise from his interview chair and walk around the holding cell. He will perform like a man telling jokes at a bar who realizes there is a bigger world to mollify. He even admits he is working in "a tough room." Mickey uses the rhetoric of performance and his own self-critique to entice his audience in the prison and the viewers at home, but viewers of *NBK* whose own critical consciousness has been ignited sense the danger unleashed in this narrative.

When Mickey starts to testify of his transformation that came about as a result of Mallory's love, Gayle knows he has a commercial break lead-in. "Only love can kill the demon," the newsman announces reverently in repeating Mickey's words. Then, he asks his viewers to hold that thought. Another Coca-Cola polar bear ad comes on, and we observe people at home in another vintage stock footage shot watching the cuddly bears cavort in the snow, reassured that they are safe from the monsters in the prison as well as the large, white, and furry ones on the frozen tundra. Returning to the interview, Gayle assumes a position of moral indignity that Mickey counters. The killer asks the journalist to consider his role in making murder, violence and fear commodities to be sold via the media. Mickey holds that he himself is more fully evolved, pure and self-aware, realizing his true calling in life. The inmates are still watching and listening to Mickey as a man, perhaps, who can lead a revolution because he has reached a stage of evolution (or, perhaps *devolution*). When Mickey boasts that the true calling is as a "natural born killer," Gayle knows he has his closer to this portion of the program. He slaps the table and looks at his crew for agreement.

With this manifest and mandate, however, Mickey has unlocked the revolutionary spirit of the prisoners who hurl objects at the TV screens and break them into bursts of sparks and glass. A riot begins in the recreation room of the prison. Alerted of the melee, McClusky tries to conclude or pre-empt the telecast and leave the interview session but Gayle implores that they're not finished because the broadcast is live! In crosscutting, we see Mickey choreograph a violent outburst as he frees himself from the hold of his guards and alternatingly witness Mallory, in another part of the prison, severely wound Scagnetti who has been harassing her throughout a sexually tinged interrogation in her cell.

Mickey collects survivors from his interview "breakout" session to go to Mallory's cell. At this point, Stone critiques external coverage of this media event of a prison riot. Channel 6-WATCH News breaks in to provide a live feed of the activities, introduced by reporter Antonia Chavez (Melinda Rama). She takes her viewers live to Batongaville Penitentiary where Wayne Gayle continues his interview in the middle of a full-scale riot. Ms. Chavez asks what is happening there and if Wayne is safe? The riot is now seen through television's eye as Gayle intones that the final chapter of Mickey and Mallory is yet to be written. When asked by the studio newswoman if he is in danger, Stone gives us one of the most intriguing insert shots of *Natural Born Killers*. It is a one-second shot of a lavaliere microphone on the white-mesh fabric of Ms. Chavez' blouse, situated between her breasts. Her nipples are clearly visible beneath the covering in this not-so-subliminal shot that juxtaposes notions of sex and violence—central ingredients in the recipe of entertainment—mediated by the camera and microphone's transmissions.

The Channel 6 News desk is a flurry of activity, most centering around Chavez who is attended by hair and make-up persons. A cue card off to the side for the weatherman even reads "Flurries, 72°". Stone cuts erratically between video (Channel 6) and film (*NBK*'s variable point-of-view shots), giving the audience an outsider/insider perspective that both engages and disorients, which is precisely the feeling of being in the middle of this violent uproar. Then, in a pre-eminent moment for fully expropriating the critical stance, Wayne Gale ventures beyond his mostly reflexive posture and into a critical one. He flails about confusedly with his camera, following Mickey as demanded, but he soon becomes an active participant in the creation of real violence more than a reporter/recorder of it.

In Mallory's cell, the emancipated Mickey finds Scagnetti. The two men compose a movie convention—the Mexican stand-off—where each points a weapon squarely at the other, both ready to fire away. It is a staple of westerns and Hong Kong action films, especially. The moment is being transmitted to Channel 6 and aired live, so its theatricality—complete with taunting dialogue—resounds with an audience. The killers play their parts and Scagnetti loses. But Stone does provide a twist to the cliché showdown here. It is Mallory, in fact, who kills Jack and gets her revenge; first, she uses a fork to stab his throat with a snake-like puncture, and minutes later she will aim a gun pointblank at the camera and finish the job. The reunited killers kiss in a reprise of the diner hug-and-swirl that opened the movie. Wayne has his cameraman frame this for the home-viewing audience, noting that the kissing couple is "doing what everyone said they'd never do again." Their embrace moves even the newswoman watching from the remote safety of the studio. Viewed through the perspective of a critical stance, the reunion is a burlesque that fulfills the needs of both television and celebrity culture.

In the Roundhouse area of Batongaville, the warden has cloistered himself and watches the mayhem unfold on several video monitors that are fed from surveillance cameras around the prison. As his world frays apart, there are intercuts of more stock footage of TV viewers gathered at their homes to witness this spectacle as live entertainment. Meanwhile, in the bowels of Batongaville, Mickey, Mallory, Wayne Gayle, and two guard-hostages are led to an exit by an inmate named Owen (Arliss Howard). This character had been glimpsed in vision-like framing earlier in the diner scene and in the prison halls; he serves a guardian angel archetype function in the plot and facilitates Mickey and Mallory's reentry into the real world where, perhaps, some hope and rebirth await them.

Wayne's meltdown is complete now. He picks up a gun and fires at the guards and rioters indiscriminately. Then Wayne raises the pistol barrel to his lips and blows away the smoke from the discharge, just like in the movies! Wayne, the newsman-cum-gunslinger, claims he is feeling alive for the first time and expresses a primal urge to kill. And now it is Mickey's turn to critique and restrict the media man, a role-reversal from their interview scene. He takes away Wayne's gun and gives him back his less-deadly camera to shoot, judging the newsman is "not centered," But Wayne still serves to make clear the way for their escape. He announces himself to McClusky and all gathered that his camera is transmitting live. Walking with the others through the mass of guards and guns he threatens to do an exposé, revealing the inhumanity and brutality that exists within the prison.

Warden McClusky, powerless in the glare of cameras and live network coverage, lets them out through the prison gate. They use TV to escape Batongaville. The demon that was infecting Mickey and Mallory—"Too Much TV"—has been essentialized in the media itself and it is used to make clear their way to freedom. Television has again trumped the real world.

Far from the prison and no longer transmitting live, Wayne Gayle is now the interview subject as Mallory videotapes him in a peaceful, forest setting to which the trio has escaped. But the newsman has outlived his usefulness and will be shot dead by the killers, with the video camera left running as the entity "to tell the tale." Gayle's fate is indeed to be no longer "live" and his last interview is a profound coup for the newsman and a fitting cap to his career. Mickey and Mallory must kill Gayle in order to further clear their path towards freedom because he represents the media—television, in particular—that they must cast off in order to be free. The persistence of the media, epitomized by this reporter who will never give up this story, must be short-circuited. Otherwise he/they will continue to find some angle for coverage of the Knox's on the run. The critical stance of *Natural Born Killers* views this bold move, this rejection of media and reconstruction of a world in new light, as an essential act of resistance.

At the close of *Bamboozled*, Spike Lee provided context to that story within the larger canvas of past African-American representations in the media and contends that the historical pattern continues. Near the end of *Natural Born Killers*, Oliver Stone allows the audience to channel-surf American television in the immediate aftermath of Mickey and Mallory's spree. A collection of real images from the early 1990s fills the screen: a WGN newsman reports on a "Wedding Day Murder" complete with color graphic of a hand gripping a knife, with a gaily-decorated wedding cake in the background; the trial of the Menendez brothers; Rodney King being interviewed; Tonya Harding skating; the Branch Davidian compound burning near Waco, Texas; Lorena Bobbitt testifying; O.J. Simpson looking shifty-eyed in his "innocence." Stone's snapshot of popular TV media during this period and its preoccupation with crime stories and tabloid journalism is backed up by statistics. David Courtright provides this data.

> From 1989 to 1991, national evening news broadcasts for all three networks averaged 67 minutes per month on crime stories. In late 1993, the amount had more than doubled to 157 minutes. The crime time kept increasing, thanks in no small part to the O.J. Simpson frenzy, which had spawned no fewer than 1,449 national news stories by 1996. Local news programs, strobe-lit with blue lights,

were worse still. One study of late-night news in Denver found that over half of all news coverage was devoted to crime, including more than two-thirds of all lead stories. Related issues such as poverty got no coverage at all. Nor was the crime mania restricted to conventional news broadcasts. Police-blotter and tabloid fare, narrowly focused on the violent, sordid and sensational, proliferated in the 1990s.[24]

In *Media Unlimited* (2001), Todd Gitlin explores how Americans are drowning in the sights and sounds and speed of the media torrent where spectators exist amidst "iconic plenitude" in which "to grow up in this culture is to grow into an expectation that images and sounds will be there for us on command, and that the stories that they compose will be succeeded by still other stories, all bidding for our attention, all striving to make sense, all, in some sense, ours."[25] Stone's film arrived before the explosion of the Internet and digital/satellite cable, which have multiplied the opportunities for media engagement. Gitlin identifies six aspects of popular culture—saturation, segmentation, sensation, scandal, synergy, and speed—that, when conflated with another recent trend, makes the media quagmire seem like quicksand rapidly overwhelming the hope. That other trend is the fact that low-end media drive the high-end media. Put another way, *National Enquirer* and *The Smoking Gun* today, *New York Times* and CBS News tomorrow! *American Maniacs* today, CNN tomorrow! Lowbrow media leads with investigative or even speculative risk-taking, their dirty work rapidly laundered but with the stains now perma-pressed to be put forth by more reputable highbrow carriers. In the aftermath of *Natural Born Killers*, audiences are confronted with even more programmed feature sensations and sidebars than ever before.

With the Knox family driving through America in their motor home as the ending credits roll, Stone scores the scene with Leonard Cohen's song "The Future." Its lyrics say "the future is murder" and later in the song state that love is the only engine of survival. Stone contends that: "*Natural Born Killers* is ultimately a very optimistic film about the future. It's about freedom and the ability of every human being to get it." Stone has verbalized the sociohistorical context of his film:

We are living at a place where all the television stations are similar, all the news is similar. Conformity is in ascendance. All of us who went to schools and colleges and worked our way into the world where we must work for employers, we all have these rules that govern our lives. We are dictated to by the welfare systems, the insurance systems, the banking systems, the television systems. And we adhere to it because it's the right thing to do. We all declare our independence in various ways. We revolt against the system with our own personal prejudices and grudges and poems. But ultimately we can't change the system. The system is a very dangerous thing. Mickey and Mallory take on the system. They kill 50-some odd people. They go to prison for it. They escape from prison. They use the media to escape, which makes them clever. But they don't take the media into the final journey which is their disappearance. They have to get into the underground. In the underground exists the anti-media virus. In the anti-media virus there is hope—hope for the 21st century in 'breaking on through'. . . getting some anti-media virus out there where you don't listen to the conformity that's sold to you. You find your own way . . . Reject the media. And be completely amoral when you reject the media, as Mickey is when he kills Wayne. Amorality? Why? Because the world is crooked to begin with. The good guys don't win. The rich guy wins. The poor guy loses. You have to be born with amorality.[26]

There is a thematic tendency encouraged by these films where the critical stance recognizes an operational intent in narrative that parallels with action of several characters. The reflexive stance is prone to readily acknowledge the restorative tendencies of the narratives and characters witnessed in *The Last Picture Show, Cinema Paradiso, The Majestic, Matinee* and *The Purple Rose of Cairo*. The critical stance, moreover, can reveal certain reconstructive tendencies of narrative and character in *Medium Cool, Network, Bamboozled*, and *Natural Born Killers*. These latter films have provided a critique of media experiences regarding television culture in particular, and strongly suggest that their structures—as well as the societies that nurtured them—need reassessment and reassembly. This is especially evident in the next film discussed, *Pleasantville*.

PLEASANTVILLE (1998)

A close analysis of the film *Pleasantville* reveals how cinema appropriates various critical strategies as it examines the role of television. The typical journey of a protagonist in storytelling can take him/her from their ordinary world to an extraordinary one, where lessons are learned and thematic imperatives driven home. They meet challenges and renew or realign perceptions in action conveyed through the tools of cinema. These include (1) establishing frames of acceptance and frames of rejection in worlds evoked with black-and-white or color photography; (2) creating literal and metaphoric interaction that inspires transformation, sometimes utilizing other media—such as literature, music, and art—as carriers of symbols for transformation; and (3) acknowledging that there is resistance to change, although *Pleasantville* affords a reconstruction of self and society as it evokes aesthetic truth through dramatism.

Kenneth Burke's theory of language known as dramatism answers the question "What is involved when we say what people are doing and why they are doing it?" (*A Grammar of Motives*, 1945). Viewers of *Pleasantville*, meanwhile, deploy engagement strategies not unlike those of David, its protagonist: interpolation, positioning and identification, along with defamiliarization and perspective by incongruity. *Pleasantville* concludes with a critical refashioning of stereotypes and expectations in the television world of the 1950s, dismantling the rigid, patriarchal society that its program construction upholds.

From the Ordinary to Extraordinary World

The natural frame of reality—the ordinary world—as presented in the film *Pleasantville*[27] is a suburban Southern California community of the late 1990s, but the first images in the movie are those of a television screen and the continuous displacement of one image with another that is the result of channel surfing. This method of watching television is anathema to the cinema experience where a single movie in a theater unfurls in an uninterrupted flow. On the contrary, here is a video wasteland of modern cable programming—24-hour sports channels, a "psychic friends" talk fest, infomercials, promotional plugs, and morning chat shows. Finally, the signal locks on a network named "TV Time!" a variant on cable favorites Nick at Nite and TV Land, and a veritable respite from the onslaught of random images. Dissonance is replaced by something conformable. We hear the soothing, mid-range tones of bouncy, elevator music that frequently underscores television situation comedy shows of the 1950s. An announcer intones this as "the only network playing lots of old stuff in nothing but black and white" as title cards flash from vintage programs such as *I Married Joan, Make Room for Daddy, The Honeymooners, I Love Lucy*, and *The Adventures of Ozzie and Harriet*. Then, the "Pleasantville" marathon is promoted for the upcoming Friday night. Viewers are advised to "take the phone off the hook and the plastic off the couch." They are promised 24 hours chocked full of pure family values epitomized by touchstone excerpts from the series such as the warm greeting (Dad voicing of 'Honey, I'm home!'), proper nutrition (Mom asking, 'Do you want some more cookies?'), and of course, safe sex (a shot of twin beds and the sound of a kiss). The teaser continues and lists memorable episodes: "Trouble at the Barbershop," "Fireman for a Day," "The Big Game," and "Bud Gets a Job." The announcer invites the audience to join all their favorites—Mary Sue, Bud, George and Betty, and Mr. Johnson at the soda shop. We learn that TV Time! is sponsoring a trivia contest, with the best-informed fan winning a trip to the Pleasantville of their choice. An animated map displays thirteen Pleasantvilles in the continental United States, randomly popping up like freckles in selected regions. Viewers are invited to flashback to kinder, gentler times on the "Pleasantville" marathon. For the audience of *Pleasantville,* and for the characters from the suburban town of time-present, this is the extraordinary world.

The commercial ends and the TV screen goes to black. Then a title card reads "Once Upon a Time. . . ." signifying the start of a fairytale, or wish-fulfillment story perhaps. *Pleasantville* invites viewers to a world within the tube. It uses cinema to interrogate that world and reveal its effects upon character-inhabitants in "Pleasantville" the TV series, and also upon the real-life watchers of the show.

Once the realm of television has been introduced, the narrative of *Pleasantville* moves to a schoolyard full of students with backpacks, busses unloading, and the requisite cliques and loners cast about. A conversation appears to be taking place between David Wagner (Tobey Maguire) and a pretty girl, filmed in shot/reverse-shot fashion. He speaks tentatively and asks her for a date. Just when it appears the girl will deliver a response, it is revealed that the two are several yards apart and that David was merely practicing words of romantic solicitation that no one else could hear. Indeed, the girl moves off with another boy as the school bell rings, leaving David alone on the grounds. A long shot of the near-deserted schoolyard has the foreground all concrete and asphalt with a few buildings in mid-frame and the sky a deep, 1950s blue in the upper half of the frame. This is, however, once upon a time . . . today.

These opening images provide the orientation, arbitrary as it seems, necessary to understand the ordinary world that film characters inhabit. It is just another morning at school. The sequence of shots where David speaks, in particular, relies on cinema's ability to solicit, provoke, and surprise its viewers and characters. There is strong identification with the youthful character in his clumsy and endearing pursuit of a date, a tendency to root for his success, and then the frustration of the reversal when it is revealed he is only capable of practicing this overture as script and not real life. The trip into "Pleasantville" will offer David the opportunity to engage with a scripted purpose at first, but ultimately be capable of actions that provoke limitless change in its characters and in him. This journey, presented by cinema, reveals the parameters of television to be limiting.

David, a fan of *TV Time!* and the "Pleasantville" series, will shift from his natural and ordinary frame of a high school senior's life within a single-parent home into the extraordinary frame of his favorite television show. The two worlds are juxtaposed in these opening scenes so that one blends or blurs into the other. The schoolyard, for instance, is filled with the children of white, middle-class families, most of who are likely college-bound. It is clean

and the sky is smog-free. The students are well dressed and apparently mindful of the cue from the bell that signals the start of their school day. Except
for the occasional pierced tongue and the automobile styles, this setting could
be the 1950s and the time-present in "Pleasantville."

The channel surfing (through 1990s TV shows) before arriving at TV
Time! reveals a postmodern, ironic sensibility in which the announcer's
commentary satirizes manners, nutrition, and domesticity, as well as the
trivial nature of small-town life that is often overly dramatized by television.
As camp, it pretends to cut through the idiosyncrasies of the 1950s—a time
when there were no answering machines or widespread use of applied fabric
protectors ("take the phone off the hook and the plastic off the couch")—by
tacitly celebrating it with Reaganesque and neo-conservative turns of phrases
such as "pure family values" and "safe sex," hinting that what we may have
thought was good for us (such as overloaded sweets) is really bad, and vice
versa (sleeping in single beds). Inferring that the culture of the past is omnipresent and considering all the Pleasantvilles around the country, the TV
Time! commercial—like the schoolyard scene—conditions viewers to the
possibility that the frames of past and present are porous and subject to rupture. Cinema's use of television as both backdrop and setting in *Natural Born
Killers* is employed to similar effect.

"Pleasantville" (i.e., the show, the town, its inhabitants) will be transformed
and reconstructed by the intrusion of David and Jennifer (his sister, played by
Reese Witherspoon) who are transported across the threshold of time and into
the frame of the TV show through the machinations of a remote control. They
become stand-ins for Bud and Mary Sue in the Parker family of the TV series.[28] This is facilitated by the appearance of a man from Reliable TV Repair
(Don Knotts), whose truck has the slogan "We'll fix you for good" painted
on its side. David and Jennifer had been arguing over their remote control,
in a tug-of-war, until it is hurled against the living room wall and breaks.
They call Reliable TV Repair and the persona of the repairman, portrayed
by TV icon Knotts (*The Steve Allen Show, The Andy Griffith Show, Three's
Company*), is an enigmatic, reflexive touch. It also introduces the notion of
magical realism to the story. David discovers that the repairman is an equally
avid fan of "Pleasantville," and is assured that he will have the set working
shortly so as not to miss the start of the marathon. Jennifer, who is waiting for
a date, becomes frustrated with the trivial pursuits of questions and answers
that the two men feed one another about the series. David's encyclopedic
knowledge impresses the old TV man, who gives him a replacement remote
control that's "got a little more oomph in it" and will "put you right in the
show." He leaves brother and sister with the tool of transport, wishing them
well on their marathon and date, respectively.

A TV repairman (Don Knotts) offers the key—a television remote control—that will create the frame-breaking experience for David (Tobey Maguire) in Pleasantville.

As David and Jennifer once again argue over control of the TV remote, the marathon has begun and a scene from the first show dispatches a similar action; "Pleasantville" characters Bud and Mary Sue are engaged in a tug-of-war over a transistor radio. David and Jennifer, in color, mirror the sibling rivalry in black and white on the tube in the background. Their argument escalates until a succession of buttons are pressed on their remote which transports them into the frame of the TV show where they continue their fight in shades of black and white. It soon dawns upon them that they have, indeed, moved through the television looking glass.

Frames of Acceptance and Frames of Rejection

Kenneth Burke in *Attitudes Toward History* (1937) orchestrates a dialectic between *frames of acceptance* and *frames of rejection*. For Burke, frames center attention on some practical or critical factors and draw attention away from others, which can be ignored or marginalized. A frame of acceptance overemphasizes what is favorable and underemphasizes unfavorable consequences. A frame of rejection will keep its focus on the unfavorable, such as the "culturally dispossessed." This tension of acceptance/rejection—cast in a narrative as assimilation/alienation, life/death, or victory/defeat—is the fuel of drama.

At the outset of *Pleasantville*, the TV community of Pleasantville exemplifies the frame of acceptance. Simultaneously, the suburban neighborhood of the present is the frame of rejection at first. By the end of the movie, both frames will have been punctured by impulses generated from the journey into Pleasantville, and it is cinema's prosecution of the TV reality that allows for reconstruction of the dual realities. Cinema upbraids the TV world, and the tension between these two environments (David's suburban world, Bud/David in "Pleasantville") will create drama. This is made especially vivid early in the film. A Wellpark Security patrol car makes its way among the rows of near-identical homes in the neighborhood. It is dusk and no signs of life are evident on the streets in this sterile setting. In their house, David slouches on the living room couch, watching "Pleasantville" and eating Cheetos from a bag while his mother (Jane Kaczmarek) is on the phone. The apparent wholesomeness of the warm and inviting world of the TV show neighborhood is juxtaposed with the dysfunctional setting in David's suburban household, as his shattered nuclear family argues about custody rights and visitation times. The real mother is a single parent. She is seen in the shadow of the dining room and pacing in the doorframe so her son, who alternates his gaze with what he sees in "Pleasantville," infrequently glimpses her. On TV, mother Betty Parker (Joan Allen) is brightly lit, poised, and speaks distinctly and directly as she deals with issues like family dinnertime and meat loaf recipes. In one shot, director Gary Ross provides both frames of rejection and acceptance with the mother in deep background on the left and Betty in the black and white TV tube image on the right. The frames coalesce in a single line of dialogue spoken by David in anticipation of Betty's sigh and delivery of the line on TV, and as a reflection of his own mom's exasperation with her ex-husband: What's a mother to do?

When David and Jennifer are whisked into "Pleasantville," viewers of *Pleasantville* are simultaneously in the world of the television sitcom as well as a nostalgia fantasy film. The siblings are recognized as Bud and Mary Sue by the parents in the TV show, Betty and George (William H. Macy). As expected, it is a wholesome, ultra-perfect, and homogenized world. Because he has become expert in the people, places, and things that comprise the narrative of "Pleasantville," David is able to maneuver through situations and even provide guidance to his sister. Although she fumes, and considers herself stuck in "Nerdville," when shown some attention by the handsome high school basketball captain, Jennifer (whom he perceives as Mary Sue) soon begins to reconsider the merits of the town and its romantic distractions.

In a pivotal scene toward the end of the *Pleasantville*, David will perform an action that is the culmination of his character's arc, or development, as well as one that sets a moral example and vivifies thematic points in the film. The black-and-white town has been imbued with some patches of color, representing the transformative power of David's action. Color, incidentally, would have been a technical impossibility for most television at the time-present of original "Pleasantville" broadcasts; this lends another weapon in cinema's critique of the video world, as will be discussed later. David's provocative actions include a major one involving the soda jerk, Mr. Johnson (Jeff Daniels), who proves to be a talented and risk-taking artist, but both his paintings and his fountain shop have been wrecked by recalcitrant townspeople. David, as the "Pleasantville" character Bud, has worked at the soda fountain with Johnson and suggests the two of them co-create a startlingly graphic mural on the outside wall of the city police station. They paint throughout the night. While the artistic process is not displayed, a gathering crowd of citizens sees its results the next morning. The purpose of this action is multiple—to express, to reflect, to honor, to incite, and to change.[29]

Transported to the sitcom world of Pleasantville, David assumes the character of "Bud" and works at Mr. Johnson's soda fountain.

As noted earlier, characters' desires for freedom and creativity often contend with powerful forces that impose rules and order, which can create tension resulting in new reconstructions of self and society. The worlds of *Pleasantville* mirror this opportunity with the film itself using the television sitcom as a flashpoint.[30]

Concurrent with an understanding of the purposeful action of David and Mr. Johnson, is an appreciation of the movie's larger themes. The images on their mural are iconographic representations of their mutual trials and pleasures that occurred in the community of Pleasantville. For Burke, the "frame" at this point in the film encompasses the tension between acceptance and rejection that must be reconciled in order to bring meaning from the drama. The townspeople, seen in black and white, mutter their disgust at the work of the two men, seen in color at the base of their mural. David/Bud and Mr. Johnson will face legal prosecution for this public display of candor, but the genie of illumination and enlightenment has already been freed from the bottle.

Defamiliarization and Perspective by Incongruity

Nostalgia fantasy films such as *The Purple Rose of Cairo, Pleasantville,* and *The Truman Show* utilize the idea of defamiliarization. The concept of defamiliarization emerged with the work of the Russian Formalists (1914-1930) and their belief that the basic function of poetic art was to challenge and renew perceptions. In autocratic or pre-revolutionary cultures, the role of the artist or critic acts in opposition to the expressions that are programmed and made habitual by the ruling elites. Victor Shkloysky contends, "The essential function of poetic art. . . was to shock us into awareness by subverting routinized perception, by making forms difficult and by exploding the encrustations of customary perception."[31] At varying levels, *The Purple Rose of Cairo, Pleasantville,* and *The Truman Show* rely on strategies of altered time and unfamiliar spaces in order to both defamiliarize and renew vision.

Another concept advanced by Kenneth Burke can be implicated in the frame-breaking transgressions of nostalgia fantasy films, that of *perspective by incongruity*. Burke discusses this in *Permanence and Change*, citing Oswald Spengler's definition of it as "taking a word usually applied to one setting and transferring its use to another setting."[32] Perspective by incongruity is established by violating the properties of the word in its previous linkages. The application of perspective by incongruity creates a new reality as it forces reorientations and reconfigurations of communication patterns.

Narrative strategies such as the "fish out of water" story apply perspective by incongruity. In this case, a character is removed from the comfort and regularity of his or her ordinary world and discovers themselves in another place or time, foreign to their ingrained attitudes, external trappings, and modes of behavior. The struggle is to understand and then accept/reject the new communication patterns which emerge from this change in perspective. In nostalgia fantasy films, it is initially the external traits—dress, language, and comportment—that draw attention and enhance a character's disorientation in the new world. Soon after, a personal or internal transformation is apt to occur that employs the system-builder of *piety*. Burke defines piety as "the sense of what properly goes with what" as a character or a spectator of film "desires to round things out, to fit experiences into a unified whole."[33] It is a scheme of orientation that results from interaction and integration. Burke allows, however, for the presence of *impiety* as a counterforce, in that former pieties can be challenged and possibly altered.

Nostalgia fantasy films that are modernist in tone (*The Wizard of Oz, It's a Wonderful Life, The Purple Rose of Cairo*) sustain the old pieties in the face of the impious and are usually restorative in their thematic tendencies (Dorothy's experiences were only dream-induced; George Bailey affirms the traditional power of Christmas-present; Cecilia retreats back into the cocoon of the movie house). Postmodern nostalgia fantasy films (*Pleasantville, The Truman Show, Peggy Sue Got Married*) situate and celebrate the presence of impiety and its contradictory concepts as a new means of organization and communication. These usually contain a reconstructive or rejective impulse in their themes.

The World in Black and White

Much of *Pleasantville*—and to a lesser degree, *The Purple Rose of Cairo*—is noted for its absence of color and the dominance of black and white tones. Television shows in the 1950s and most movies made in the 1930s were photographed in black and white, so it is a realistic expectation for the audiences to view images of the past this way. But *Pleasantville* utilizes color and shadings in metaphoric fashion, much more than *The Purple Rose of Cairo* or *The Last Picture Show*, which deploy black and white to primarily qualify an era. For audiences of the moving image today, the black and white world is not the most vivid recreation of reality. It is a representation of reality and a reminder of being in a fictional medium, in this case 1950s television. Viewing black and white films then, arguably, is more challenging for a contemporary audience that is surrounded by color in most mediaplay.

So, it is not unusual for the characters in "Pleasantville" to see themselves in black and white—with all its metaphorical connotations of rigidity, including racial and class distinctions, and its failure to grant space to alternative shadings—because the technology of color was not yet available to their world. Ross sets the film in the days when color television was itself barely emerging as a reality. In a scene near the conclusion of *Pleasantville*, after David is acquitted in his trial and the town has transformed and broken out into splashes of color, he approaches a department storefront window. The display has a television cabinet and TV images of the Sphinx of Egypt, the Eiffel Tower, and the Hawaiian Islands are presented in color. The shots only last 18 seconds, but there is a sign in the window ("See What a Difference Color TV Can Make") as the tube shows a rainbow of horizons beyond the town of Pleasantville. Literally, the world is opening up to the people of this town as color TV soon becomes a viable consumer commodity. Now, black and white represents the anachronism, and enhances cinema's ability to deliver a narrative lesson that also, ironically, acknowledges the surrender of the new technology of color to television. *Pleasantville*'s critique of television culture at this time suggests, at its most simple, that the injection of color will make the TV world more real and authentic. But it also broaches issues of identity and individuality that films can explore, using the television-wise environment as showcase or backdrop.

Pleasantville conditions its viewers to embrace nostalgia and accept the black and white environment as the grounding for David and Jennifer in this extraordinary world. When real color is injected, at first in bits and pieces (a rose, a fire, a pink bubble blown with chewing-gum, an apple), one realizes just what is missing from this world, and others that resemble it—knowledge. Knowledge is brought into this sealed and pleasant utopia through the actions of David, Jennifer, and the "Pleasantville" characters they affect. This is particularly evident as sexuality and free will are introduced as parts of unscripted action.

Jennifer, especially, brings a higher consciousness and sexual awareness to the community and toys with the 1950s ethos of sex because she is a confident, modern girl and because the basketball player, Skip, is reticent and unsure of himself when she takes him to Lover's Lane. *Pleasantville* confronts both the clichés of the 1950s and society's elevation of them as a standard by which the present may be judged. And it provides color as a leveler and antidote. When Skip drops Jennifer off at her house after their passionate embraces at the Lane—which were accompanied by his nauseous reaction to an erection—each has been charmed by the other. Skip now pauses alone in his car and notices a single, bright red rose in the bushes amongst a black and white moonlit scene.

Interpellation, Positioning and Identification

When we observe the events in "Pleasantville," it is as viewers rooted in the 21st century postmodern perspective and managed by the critique of cinema.

Interpellation, positioning, and identification are three considerations that are integrated into the production strategies of the cinema-maker and engagement strategies of the cinema-watcher. The French Marxist critic Louis Althusser has written about ideology and representation. His theories apply to the culture of cinema since movies invite people to recognize themselves and identify with positions of authority and omniscience, or subservience and marginalization, while watching films. Interpellation is the process by which ideology addresses the individual subject, thus producing him or her as an effect. Through their texts, ideologies recruit us as authors, as "always already" subjects. Christian Metz describes the process of spectatorship.

> The viewer suspends disbelief in the fictional world of the film, identifies not only with specific characters in the film but more importantly with the film's overall ideology through identification with the film's narrative structure and visual point of view, and puts into play fantasy structures (such as an imagined ideal family) that derive from the viewer's unconscious.[34]

The way in which a cinema spectator is positioned within a film-viewing environment— in a darkened room, eyes focused towards the screen with the projection of film coming from behind the head—forces an identification with the camera. The camera had "looked," before the spectator, at what the spectator is now viewing. The spectator is thereby interpellated by the filmic text. The film constructs the subject. The subject is an effect of the film text (i.e., the spectator as subject is constructed by the meanings of the film text). Here, cinema provides its most genuine representation and invitation to engage in the interrogation of the image and, by extension, of the self and society. Images promoted by television, as noted, are especially ripe targets for this prosecution. The role and influence of television in the political, corporate and media-related worlds have prompted other films to expose those areas. While these realms will be further explored in the next chapter, it is important to understand how cinema grants authority to both itself and its spectators to pursue this critique.

Leo Braudy identifies three central elements of film experience: "its visual and aural form, its context of social myth and reality, and its psychological relation to the individuals in the audience."[35] These elements commingle and evoke a critical stance regarding, in the cases of films in this chapter, television's cultural impact. Jean-Louis Baudry, meanwhile, considers two levels of identification for the spectator.

> The 'reality' mimed by the cinema is thus first of all that of a 'self.' But because the reflected image is not that of the body itself but that of the world already given as meaning, one can distinguish two levels of identification. The first,

attached to the image itself, derives from the character portrayed as a center of secondary identifications, carrying an identity that constantly must be seized and reestablished. The second level permits the appearance of the first and places it 'in action'—this is the transcendental subject whose place is taken by the camera, which constitutes and rules the objects in the 'world.' . . . . Just as the mirror assembles the fragmented body in a sort of imaginary integration of the self, the transcendental self unites the discontinuous fragments of phenomena, of lived experience into unifying meaning."[36]

The notion of cinema-watcher as transcendental-self is underpinned by what can be termed the process of frame-breaking. Christian Metz explores the gift of "ubiquity" that film makes to its spectator, conferring a status of "all-perceiving." For Metz, film is like the mirror, but differs from the primordial mirror in that "Everything may come to be projected, (but) there is one thing and one thing only that is never reflected in it: the spectator's own body. In a certain emplacement, the mirror suddenly becomes clear glass." The filmgoer, then, identifies with herself, as a pure act of perception, as "the condition of possibility of the perceived and hence as a kind of transcendental subject, which comes before every *there is*."[37]

Jacques Lacan, the French psychoanalyst, conceptualized the "mirror phase" of childhood development when infants establish their egos through looking at a mirror body-image, either their own or that of another figure such as a parent. This image is recognized to be both their self and another (something of difference). The contradictory relationship to the image—an infant seeing that she and the image are the same, yet at the same time an ideal (not the same)—infuses the mirror stage with sensations of recognition and misrecognition. Lacan views this as an important step in understanding how we become subjects and forge identities. Baudry allows that the darkened theater of cinema and the conditions of watching a mirror-like screen encourage a regression to a childlike state. Frame-breaking by a character in a film with whom a viewer identifies is an attempt to negotiate the state of alienation that results from this split between seeing the image as oneself and also as an ideal. David inhabits the character of Bud in "Pleasantville" but his attributes of self are in a struggle with the pretensions of the sitcom world. The viewer experiences dislocation as well, striving with David to first, comprehend (make sense), and then influence (make right) that world. Assimilation can then triumph over alienation in the narrative. In *Pleasantville*, interpellation, positioning, and identification ground the filmmaker and the viewer in preparation for frame-breaking that allows the critique of television to emerge.

The connections among mirror, glass, and frames are further embodied in mise-en-scène. Within mise-en-scène we can speak of the elements of set design as they inform and invoke plot and character in a narrative. Consider them as aspects of the frame-within-a frame discourse, the encased pictorialization of a posture that itself is a frame of film. Cinema examines the culture of television (itself a frame, literally a frame or tube within another box or framed cabinet) with the frequent use of frames and mirrors in *Pleasantville*. It reflects a world that is, at first, boundaried but capable to both contain and inspire expressions of limitlessness. As part of her own transformation, Betty spends the night with Mr. Johnson and even poses for a nude painting he makes of her. That representation is hung on the outside of his shop, in display for all to see, as a public statement of their love and their liberation from the town's traditions and confinements. Betty leaves the fountain and begins to walk home. Meanwhile, David has seen the mural and as he runs past a windowed storefront of TV sets, he halts upon hearing the voice of the TV repairman coming from all the televisions that are turned on in the store. The voice asks David what he thinks he is doing? David has remained in black and white, even as his agency has brought small visages of color to Pleasantville. He enters the store, and is now surrounded by several small images of Don Knotts as the repairman standing in front of a TV test pattern, voicing firm regrets at having sent David to Pleasantville. When the young man confesses he feels he has done nothing improper, the repairman's image is replaced on the TV screen with a flashback to a lakeside scene in the moonlight between Margaret and David. She is handing the monochrome David a large, red apple. He takes a bite and the picture freezes, while the repairman uses white line markings to compose what is familiar to TV football fans as a sketch of play-by-play analysis. He draws an arrow to the apple and circles it in a spiral, describing the transgression in God-like fashion as an act of temptation that demands David's removal from the paradise in which he lives. Here, cinema uses variants on TV strategies—the instant replay, file footage, graphics and analysis from sports and weather reporters—to advance its argument for a world free of TV's rules and restrictions. The repairman points a finger at David, but it bumps against the glass of the lens/TV tube with a "thunk". David quickly departs, knowing the repairman is trapped in his own frame. He is limited, even imprisoned by his medium; David, meanwhile, is liberated and capable of further activity in his cinematic one.

David runs outside, and on the soundtrack a voice is heard: "Hey, where you going in such a hurry?" It is a filmmaking strategy of transition and montage to ease the viewer from one scene to another. In this case, the line could be coming from the repairman and thus closing the previous scene, but the visuals reveal it to be the start of the next scene. The scene that follows is one of the most significant in the film. It represents a pivotal moment of character action that alters the narrative flow, but it also utilizes the spectator's combined awareness of the attributes of film and television, to realize its thematic

points. The closed world of Pleasantville is about to be further transformed
by the vision of *Pleasantville*.

Color and Consequences

On the sidewalk in Pleasantville, Betty walks briskly to avoid a group of boys
who have gathered to rebuke her for her dalliance with Mr. Johnson. A full
body-armor of color covers her—blue dress, red lipstick, and shades of make-
up and flesh tones. The rest of the town landscape, as well as the young thugs,
are in black and white. The bullies taunt Betty, noting she's "not real friendly"
and wondering aloud "if she looks like her picture" as they ask to see what's
under her blue dress. As she runs from them, David hears the commotion and
hurries to intervene. The boys corner her and continue the verbal abuse. Ross
shoots this with hand-held camera for the first time in a film that, up to this
point, has been documenting a world-model of stability and rationality, using
locked-down cameras. Here, he also uses brief close-ups to further the jag-
ged intensity and peril of the moment. Both the internal and external rhythms
are brisk. One of the bullies, the aptly nicknamed Whitey, puts his hand on
Betty's collar and menacingly compliments the dress and its shade of blue.
Just at that moment, in cavalry-to-the-rescue fashion, David whirls Whitey
around and slugs him in the face much to the surprise of Betty, the bully, and
even David himself. Whitey goes down and when he turns to look at David,
there is a smudge of blood at the corner of his mouth. Neither he nor his pals
seem to know what to make of this trickle of red. They appear equally confused and enlightened, running away in the midst of David's order for them
to leave the scene. He asks his TV mother if she is O.K. and, nodding, Betty
notices a change in Bud/David. His face reflects color and flesh tones. She
reaches into her purse, retrieves a compact and opens it so David can see his
face in the round mirror. They smile and embrace to close the scene.

This moment represents an intrusion of naturalism via an infusion of color
in a film that, heretofore, has been absent of the genuine consequences of sex
and violence. This is real as red blood can be, and not the chocolate syrup
prop used in black-and-white television. Color, as noted, is a primary device
by which cinema is interrogating TV culture and nowhere else in *Pleasantville* is this as apparent. The bloodletting is extremely significant and serves
to illustrate the levels of critique and interpretation invited through use of a
sign or symbol, in this case human blood. There are four levels that this critical stance engages simultaneously: literal, symbolic, intended, and personal.

Literally, blood is the fluid that sustains life, provides a measure of one's
health, and contains information that signifies mammalian and human com-

position. Blood is lost, more often than not, unwillingly. In this case, it is the result of a violent punch.

Blood is a symbol in various arenas of culture—the religious, the medical, the occult. The spilling of blood can incite vengeance or sorrow in those who witness it. It can prompt death, disfigurement, or embarrassment to those who suffer its loss. In nonscientific terms, blood is a mystery to many. Surely, that is the case in this moment from *Pleasantville*. When David brings violence to the town of Pleasantville with his action, he reveals a force that its citizens have never had to recognize. The action and its repercussions never existed before. By unleashing that passion in as direct and impulsive a manner as he can—a tendency that David has inspired but never personally enacted up to this point, content as he was to bide time in Pleasantville—David, too, attains real transformation as color flushes his cheeks. For the intended meaning of this scene, Gary Ross offers an explanation.

> Passions always have a good and a bad side. Living life in a truthful or honest way—in all of its complexities and all of its hues—is going to have positive and negative effects. (Bud/David) stands up for his mother and he comes into himself, so much so that he literally turns into color at that point when he completes a long journey for himself, which is a reunification and invulnerability and a reunification with his mother that is profound for him after being distant, withdrawn and disengaged.[38]

David will return to his suburban home and likewise become involved and re-engaged with his real mother in the contemporary world. Back in Pleasantville, however, one act of violence begets another as an angry mob breaks the publicly displayed mural painting of the nude Betty and proceeds to wreck Mr. Johnson's fountain and art studio. Ross continues.

> David has brought violence to this world and there are ramifications to that. It isn't that peace is good or violence is bad, or openness is good and fascism is bad. It's that many of these things are flip sides of the same coin, which is what happens when we try to repress versus the pain and the difficulty of being open. These things may happen, but they are ultimately worth working through.[39]

Symbolic Interactionism and Character Transformation

The personal level of engagement depends largely on the cinema spectator's life experiences and worldview. With who can or will the viewer identify in this scene? David? Betty? Whitey? The townspeople? Recalling the strategies of interpellation, positioning and identification, perhaps all at any given moment. Regarding the exact moment of the punch, there is likely dramatic and emotional satisfaction, which overrides these more thoughtful and digressive concerns. It is, after all, a rescue not unlike those enacted in captivity narratives so it is a tried and true cinematic storytelling strategy. But symbolic interactionism asks that we go beyond the obvious and these four levels of interpretation provide a framework.

Within the narrative itself, a character's engagement with a symbol or symbolic action forces an interlocking with other symbols and actions that propel plot and character development, as well as ensuring the spectator's continued interest. In *Pleasantville*, it is quite profound with Mr. Johnson, who faces an existential crisis. Since he has stopped wiping the counter at the fountain, he now begins to question the meaning of his whole existence. Indeed, he performs routine tasks that are always the same: grill the bun, flip the meat, melt the cheese. Things never get better nor worse. But Mr. Johnson confesses a thrill when he closed the shop by himself the previous night, a simple variation from the norm that has larger implications in the feeling it creates.

David senses the ruptures in the Pleasantville world and acknowledges this as a major crisis. He must decide whether to enable Mr. Johnson in the maintenance of this world or liberate him from it, thereby forcing a reconstruction of that world. Cinema presents David—the penultimate "Pleasantville" viewer who would likely welcome a restored sense of the show's traditions and characters—as one who still aspires to be a fixer for the ways of the old despite the relentless intrusion of the new. His hesitancy as the hero in narrative is an important component that gives the viewer of *Pleasantville* a moment to also take stock in the present and in the potential consequences of action/inaction and the risks in commitment. David is still conflicted, and he tries to convince Mr. Johnson that his job is to perform those necessary functions, even with feelings of unfulfillment, because the townspeople need hamburgers! But what Johnson really wants is to be an artist. He shares pictures of some of the past window paintings with David, who is impressed.

If there is a "child as father to the man" sensibility in David's counsel to Mr. Johnson, then it is further evident as an educative strategy with Mary Sue/Jennifer and her mother Betty. The two are washing dishes in a scene just after the bridge game. Betty, like Mr. Johnson, is one of the two adults in the town who is beginning to change. Johnson queries David about artistic expression, but Betty pursues a line of questioning about sexual expression and asks what goes on at Lover's Lane. Jennifer ends up giver her mother a lecture on sex education and the camera cuts to a full shot of the house from the outside. The viewer is not privy to the full exchange between Jennifer and her TV mom, but we return inside the house as they are finishing their talk over milk and cookies. Betty seems flushed with worry over what she has heard and notes that her husband "would never do anything like that." Jennifer informs her TV mom that there are other ways to enjoy herself, without Dad.

And now, it is time to witness the Parker bedtime ritual—with a new variation. Betty is running a hot bath as George downs a glass of milk and turns back the sheets on his twin bed. In the bathroom, Betty observes her own naked body in a mirror and gets into the tub. Jennifer, in the spirit of sisterhood, has explained that Betty can experience gratification without her husband. What *indeed* is a mother to do? If you feel sexual in "Pleasantville" and there is no one in Pleasantville to have sex with, then masturbation seems a logical choice, or at least the result of not having a choice at the moment. Cinema introduces this as a solution, one that TV culture would never explore or even acknowledge during the 1950s. For Betty in the bathtub, change occurs; "like water coursing downhill, it will find an outlet and its own path," admits Ross. Elements within the room are colored to life as she soaks and sighs: beige flowers and green leaves on the wallpaper, brown towels on the rack, an emerald green glass swan-dish filled with bath beads that are all hues of the rainbow, a grey owl on a branch outside the window seen past a shelf of bottles with lotions and liquids of different color.

The camera rotates and the ducks on the wallpaper seem to swirl in the pool of water on the wall. Meanwhile, Betty swoons to orgasm and the large tree outside the Parker home bursts into orange flames. The passion has created a kind of spontaneous combustion! It wakes the sleeping George and alerts David, who has been watching television, to run for the fire station. Betty's passion has brought the new element of fire to the town. The fire department, seen earlier, merely provides the service of rescuing cats from high atop neighborhood trees! Another fundamental, transforming event is being incorporated into the prosecutorial narrative of *Pleasantville* as it critiques and changes the world of Pleasantville. David finally convinces the volunteers to respond to his alarm not by shouting "Fire!" but by announcing "Cat." He, of course, must also demonstrate the manner of dousing the flames with the hose. Holding his nozzle rigidly before him and pointing a gusher of water toward the blaze, a fireman is astounded at the discovery of "what these things do."

Places of Transformation in *Pleasantville*

Settings in Pleasantville serve both the affirmation and the fracture of stereotypes. *Pleasantville* illuminates and skewers them in TV culture and in America of the 1950s. These locations, familiar to anyone aware of small-town life in America, include the barbershop, the suburban kitchen and living room, the soda fountain and public library. They combine with other settings such as the neighborhood streets and the front yard, the schoolroom, the public park, small retail shops, and later in the film, a courtroom, to provide backdrops for character transformation.

One such vivification occurs in the crosscutting between the barbershop where the men of the town gather, and a bridge party at the kitchen table of one of the women. The men talk about the school basketball team and their record of never losing a game, wondering if the predictability of always winning diminishes the excitement of the contests. Then the mayor (J.T. Walsh) allays any fears of disconsolation because their team is unbeatable. This always has and always will be so. It is the hubris of Manifest Destiny evidenced in small town America. Patriarchy, order, and victory will be maintained and passed on to the next generation, exemplified by a young shoeshine boy working at the foot of the mayor who has just settled into the barber chair. Across town at the bridge game, the mother of a girl who had the visible symptom of a reddish tongue assures her card mates that the doctor promised it would clear up on its own if she just stayed away from fried foods and sweets. At this point the camera dollies toward the table, in a shot that had begun with a heaping plate of sweet baked goods in the left of the frame's foreground. The mothers are, perhaps nutritionally and unwittingly, catalysts for change in their daughters. The women giggle with nervous self-assurance that the male doctor's advice is sound, but then the patient's mom quietly adds that the color has spread to her child's lips, too. At this point, the camera begins to favor Betty as the other players get more inquisitive, especially about the presence of the occasional color in other parts of town, notably at the soda fountain. The camera pushes in closer to Betty, who has experienced an inexplicable attraction to Mr. Johnson. She looks down at her hand which has just a hint of color in her fingernail polish but upon turning over the playing cards we see the bright red of the suit of hearts, a bouquet of valentines.

The Pleasantville Chamber of Commerce and the mayor himself recognize Bud/David as a hero, thanks to his actions in putting out the fire. His fame encourages Margaret to approach him with a plate of oatmeal cookies she claims she baked for him. But David attempts to set her straight and, being a devout fan of "Pleasantville," reminds her that the cookies are meant for Whitey. Margaret is insistent and when David accepts the gift he is, again, directly breaking the scripted television narrative of "Pleasantville" in service to the cinematic critique *Pleasantville*.

In the soda shop now, David notices not only jazz music coming from the jukebox, but random spots of color in other characters and props. Jennifer tells her brother that the students have questions for him. An air of seriousness pervades the soda fountain, which seems to have taken on the tone and ambiance somewhat of a coffee house, a hint of bohemia in the air. This setting is a focal point of transformations where the youth are unfettered by adult norms and seem free to ask questions not entertained in school, on the street or at home. Their intellectual curiosity is aroused and they wonder, specifically, how Bud knew to extinguish the fire. But their interests are more expansive. Margaret asks the most dangerous question yet: "What's outside of Pleasantville?"[40]

For if we are to presume that Pleasantville is a utopia—which it is not, in fact it has dystopian markings—then we have characters at Mr. Johnson's fountain who lack knowledge in the real sense. They are, however, characters that *desire* and will accept the consequences of knowledge. In this way, *Pleasantville* is not merely about the 1950s or functioning only as an Edenic parable, but it is about the attainment of all kinds of knowledge and enlightenment. There may have been a benchmark moment in mid-century American towns like Pleasantville that historicized change, such as the removal of the "No Coloreds" signs at segregated businesses, but there is no single historical moment for the liberating consequences of knowledge. It should be an ongoing process. Thus, *Pleasantville* speaks critically in a broad and mindful way. Cinema helps re-envision this era in America and in television's history, and illustrates both the roadblocks to progressive action along with their dismantling.

One student presents Bud/David with the library book *The Adventures of Huckleberry Finn* which is not fully realized with printed text; indeed, the last half of the book's pages are blank! The partially reconstructed narrative of Mark Twain in this book represents the town's process of transformation. Frame-breaking narratives such as *Pleasantville* display their reflexivity where one interior story is surrounded by another and then another. *Huckleberry Finn* deals with a young person's quest for maturity and freedom, a process that longs to be enacted by the students in Pleasantville, and a process in which David and Jennifer are engaged in the film *Pleasantville*. Spectators who identify with the film's protagonists represent another, outer rim of the framing. David knows Twain's story, just as critically conscious viewers know the *Pleasantville* narrative and can apply it in their own lives as what Kenneth Burke terms "equipment for living."

Outside the barber shop, some city fathers in black and white witness a large group of young people lining up to borrow books at the public library. By recounting the stories of *Huckleberry Finn* and *The Catcher in the Rye*, David has not only "talked" them into existence, he has inspired the others to read more themselves. The film visualizes and celebrates this new trend among the young people by highlighting certain props in color—books, a sweater, and soda in a glass. More kids are breaking out in color as the germ of knowledge is transmitted and transforms them.

The mayor visits George at his home, and at this point the spectators of *Pleasantville* are positioned within the interior lives of fictional characters—indeed, sitting in the living room with them in this segment—effectively, behind the scenes of a situation comedy as the actors struggle with their motivations and fabricated narrative whose internal logic is being disrupted. Here, *Pleasantville* the film eavesdrops on a crisis-motivated strategy session of community leaders in suburban America and, simultaneously, those channeling the sentiments of television sitcom writers of the same era. The mayor notes certain changes in the town. There is a colleague's wife who wants her husband to buy a new, double bed! Another friend's son has just quit his job at the supermarket for apparently no reason as the man recalls, "right in the middle of an order" and with groceries all over the counter! George, meanwhile, is invited to be a member of the Pleasantville Chamber of Commerce and given a pin by the mayor. He is overwhelmed and grateful to belong to this select group of leaders and opinion-shapers in the town, a cabal that will soon turn insidious.

After receiving the fellowship pin, George enthusiastically and confidently calls to the kitchen for Betty to bring out some of "your great hors d'oeuvres." But there is a long pause and no response from Betty, who is leaning over the kitchen sink, her back to the camera. Bud, instead, responds to George's request and offers to get her attention. Approaching Betty, he gently puts his hand on her back and she turns, her face now in full color. She is tearful and distraught, wondering what to do and how to face her neighbors. Bud/David suggests putting on some makeup, which returns her face to monochrome. This reference to minstrelsy—a kind of "greying up"— allows Betty to mask her true self and become the exaggeration of the stereotyped housewife role that George and the mayor expect in her "performance" of delivering the hors d'oeuvres. Adjusting her housedress and replacing the tears with a smile, Betty warbles a cheerful greeting and heads for the living room.

Carriers of Symbols for Transformation: Literature, Music and Art

Pleasantville uses art, literature, and music as recurrent carriers of symbols. They aid in reorganizing orientations of the characters and of the film viewer. Earlier, it was noted how blood contained symbolic significance; most audiences confront that significance through media representations that provide literal or metaphorical manifestations of blood. Books are the most obvious symbol—and carrier—of knowledge and, as we have seen, it is significant that the high school students begin to take on color when they are gathering

Knowledge and self-awareness are evidenced by the emergence of color in Pleasantville. *Bud/David helps his TV mom Betty Parker (Joan Allen) conceal those traits by camouflaging her spots of color and flesh tone with face powder, restoring her black-and-white visage until it can fully flourish.*

outside the library. David whetted their appetite for edification when he told them the story of Huckleberry Finn, and the white pages of *The Adventures of Huckleberry Finn* filled in with text as he recounted the picturesque tale of a journey toward freedom and maturation.

Pleasantville acknowledges the rigidity of the television world created in "Pleasantville," as well as the real world of 1950s America. However, through cinematic appropriation and representation of some of these carriers of symbols in *Pleasantville,* its audience comes to understand how historical forces of conformity and oppression were challenged. When the students at the soda shop hunger for more details, David begins to "fill in" the pages from J.D. Salinger's *The Catcher in the Rye.* There is also the symbolic presence of music in that scene. It begins with The Dave Brubeck Quartet's "Take Five" on the jukebox—a simple, even soothing jazz selection. As the camera pulls back and moves out to the street and a wider view of the soda shop in the town, the music heard is Miles Davis' "So What"—an infinitely more complex representation of the jazz idiom. When David brings an art history book to Mr. Johnson at the fountain counter, the first image is Masaccio's "Expulsion from Paradise," the first real painting of the Italian Renaissance.

Besides connecting with the movie's Edenic allegory, this painting itself represents a great leap forward for artistic expression, as it was an early example of realistic portrayal of the human form in a Biblical setting instead of the flat, iconographic styles of prior times. Notably, it is also one of the first paintings to display a single light source, a further connective to realism and its cinematic representation. The work emerges from a period that enlightened the Dark Ages that had just passed before its creation. Mr. Johnson slowly turns the pages of the book, quietly absorbed in paintings by Titian, Monet, Van Gogh and others extending into styles of cubism which will influence Johnson's own work to come. Indeed, Picasso's "Weeping Woman" will provide a model for Mr. Johnson's later portraiture of Betty.

David, who provokes an understanding of the power of literature, music and art, finally musters the courage to ask Margaret for a date and she accepts. Bounding joyfully into the Parker house, he is diverted by the TV repairman's image on the set in the living room. The mentor who provided the key to David and Jennifer's transportation to Pleasantville has been testily observing their rupturing of the town's "reality" and wants the pair to come home to the present. When the repairman admonishes Bud/David for taking Margaret's cookies meant for Whitey and altering the narrative, David turns off the set in defiance. The stage is set for the traditional values of Pleasantville to be restored, or else altered and reconstructed.

Upstairs, David notices that Jennifer is reading a book, a past time not normally associated with her character. She can't believe her brother started what she calls, in mock-fury, such a "dorky fad." Her book by D.H. Lawrence, she admits, seems kind of sexy. But Jennifer is still dismayed that she is in black and white, equating only sex (which she has experienced) with the coming of color. David suggests that perhaps it is not simply sexual activity that brings transformation. Gary Ross has said that *Pleasantville* "is one of the few movies that has been called amoral and moralistic, a contradiction which I embrace."

When Bud drives Margaret to the lake, the road takes them through orchards of cherry blossoms that gradually turn pink and fall on the couple in their open convertible. The libidinous impulse, which the young people initially experience but perhaps do not fully understand, is able to blossom and evolve into other fulfilling tendencies. By the time the car pulls lakeside where other couples are gathered, the entire frame appears in full color. Only Margaret and Bud, and the occasional "unenlightened" students, are monochrome. An associative edit—two different images linked in a literal or metaphorical fashion—occurs between the Technicolor rose bushes at the lake and a black-and-white flower arrangement in the window of a flower shop in Pleasantville, a move from the blossoming of youthful love (for Bud/David) to the hint of its first-time potential (for Betty). It is evening and Betty, still masked with her make-up that hides the hint of color on her face, observes the florist storefront through her monochrome veneer. Both mother and TV-son experience an unfulfilled longing at this point in the story.

Strolling past the soda fountain, Betty sees that Mr. Johnson has painted his front window with Christmas decorations as he has done in the past, only this time the image is of a cubist-style Santa Claus. She enters the shop to find Mr. Johnson working on another canvas, and scattered among the booths and on the walls are other colorful paintings from his hand. He, like Betty, is still a vestige of black and white. Upon sharing some of the beautiful artwork from the pages of the book Bud/David brought him, Mr. Johnson notices a tear on Betty's cheek and when she wipes it, a smudge of her flesh tone is revealed. The artist recognizes the beauty in her reality beneath the surface, and dabs a napkin in water to assist in uncovering more pink flesh. While Johnson is enthralled by the color, Betty desires to know what it means.

Threatening Patriarchy

The respective journeys of characters in *Pleasantville*—Betty and Mr. Johnson, Jennifer, David—are now advanced in crosscuts from the soda fountain where housewife and artist romance, to the Parker household where Jennifer puts on glasses and becomes more like the studious Mary Sue, to the lakeside where Margaret continues to press Bud/David on what it's like "out there." But there is another character whose journey cannot be neglected, and as one of the patriarchal symbols in the film it is his transformation that, if not insured, is at least implied as a possibility. Men like George Parker have the most to lose in terms of power when the structures of Pleasantville are disrupted. They can either face and admit defeat, or accommodate the coming changes as others have done in this emerging plurality.

Still mired in his stock-character role, George opens the front door of his house and intones, "Honey, I'm home," as he has done every evening and in every episode. This time, however, there is only silence, interrupted by a bolt of lightning and thunder that lend his entry an ominous feeling. He repeats the line a few more times, as he wanders through the dark and quiet rooms. George replays his role and his dialogue line in the hope of restoring order. But it is not to be. Betty is currently at the soda fountain posing for a painting by Mr. Johnson, which reveals her in full color. At the lake it begins to rain, another new experience for the town and although the young people are fearful, Bud/David encourages them to embrace this elemental force of nature. Jennifer, meanwhile, has politely rebuked Skip who wanted to entice her from D.H. Lawrence with some sexual play of his own.

George's frustration continues when he notices that his dinner is not ready and waiting for him, as is the expected custom. He ventures out into his front yard, getting drenched by the rain but not receiving an answer to his query, "Where's my dinner?" A stunned George stumbles into the town's bowling alley where the mayor—finally identified by the name "Big Bob" stitched on his bowling shirt—is making short work of a 7-10 split. Like the barbershop, this male bastion provides brotherhood and support, but not without some bewilderment, as the men of Pleasantville consider George's triple predicament of no wife, no lights, and no dinner. While the film satirizes abandonment at this point, it should be noted that George does not suspect Betty of sexual infidelity; it is the dereliction of her custodial wifely duties—which overtly affirm his patriarchy—that so disquiets him and his fellow men. The gathering turns to their leader, the mayor, for guidance. There is a low angle shot of Bob and behind him the projection of the men's bowling score sheet, indicating only strikes and spares; George's bombshell of abandonment is like a gutter ball to them, something unfathomable, to be destroyed or denied.

The mayor tries to calm his men with logic that politicians and persuaders have always used to mobilize the threatened: If George doesn't get his dinner, any one of them could be next. Then Bob singles them out by name, forcing a more personal reflection of the consequences from each man present. He encourages one of the men, Roy, to come forward and expose the mark of a wife's failure-of-duty in his own household—the burned-on imprint of an iron on the back of his bowling shirt. Bob parlays the group's support, moving from dismay over George's dinner and Roy's blemished shirt into a fighting spirit to sustain the values they cherish. As the men chant "Together. . . Together" to affirm their solidarity, Ross takes us outside the bowling alley amidst the rain and thunder and includes three one-second shots of activities that signify obstacles to that solidarity and hegemony: Jennifer reading and preparing to intellectually compete in a man's world, Betty and Mr. Johnson passionately kissing at the soda fountain, and the colorful young people sheltered by the gazebo at the lake enjoying the rainstorm.

Challenging Resistance to Transformation

The next morning finds Mr. Johnson's soda fountain, doubling as his artist's studio in full color, and he lies with Betty in his arms. Jennifer had fallen asleep while reading in monochrome, but as daylight enters her bedroom window, she is revealed in full color as well. At the lake, Bud/David sits isolated from the others; he is the only monochrome-toned character in the scene. As the town's milkman makes his deliveries, the camera lands on a placard posted on a tree. It heralds a Town Meeting that night for "All True Citizens of Pleasantville." By now, Betty has returned home. George is willing to forget the domestic mistakes of the previous evening and urges her to attend the meeting, but the fully colorized Betty refuses to go. Her husband's stern warnings and his demand that she return to the old ways of black and white do not wash with the emancipated Betty who, dutifully, has made a dinner for George and leaves him with instructions on how to heat it. She has also taken time to prepare his lunch for the next day. Betty articulates her agency and intention by telling George she is leaving. With the breakdown of stereotypes comes the fraying of their relationship. Distraught, George remains at the kitchen table. Betty has packed a suitcase and goes to be with Mr. Johnson.

Later at the town meeting, George sits on the dais as Bob attempts to calm the citizens who note the changes of color in their community. The racializing of this transformation is, of course, another metaphor at work. "Pleasantville" takes place during the Civil Rights era in the United States, as demonstrations and rallies became a mainstay of the movement. Resistance to change displays a recalcitrant public face in the town meeting. Mayor Bob seizes the political moment, recalling how things once "pleasant" have turned "unpleasant" and the need is to separate out the things that are pleasant from the things that are unpleasant. He sounds not unlike the politicians who wish to distill compli- cated notions of truth and reality into pithy and simplistic sound bites. Just as the "War on Terrorism" inspired the rapid passage of the Patriot Acts and various other applications of homeland security preparedness in the United States after the events of 9/11, the city fathers of Pleasantville quickly draw up a Code of Conduct in their attempt to calm fears and maintain their vision of control and hierarchy. The list begins with applications of universal truths and desires, but soon develops into negative directives that will preserve what the men of the town presume to be preferred traditions and values:

1. All public disruptions and acts of violence are to cease immediately.
2. All citizens of Pleasantville are to treat each other in a courteous and pleasant manner.
3. The area commonly known as "Lover's Lane" as well as the Pleasantville Public Library shall be closed until further notice.
4. The only permissible recorded music shall be the following: Johnny Mathis, Perry Como, Jack Jones, the marches of John Philip Sousa or *The Star Spangled Banner*. At no event shall any music be tolerated that is not of a temperate or pleasant nature.
5. There shall be no public sale of umbrellas or preparation for inclement weather of any kind.
6. No bed frame or mattress shall be sold measuring more than 38 inches wide.

7. The only permissible paint colors will be black, white or gray, despite the recent availability of alternatives.
8. All elementary and high school curriculum shall teach the "non changes" view of history, emphasizing continuity over alteration.

A nude painting of Betty in Mr. Johnson's soda shop first intrigued and then enraged the townspeople. The shop's front glass window is shattered by the mob, which proceeds to destroy the interior as well. Later, when the young people gather among the debris, Bud/David reads the new rules of order to them. They are in what Kenneth Burke would consider a state of transition, and "the conditions of such transformation involve not merely intellectualistic problems, but also deeply emotional ones" which can be invoked through piety. Piety, as noted, is a schema of orientation accomplished through the putting together of experiences. It is the yearning to conform to the sources of one's being, "the sense of what properly goes with what." For Burke, piety is connected to childhood experiences and its elocution "can be painful, requiring a set of symbolic expiations to counteract the symbolic offenses involved in purely utilitarian actions."[41] The Code of Conduct appears before them as a purely utilitarian affront, an impiety that requires a response in turn.

So, their new pieties challenged, it is now time for the renegade youth to be impious. A boy walks to the jukebox and plays a Buddy Holly song that exhorts listeners to "Rave On." Again, music becomes a carrier for symbolic action. Tom-toms measure the beat and the lyrics focus on the self-expression of the individual, perhaps someone "raving" outside the norms of society. And in the desolation of the dismantled soda shop, the decision is made to take back the night through poetic expression—music, at first. Then visual art as Mr. Johnson, assisted by Bud/David, paints the mural on the side of the police station—a creative, incendiary, political act that both literally and symbolically expresses who they are and how far they have come since Mr. Johnson stopped wiping the counter and David accepted the cookies from Margaret.

The town has been divided, and a scene reminiscent of Nazi Germany, where a marauding crowd breaks into the library and begins to extract books for burning, best epitomizes the gulf between enlightened and unenlightened. A huge bonfire is set on the library grounds, and the scene in photographed in a style reminiscent of the newsreels of the 1930s. Earlier images of the angry mob's destruction of the soda fountain evoke recollections of news footage of the Civil Rights riots of the 1960s. Against these fictional events cast as shadows of historical ones, *Pleasantville* continues its societal critique but still maintains a focus on its individual characters. Jennifer has a tug-of-war over her D.H. Lawrence book with a bullyboy who wants it burned; the TV remote control over which she and David had argued has become a novel that she must retain to insure her personal evolution. She wins its possession. Margaret has apparently escaped from the clutches of a taunting Whitey and his gang; her clothing is ripped but Bud/David now comforts her. Betty has been watching the chaos from a side street before returning to the demolished soda fountain to witness Bud/David's reading of the Code to colorful, enlightened, renegade youth.

The Code of Conduct contains measures that are satiric and absurd, but also rather pointed and even grounded somewhat in history. Its eighth rule regarding "the 'non-changes' view of history" is not very different from the tone surrounding the Scopes Monkey Trial in the 1920s and even evokes the anti-evolution intelligent design sentiment found in some contemporary classrooms. The force of an official document and rules that must be followed causes some of the young people to shudder. One red-sweatered girl demands that the jukebox be silenced when Holly's "jungle music" comes hiccupping from the box: "Weh eh eh eh ell . . . Little things that you say and do . . . " Later, firemen shovel the embers of the charred books while most of the town sleeps. Mr. Johnson and David, meanwhile, paint their statement in muralist form. When the townspeople gather to mutter and criticize the painting, the two men stand against the wall as if before a firing squad. This is the logical expression of Johnson, who confessed he would not know what to do if he couldn't paint anymore, and also Bud/David, who has set a moral example by both plugging in the jukebox after the girl's fearful warning and by encouraging and assisting Mr. Johnson.

But the Code is in effect, and its violation lands the two provocateurs in jail where they await Pleasantville's "very first trial ever," according to an advertisement in the town newspaper. Indeed, the Edenic parallels persist if this is the first transgressive act with which the town has had to contend. Will the rule-breakers be punished and banished? George visits Bud's cell and confesses his confusion at the disruption of their lives. He asks his "son" what went wrong. Bud/David answers that nothing went wrong, but that people change. George bemoans the unfairness of this, preferring life as a scripted narrative.

Refashioning Patriarchy

The trial of Mr. Johnson and Bud/David takes place in the town hall, overseen by Mayor Bob. The defendants are seated before the bench. They are the only evidence of color on a main floor filled with Pleasantville citizens in black and white, including George who appears to be a juror. In the balcony sit the "colored" townsfolk, including Betty, who looks down at Bud/David with a smile of encouragement. Bob reads the indictment and, in kangaroo court manner, the defendants are disallowed a lawyer in order to keep the proceedings as pleasant as possible. When given a chance to speak in his defense, Johnson simply admits he didn't mean to hurt anybody, and that perhaps he could paint something different or use less colors. He babbles on and even suggests that the mayor could choose the colors, getting himself sidetracked until Bud/David stands up and interrupts. Mayor Bob reproaches him, but the young man begins to assert and defend himself, going up to George and imploring his TV father to look at a Technicolor Betty in the balcony. They wonder at her inner and outer beauty. Bud/David persists with questions about their needs and desires and they strike a sentimental chord in George. Soon, Bud/David is whispering just inches from George's face. He nods again. From behind the boy, we see him wipe the cheek of his father. Then, he moves to reveal a George that has transformed into color. Mayor Bob's gavel comes down at this new transgression. He fumes that he is not going to let the courtroom turn into a circus. However, Bud/David does not feel this is a circus, and apparently neither do others. He turns and gestures to the townspeople on the mezzanine who, one by one, are gaining color.

David affirms the intrinsic capability of everyone to change, to feel, and to evoke color and new perspective. The external repressions are surmountable, especially those that deny challenges to the norms. For Mayor Bob, the norm is his control that he seems to be losing in light of everyone changing to color. Bud/David leans against the front of the mayor's elevated desk, looking up at a seething Bob and goading him about the changes in Pleasantville. It's a long list, and when Bud/David comes to "soon, the women could be going off to work while the men stayed at home and cooked" Bob roars an angry denial of this last point, and the furor of emotion flushes color to his face and body. Embarrassed and afraid, he rushes out of the courtroom where now the only monochrome images are the walls and furnishings. And when the doors to the courthouse are opened, the city of Pleasantville itself is awash with color. People walk outside and observe their surroundings as if they were works of art. In a sense, the town is just that—a work created by them and willed into existence by their own transformations. Now all citizens—adults as well as young people—wander the streets of what appears to be a new community.

Reconstructing Self and Society: Aesthetic Truth Through Dramatic Play

The denouement of *Pleasantville* begins as its characters ponder how their transformations will aid them in reconstructing their worlds. Jennifer elects to stay in this extraordinary environment, and plans to attend college at a nearby town, the ubiquitously named community of "Springfield." She and David have put their sibling rivalry behind them. Jennifer's journey continues as a Greyhound bus pulls up, its door swings wide open in the foreground-left of the frame while she walks from across the street in background frame-right carrying her suitcase. She approaches and enters the bus as the door closes and there is a match cut to another door, that of the Parker household. Inside the living room, Bud/David holds the remote control that powered him and Jennifer to this television world. He is saying goodbye to Margaret who gives him a lunch bag for his own return trek. From the kitchen, we hear Betty list some things she has included in the bag as well. While neither of the women can or need to fully understand the world from which David came—it is, after all, his effect on their world that matters most in *Pleasantville*—this scene enables both cliché and closure. David can, indeed, still be perceived as Bud to them anyway. Margaret is Bud/David's girlfriend; their relationship is apparently a chaste one and she serves as the girl he leaves behind, with Margaret inviting him back someday and hoping aloud that he will not forget her. Betty, the mother, grants her "son" his freedom with her blessing signified by the symbols of the foodstuffs and a sweater. Bud/David has provided her with a new exterior dressing and a new outlook as well. In departing the past, fictional world of a reconstructed Pleasantville, the film *Pleasantville* offers a poignant moment that acknowledges cross-generational giving and learning that concludes with an embrace between Betty and Bud/David.

Transported back to the present, David is unaware that the TV repairman's truck is positioned outside his house. From inside the cab, the repairman seems content that David has been returned safely and he drives away. In keeping with the archetype and mythology of the hero and his journey, David returns with knowledge that having faced uncertainty he can now live a more fulfilled life. He finds his real mother alone at a dining room table, crying. She is embarrassed by her inability to provide a stable household and for dating a younger man as an inopportune panacea for not having "the right house, the right car, the right life." David wipes her tears, tenderly and calmly giving solace and assurance as he did to Betty. His mother wonders at his source of strength and wisdom, but David just admits he "had a good day."

Stripped of its context, this simple scene in *Pleasantville* seems trite. But within the narrative, the actors' delivery and performances inform it with profundity. Once again, the adolescent David is parenting an elder. He displays compassion and understanding that is the result of his "good day" in Pleasantville. For his mother, the way things are "supposed" to be is illuminated by the narratives in film and television which establish and affirm stereotypes and presupposed solutions—if not "Pleasantville" then hundreds of other texts that showcase middle-class American values and expectations. Admittedly, the TV Time! show "Pleasantville"—like *The Purple Rose of Cairo*—exists as a restorative narrative, affirming traditions and the status quo. An inversion and rupture of those stereotypes and suppositions included in the 1950s sitcom enables David to cope with the reality of living that includes rewriting one's life-script in order to deal with the unpredictable and unexpected, then forging ahead to reconstruct one's world. *Pleasantville* acknowledges the presence of Burke's aesthetic truth,[42] created through dramatic play, as a counterbalance to that which is seen in the TV show "Pleasantville."

The cinema experience depends largely on subtle negotiations between the predictable and the unexpected. Nostalgia fantasy films are no more vulnerable than other genres but because they inherently deal with the notion of time, the past usually, they offer narratives already committed to some forms of closure. Since the past cannot be changed, what is the use in remembering or revisiting it? Indeed, Scott Maguire (*Visions of Modernity*, 1998) turns attention towards what he calls the "emergence of 'amnesic cultures': societies entranced by spectacle and immediacy but lacking any sense of history. He notes the transition from a rural, cyclical idea of time to a modern, urban idea of linear time that moves like a train down tracks towards a specific destination. This creates a "crisis of memory," in that memory has to be controlled in order for time to move forward teleologically. McQuire quotes Focault: "If one controls people's memory one controls their dynamism." Like all new orderings of human experience, Leo Braudy contends that film allows us to reevaluate the past, to establish new continuities and new connections—in itself and within ourselves. The critical stance in films about TV considers these new possibilities of connection. Cinema manages this in *Pleasantville* through a prosecution of television production and spectatorship demands in the 1950s, as seen through contemporary eyes.

Pleasantville concludes with a montage of life in the newly minted Pleasantville. In the final shots we see George and Betty Parker, still married but adrift from one another, as they sit on a park bench and he wonders what's going to happen now. She responds that she doesn't know, and asks him likewise. In a close-up, George laughs sincerely and concurs that neither does he know what the future holds. The camera pans to the right and Betty laughs as well. It stays on her for a moment, then pans left to where George was sitting, only now the space is occupied by Mr. Johnson who agrees: "I guess I don't either." This open-endedness at the film's conclusion regarding character choice signifies the limitless nature of the future when free will is exercised and the discarded script of the TV show "Pleasantville" is not followed.

Pleasantville is a transformative narrative in the nostalgia fantasy genre that concludes with a sense of reconstruction. By focusing on a character's participation in a contrived TV narrative, it reveals how stratified and stifling that structure and environment can be. It embraces the cinematic possibilities for critical exploration that ultimately rehabilitate the mythical town of Pleasantville, and likewise have an effect on the suburban setting from which David and Jennifer traveled. As the rules of the interior story ("Pleasantville") are challenged and broken, boundaries are exceeded and new territory is claimed and inhabited. Change is first internalized, and then manifest in the external, for widest possible effect on dual worlds.

In *Pleasantville*, specifically, characters from the real world (David, Jennifer, their mother) as well as those from the TV world (Betty, Mr. Johnson, George, and all the townspeople of Pleasantville) are allowed to blossom and develop when stereotypes and suppositions are broken apart. In the end, David reconstitutes a meaningful and profound relationship with his real mother, and if Betty reconnects with George it will be under new terms of agreement. Some characters are more in process with this reconstructive tendency. Jennifer begins life as a college student and feels unprepared to leave the TV world just yet. When George visits the jail cell and has a moment of reconnection with Bud, it allows a new relationship to germinate that eventually works to liberate him from the conformity of the town; but George knows he has miles to go, as do Mr. Johnson and others. The reconstructive tendencies have taken root, however.

In *Pleasantville*, the critical stance consumes movies about the television experience with an eye toward reconstructing the world represented and shaped by television. Sometimes in the films we have explored, a character in the narrative is unable to assume responsibility for reconstructing that world and it is up to the spectator to act; John in *Medium Cool*, Howard Beale in *Network*, and Pierre Delacroix in *Bamboozled* are dead at the conclusion of those films. A character's reconstructive designs can be radical (Mickey and Mallory in *Natural Born Killers*) or comparatively restrained (David and others in *Pleasantville*), though no less effective. In all these cases, the critical stance challenges film characters and spectators to go beyond traditional, conservative, restorative strategies as they re-envision a world made by television.

NOTES

1. Auster, Albert. 1994. "Television as Seen by Hollywood" from *The Political Companion to American Film,* Gary Crowdus, ed. New York: Lakeview Press. 433.

2. Ibid. 434.

3. See *Understanding Media: The Extensions of Man* by Marshall McLuhan, originally published in 1964. McLuhan distinguishes a hot medium like radio from a cool

one like the telephone, or a hot medium like cinema from a cool one like TV. A hot medium extends one single sense in high definition. High definition is the state of being well-filled with data. A photograph is, visually, high definition. A cartoon is low definition simply because very little visual information is provided. The telephone is a cool medium, or one of low definition, because the ear is given a meager amount of information; of course, cellular phones with text, games and other data approach a hot status. And speech is a cool medium of low definition, because so little is given and so much has to be filled in by the listener. On the other hand, hot media do not leave so much to be filled in or completed by the audience. Hot media are, therefore, low in participation, and cool media are high in participation or completion by the audience. *Medium Cool*—a film about television—is in the middle. The TV style of low definition that has to be filled in or completed by the spectator is cast against the high definition of film style that pushes the spectator, reflexively and critically, to a state of being well-filled with data. For a brief foray on McLuhan, see "Thawing Out Media: Hot and Cool" by Gordon Gow at *Critical Mass*, http://www.peak.sfu.ca/cmass/issue2/july.html

4. Wexler, Haskell. 2001. *Medium Cool* DVD commentary track, Paramount Home Video. Wexler's quotes are sourced therein unless otherwise noted.

5. Katz, Valentin. 2002. "The Whole World Is Watching!" http://valusha.tripod.com/mediumcool.html

6. Mark Kulansky interview, "Why 1968?" at barnesandnoble.com/booksearch

7. Ibid.

8. This incident is based on reality. In New York City, a well-know politician named Carmen DiSappio had left $10,000 in a cab. Because he could not really explain where he got the money, he never initially fesses up which left the police questioning the honesty of the cabdriver collected.

9. In some cases, they did more than ask. Some 20 hours of the footage that Haskell Wexler shot of the riots and demonstrations was subpoenaed by the federal government in the Chicago 8 Conspiracy trial.

10. Television routinely utilizes close-ups and medium shots. The size of the TV screen, as opposed to the larger canvas of cinema, allows such compositions to have the greatest impact. Cinema, meanwhile, can convey certain sensations and material through effective use of long shots and extreme long shots in addition to close and medium shots. Lighting is more flat and evenly dispersed, especially in TV news. Cinema invites atmospheric applications of light to create particular tones or feelings. *Medium Cool*, because it is a film-about-television and viewers know that, has license to use production strategies from both media. In a similar fashion, films-about-television regularly mix their photographic stock to quickly convey the softer texture and depth of 35 mm or 16 mm film, or the crispness and flatness of analog videotape. Now in the digital age, it is getting harder to discern celluloid from digital tape, especially when the showcase on which one is viewing is a video screen. The point being that just as the language of film or TV is transposed one into the other, so are the traditional recording stocks more malleable and applicable one into the other. Even a film not located in this sub genre, *In America* (Sheridan, 2003), comfortably mixes 35 mm stock with home camcorder to achieve its narrative purpose.

11. *Medium Cool* was produced by Haskell Wexler with $800,000 of his own financing, and then sold to Paramount Pictures for $600,000 and a 50/50 split of the profits. Studio executives were not pleased with the results and delayed the release of the film for a year. The eventual release was curtailed somewhat as well; Wexler explains that the film was "not commercial enough." It's X-rating (for nudity and language, but more precisely for political content) made some exhibitors skittish. The film has been revived, most effectively on DVD, and stands as "a vital late '60s film for its incisive narrative and formal dissection of the visual politics of 'truth,' and its awareness of how coolly seductive televised violence might be as entertainment, especially in a historical moment marked by incendiary images of political assassination, the Vietnam War, the civil rights movement, and counterculture protests." (Lucia Bozzola, *New York Times* All Movie Guide). Wexler's original plan was to make a film called *Concrete Wilderness*, about animals and a young boy in a major city; the subplot with the carrier pigeons reflects that genesis which, of course, was not fulfilled.

12. Palmer, William J. 1987. *The Films of the Seventies: A Social History*. New York: Scarecrow Press. 69-70.

13. The term "controlled nonconformity" has several applications in consumer culture. See *Cute, Quaint, Hungry and Romantic: The Aesthetics of Consumerism by Daniel Harris* (New York: Da Capo Press, 2000).

14. On January 22, 1987, Pennsylvania state treasurer R. Budd Dwyer called a news conference to discuss his conviction for embezzlement. He read a short statement, and then revealed a gun that he placed in his mouth and killed himself. Some stations broadcast all or part of the event, and many used audio portions of what has become a textbook example of how or when the line is drawn in broadcast standards and practices. Earlier in 1974, a Sarasota, Florida, news anchor named Chris Chubbock shot herself in the head during a live broadcast on WWSB-TV. A much less compelling but more highly disseminated rupture occurred on February 1, 2004, during the half-time show live telecast of the Super Bowl when singer Janet Jackson allowed her dancing partner, Justin Timberlake, to rip a portion of her dress to reveal a bare breast. The outcry among watchdog groups, network officials and show sponsors was so great that several subsequent "live" telecasts are being scheduled with 5 seconds or more of transmission delay.

15. Macdonald, David. 2000. www.angelfire.com/movies/davidsmovies/network.html

16. Palmer. ibid. 81

17. Bagdikian, Ben H. 2004. *The New Media Monopoly*. Boston: Beacon Press. 16.

18. Butters, Gerald R. 2000. *Bamboozled. Scope: an on-line journal of film studies.* Institute of Film Studies, University of Nottingham. http://www.nottingham.ac.uk/film

19. The ploy of mounting a hoped-for failure is a referent to Mel Brooks' *The Producers* (1968, 2005) where a struggling Broadway producer and his accountant join forces to find an overabundance of gullible investors for a surefire theatrical flop. They create *Springtime for Hitler*, which they feel is an offensive, horribly acted,

musical about Nazis. When it becomes a surprise smash hit with audiences and critics, the two must deal with investors who cannot be compensated as well as a despicable work of "art."

20. Lee's insights and quotes are taken from the audio commentary on the *Bamboozled* DVD release. 2001. New Line Home Entertainment, Inc.

21. A poll taken by Harris Interactive in January 2004 indicated that two-thirds of Americans support the idea of televising executions. While the case of Manray does not move through legal trial and conviction, the willingness to allow witnessing of a live broadcast of torture and death seems apparent in reality.

22. Production information about *Natural Born Killers* is sourced to director Oliver Stone and can be found on the audio commentary track to the DVD release, 2000. Warner Brothers Pictures. In addition, the author has incorporated information from public forums, panels and seminars with Stone at the Austin Film Festival in October, 1997.

23. The prison scenes in *Natural Born Killers* were shot at a real penitentiary, the Stateville Prison in Illinois. Located just outside of Chicago, over 80% of its inmates are incarcerated for violent crimes. Several real prisoners and guards were cast as themselves to add veracity to the shoot.

24. Courtwright, David T. 2000. "Way Cooler Than Manson" from *Oliver Stone's USA; Film, History and Controversy*, Lawrence: University Press of Kansas. 198.

25. Gitlin, Todd. 2001. *Media Unlimited: How the Torrent of Images and Sounds Overwhelms Our Lives*. New York: Metropolitan Books. 14-15.

26. From the closing to the *Natural Born Killers* audio commentary track.

27. Throughout this text when discussing the film *Pleasantville*, there will be three different type-settings that refer to three distinct but overlapping territories in the narrative. *Pleasantville* is used to identify the movie itself. "Pleasantville" as set off in quotes refers to the television show on the TV Time! network. And Pleasantville, with no type alteration signifies the town itself as the setting that is within the TV show.

28. David's character will be referenced in three ways throughout this text. He will be referred to as David when in the frame of time-present and his California setting, as Bud when he is interacting with members of the "Pleasantville" community who have little or no awareness of his dual nature, and as Bud/David when he represents the potential of forceful changes in the community or is in a setting where some characters see him as Bud and others as David.

29. Burke, Kenneth. (1931). *Counter-Statement*. Berkeley: University of California Press. 124.

30. This incident reflects upon the use of art—in this case, large-canvas art—for political purpose. It recalls a real-life event dramatized in *The Cradle Will Rock* (Robbins, 1999) when artist Diego Rivera infuriated Nelson Rockefeller in 1938 with a mural of revolutionary images that was to hang in the lobby of Rockefeller Center. Like the David/Bud-Mr. Johnson collaboration, angry reactionary forces destroyed Rivera's work. This scene in *Pleasantville* affirms the role of art as incendiary and the artist as provocateur.

31. Stamm, Robert. Burgoyne, Robert. Lewis-Flitterman, S. (1992). *New Vocabularies in Film Semiotics: Structuralism, Poststructuralism and Beyond*. London: Routledge. 10.

32. Burke, Kenneth. (1935). *Permanence and Change: An Anatomy of Purpose.* Berkeley: University of California Press. 90.

33. Ibid. 74.

34. Sturken, Marita and Cartwright, Lisa. (2001). *Practices of Looking: An Introduction to Visual Culture.* Oxford: Oxford University Press.

35. *The World in a Frame; What We See in Films.* Braudy, Leo. (1976). Chicago: University of Chicago Press. 17.

36. Baudry, Jean-Louis. (1975). "Ideological Effects of the Basic Cinematographic Apparatus." *Film Quarterly,* Volume 28, Number 2

37. Metz, Christian. (1975) "Identification, Mirror" from *The Imaginary Signifier. Screen.* Vol. 16, No. 2.

38. Ross, Gary. (1999), *Pleasantville* audio commentary track. New Line Home Video Productions. The author gathered additional insights from Ross in seminars and public forums with the director at the Austin Film Festival, October 1998.

39. Ibid.

40. Earlier, in fact, there was a classroom scene shot like a black-and-white 1950s propaganda film with regimented students in neat rows of desks listening to a teacher discuss the geography of Pleasantville. On the chalkboard is a drawing of the main streets in the town that has clearly marked limits and from which there is no road out. Jennifer stumps her teacher, dumfounds her fellow classmates and closes the scene by asking, "What's outside of Pleasantville?"

41. *Permanence and Change.* 74.

42. Aesthetic truth is "the exercise of human propriety, the formulation of symbols which rigidify our sense of poise and rhythm. Artistic truth is the externalization of taste." (Kenneth Burke, *Counter-Statement.* 42).

Chapter Four

Movies About the Surreal in Media: The Ironic Stance

Previous chapters looked at the reflexive and the critical stances in films that deal with media making. Examples that follow position an ironic stance that engages with film narratives about the surreal in media. Cinema can provide explorations of social-political arenas and reveal dissonance that emerges. These areas of play are, significantly, reliant on media to encourage compliance and coercion among spectators who are also consumers and voters since the managers of the message frequently advance a particular ideological agenda. For French Marxist theorist Louis Althusser, "ideology represents the imaginary relationship of individuals to their real conditions of existence."[1] The ironic stance acknowledges the importance of representation in cinema (how to recognize ourselves and others), accepts the possibility of interpellation (that we can become/are the subject that we are addressed as), but additionally, considers that we can resist or reject the ideological agendas as a result of evaluation/reevaluation of the arena.

The "surreal" suggests qualities associated with surrealism, an early 20th century movement in art and literature that tried to represent the subconscious mind by creating fantastic imagery and juxtaposing elements that seem to contradict each other. Films examined in this chapter presume a gullibility of the audience to accept as reality that which is presented in major media forms such as movies or television, in spite of their moments of surrealism. For example, a character walks on water in *Being There*, a war is fabricated and sold to the American public in *Wag the Dog*, political candidates use extreme rhetorical tactics in pursuit of votes in *Bob Roberts* and *Bulworth*, and the mesmerizing effects of reality television are excavated in *The Truman Show*.

Since most of these films deal with the political process, itself part of a system of participation, strategies of creation and appropriation seem particularly relevant to the making of reality using the tools of media. In addition to critique-by-participation, these films offer perspective by incongruity. Discussed in the previous chapter, this especially applies to *Bob Roberts* and *Bulworth.* Both films invoke a spirit of hope and change that flickers momentarily in *Being There* and is extinguished in *Wag the Dog.*

The movies in this section utilize satiric-parodic frameworks. Satire blends a critical attitude with humor and wit in an effort to improve society. Satire assumes that an implicit moral code is understood by the audience, such as 'good men and women should lead us' or 'majority rules.' The satirist's goal is to point out the hypocrisy of the target/subject in hopes that either the target or the audience will return to a following of the code. Stories, for example, in which corrupt or complacent men and women are given authority, and where expediency rules, can incorporate satiric strategies because they present a negative variant on the implicit moral code. A presence of irony, naturally, informs the ironic stance. Irony—the recognition of a reality that is different from its masked appearance—is frequently marked by a degree of grim humor, and a detachment or cool and diffident expression. It is most often achieved through the use of hyperbole or understatement.

Chauncey Gardener in *Being There* is a simple-minded fellow whose meticulous nature is mistaken for profundity. He has absorbed the rules of reality from limited exposure to the outside world and through the omnipresence of television in his living quarters. Gardener will end the film as a close confidant of the President of the United States and, perhaps, his successor.

Wag the Dog satirizes the relationship between electoral politics at America's highest level and the media that was also a theme in the serious documentary *The War Room* (Pennebaker, Hegedus, 1992). Both are less about the candidates and the issues than the process of what it takes to get them elected. Both films show the relentless intensity of political operatives and their media specialists in pursuit of specific goals. In *Wag the Dog*, Conrad Brean is a political fixer called in by presidential adviser Winifred Ames to divert attention from an imminent personal and political scandal involving the Chief Executive. Brean enlists the help of Hollywood producer Stanley Motss and, together with other media professionals, they conspire to create a series of fabricated stories about war and heroism that effectively displaces the scandal story from center-stage and ensures the reelection of the President. When Motss desires some public acknowledgment of his role in presenting the show-lie of war, the strong-arm tactics of his co-producers eliminate him, in the name of national security.

Shot and directed like a documentary film, *Bob Roberts* presents, in contrast to Wayne Gayle in *Natural Born Killers*, a more understated British journalist as he covers the Pennsylvania senatorial campaign of "rebel conservative" candidate Bob Roberts. Spectators familiar with the conceits of nonfiction filmmaking will note parodies of certain documentary production tactics, but the unfolding narrative provides all viewers with a behind-the-scenes portrait of campaign dynamics that favor certain media outlets and tendencies as they simultaneously marginalize others. After faking an assassination attempt and winning the election, Roberts' and his supporters dispense with dissenting voices. The film calls for wide-eyed vigilance when observing the political process in a media age that encourages the use of buffers and blinders.

Bulworth is an oppositional film as well. Unlike *Wag the Dog* wherein the media is allowed to prevail but on terms set by the Political-Corporate-Media (PCM) state, it is an individual, J.B. Bulworth, who presides over a campaign landscape where he alone sets the pace and tone. In a way, he resembles Mickey and Mallory in *Natural Born Killers*, forcing coverage of his exploits because he is effective media material—a charismatic Senate candidate in California whose provocative statements and positions make him popular and/or intriguing to the working press and viewing public but threatening to the PCM state. When the senator lies near death at a hospital after an assassination attempt, *Bulworth*'s audience is asked to consider his spiritual presence and suggestions for political/media deconstruction as a force, an anti-media perhaps, to countermand PCM power.

The Truman Show celebrates, then explodes, the narcoticizing tendencies of reality television programming today. "The Truman Show" as a TV program succeeds due to the malleable nature of spectators who are spoon-fed the daily minutiae of a prefabricated character's life, and asked to consider it a worthwhile and engaging activity. When Truman Burbank finally escapes the scripted narrative of his programmed life, it is an instruction to his dedicated audiences to do likewise and pursue an existence that rejects the dictates of political, corporate and media forces that corral them.

By invoking ironic stances, these films illustrate how some characters transform from passive observers-reactors of mediaplay to self-aware, participant-players (*The Truman Show*) or those whose example and fortitude suggest a more life-affirming path of existence (*Bulworth*), or where resistance can be ennobled or extinguished by powerful forces (*Bob Roberts, Wag the Dog*), and where coping strategies are guileless and not duplicitous (*Being There*). Herein cinema interrogates various media-making structures dependent on the moving image—reality television, advertising, documentary film, music industry, TV news, and others—as they interplay with political and corporate forces to examine the process by which audiences define and understand themselves.

BEING THERE (1979)

At the outset of *Being There*, Chauncey Gardener (Peter Sellers) declares that he cannot read nor write but likes to watch TV. He is not a five year-old child but a middle-aged adult man who finds himself the houseguest of a politically connected, millionaire-adviser to the President of the United States. Negative instincts, such as illiteracy, are ironically enabled and excused by the simplest acts and phrases. When Chauncey says he can't read, the Chief Executive merely responds in agreeable, small talk fashion, wondering aloud if anyone has time for reading these days?

Written by Jerzy Kosinski and based on his novel of the same name, *Being There* identifies television as the central, shaping influence on Chauncey. The film's satiric tone is low-key and subtle, rather than broad or slapstick. Like *Network*, it arrived for audiences of the late 1970s who were just beginning to experience the boom in electronic media choices, not quite overwhelmed by them and thus, perhaps not conditioned to fully assimilate their flood of sensations and affect. The spectator Chauncey can be considered part of Howard Beale's great, unawakened audience, made somnambulistic by television and little aware of life outside its confines.

Chance, as he is called, is a simple gardener who has never left the urban estate where he works until his employer dies. On that fateful morning, his TV-timer acts as an alarm clock and awakens him. Chance is expressionless as he flips through the channels. The housekeeper informs him of their boss's passing but Chance is lulled by television images of Big Bird and Captain Kangaroo, and the real news does not seem to register. Chance goes into the old man's room, sees that he is not there, and then turns on the TV set in that space. A commercial for Sealy Posturepedic mattresses plays, and Chance mimics the spokesman as he reclines on the empty bed. Mimicry of what shows on the tube comes easily for Chance regardless, or in spite of, the context. When the President of the United States next appears in a news clip, Chance notices how he clasps the hand of a visiting dignitary and practices the gesture himself until he replicates it perfectly.

Lawyers handling his employer's estate require Chance to vacate by the next day. He dutifully agrees, even though he has never been allowed outside this house in Washington, D.C., never been in an automobile, nor allowed to listen to the radio or electronic media until the old man gave him a television set. Chance's origins are unclear and unimportant. He lives exclusively in the moment with TV his window to the world. Leaving the estate, he walks through inner city bleakness: fenced lots, pawnshops, kids playing basketball, men gathered around a burning garbage can. Chance, dressed in a dignified but outdated suit and overcoat, carries an umbrella like a guide stick for the blind, or perhaps a divining rod. He is, in fact, looking for a garden to tend and water. Metaphors of new growth—seasonal changes, nourishment and fertility— are frequently invoked in *Being There*, and instinctively understood by Chance. They can, however, be misunderstood by others in the real world. When the gardener approaches a group of tough, inner-city kids and politely asks them where he could find a garden to work in because "there is much to be done during the winter," they take Chance as an emissary for a rival gang. One thug pulls a knife and threatens Chance, who calmly retrieves a TV remote control from his pocket and clicks it at the boy. The threat of a real hoodlum with a weapon fails to transform into a media image from another channel, and the gang dismisses Chance as dim-witted and harmless.

Like any hero who leaves his comfortable and ordinary world, the journey through new territory brings an opportunity to learn new rules and change outlook. In *Being There*, Chauncey is a catalyst hero who changes very little

Chauncey Gardner (Peter Sellers), on his first day away from hearth and home and TV, is threatened by a street gang in Being There. *He responds by clicking a television remote control at them.*

and instead affirms change or agreement in others. He has been programmed to his human limit within the operating system of television. Like a good consumer, he responds to cues, can adapt and learn from them, but offers no real resistance to personal affronts. He seems, moreover, to merely absorb them and lets those who confront him project their own expectations and prejudices onto his reactions.

Appearance *is* reality for Chance, and for most persons who interact with him. Thus, an ironic stance is mostly absent from the players in the film, although the spectators of *Being There* are invited to embrace it. Walking past the gates in front of the White House, Chance stops and inspects a tree that looks sickly. Dressed like a bureaucrat and speaking in short, measured phrases, he informs a uniformed guard that the tree needs attention. The guard responds immediately, with serious deference to the authority figure Chance appears to represent. As night approaches, Chance strolls before a store window that displays big-screen TVs connected to home camcorders pointed at the passing crowds so they can see themselves on the television sets. This is a marvel to Chance, who is so mesmerized with his own image on the screens that he accidentally backs away and off a curbside, getting pinned between two parked cars as one tries to leave its spot. Plot-wise, this event serves to rescue Chance from the street and facilitate his entrance into the influential circles of power.

Inside the limousine that backed into Chance is Eve Rand (Shirley MacLaine), the wife of a dying millionaire and she is, at first, merely fearful of lawsuits that the distinguished-looking Chance could possibly lodge. But she soon becomes intrigued with him. Introducing himself as "Chance the gardener," Eve hears it as "Chauncey Gardener" and the sophisticated sounding moniker sticks. Significantly, Chance never misrepresents himself; it is observers of the 'spectacle' that is Chauncey who inform his words and deeds with profundity, a further application of the ironic. Chauncey ingratiates himself with Eve and her sickly husband, Ben (Melvyn Douglas). Invited to stay at their suburban mansion for a few days, the industrialist Ben begins to interpret Chauncey's naive and soothing ramblings as applications to the gospel of business. Eve perceives their guest as "very intense" and Ben agrees, admiring Chauncey's balanced and peaceful nature. Arguably, this Zen-like simplicity could function as a viable political strategy in certain situations.

One afternoon, Ben gets a visit from the President (Jack Warden), to whom he is a confidant and adviser. Chauncey meets him as well, and with no trepidation is soon on a first name basis with President "Bobby." Also intrigued with the gardener's persona, he commissions a background check which reveals no data whatsoever. In a press conference, the president references the enigma that is Chauncey. He even calls the gardener a most intuitive man who counseled that "as long as the roots of industry remain firmly planted in the natural soil, the economic prospects are undoubtedly sunny.'" Chauncey's metaphor both oversimplifies strategies of world economics and makes certain aspects of it palatable to most untrained observers. Chauncey's outlook and the reaction he prompts is an embodiment of media manipulated structures and audiences.

Chauncey is nonplussed by his celebrity status. He is unable to fathom the power he exerts, and it will be up to others to do so and to manipulate him for their ends. His short, pithy declarations are taken for words of wisdom by the press, politicians and the public. Critic Roger Ebert considers it fitting that Chauncey's simple, TV-informed utterances are mistaken for profundity.

> The hero survives a series of challenges he doesn't understand, using words that are both universal and meaningless. But are Chance's sayings noticeably less useful than when the president tells us about a ``bridge to the 21st century?'' Sensible public speech in our time is limited by (1) the need to stay within the confines of the 10-second TV sound bite; (2) the desire to avoid being pinned down to specific claims or promises; and (3) the abbreviated attention span of the audience, which, like Chance, likes to watch but always has a channel-changer poised.[2]

Within the narrative, media practitioners bow and genuflect to Chauncey's laconic persona. A *New York Times* financial reporter concludes that he plays his cards very close to the chest, and that unconfirmed reports say he is a strong candidate for a seat on the board of First American Financial. In *Wag the Dog*, the ironic stance will reveal a more sophisticated version of this sort of media-manufactured maelstrom.

Three exchanges represent cinema's ability in *Being There* to ironically assess the random but co-optable (shown through a false sense of security with the Russians), addictive and narcotizing (shown with a distraction from the reality of death), displacing and de-socializing (shown by unfocused sexual play) tendencies of television. In the first example, Chauncey escorts Eve to a dinner party with the Soviet ambassador. The Russian notes that the two men are not so far from each other. The gardener agrees, noting that their chairs are almost touching. It is like a television moment taken from a spree of channel surfing. That can be said of most of Chauncey's pearls of wisdom. They lack context amidst the swirl of other activity but are nonetheless comforting and seductive to many. A second exchange has Ben discussing Chauncey's trustworthiness and how being around him makes the ailing man feel better. The thought of dying, he confesses, has been much easier since the arrival of Chauncey. And in a third example, Eve eventually develops a romantic attraction to Chauncey despite him being a neophyte at the game of love. She

Chauncey Gardner, a savant nurtured by television, becomes adviser to the rich and powerful.

enters his bedroom one night while he watches TV. Onscreen, a couple is kissing. Perhaps, finally, some human, sexual dimension and break-through to the reality of living can be manifest in the gardener, albeit once again via TV's instruction. Eve, a little drunk, asks him what he likes. Chauncey responds, "I like to watch." Mistaking this for the gratification desires of a voyeur, Eve masturbates while Chauncey watches . . . TV.

When Ben ultimately dies, the pallbearers at his funeral are all men of great power. They discuss who might be the next person they'd like to manage and manipulate, looking toward the figure of Chauncey Gardener. These men, members of the Political-Corporate-Media elite, represent institutions that wish to maintain superficiality in public discourse. To do anything less would encourage the public to begin to think and challenge the agendas of those men. Television and its apparatus of news and personality-making is the tool that primarily establishes and sustains the holding pattern, forever seeking individuals with the right look and sound, offering platitudes on behalf of their proper friends in high places. The ironic stance in *Being There* acknowledges this intention.

WAG THE DOG (1997)

The metaphor that animates the title *Wag the Dog* is explained in its opening placards that pose the question and answer: Why does a dog wag its tail?

Because a dog is smarter than its tail. If the tail were smarter, the tail would wag the dog. This conjures a confounding, preposterous word-picture arrangement that, the film seems to tell us, is ironically true. The tail (or tale, i.e. fabrication) wags or controls the dog, which is reality. Media forces represent the tail, which wags both information and audience.

Wag the Dog resonates with the contemporary historical record. Just a few weeks after the film was released, President Bill Clinton was accused of having an affair with a White House intern. The photo of the President in *Wag the Dog* that is used to break the story of his alleged dalliance with a "Firefly girl" who was touring the White House with her scouting group is staged with obvious similarity to one of Clinton greeting intern Monica Lewinsky taken by a *Newsweek* photographer and widely circulated in the wake of the ensuing "Monicagate" scandal.[3] Director Barry Levinson never shows nor names the President in his film. *Wag the Dog* is more about the Presidency as an office than the personality that inhabits it, with a special regard for the Political-Corporate-Media forces keeping guard over their own interests at the expense of truth and authenticity in the face of the electorate.

The film begins, as does so many of these analyzed, with an image from TV. In this case a political commercial is shown of two jockeys who, presumably, are talking about their trade. They parlay into the cliché line, "Don't change horses in midstream," and we realize this is a political advertisement for the incumbent President of the United States. It is a hackneyed, cheap-looking spot, the kind that causes Hollywood film producer Stanley Motss (Dustin Hoffman) to label its effort "amateur." After the commercial the camera cuts abruptly to a vacuum cleaner in close-up at ground level. In the collision of these two shots, the movie implies that dirt, or untruth, is the fallout of political machinations; it must be spread, exhumed, and removed or concealed. Shortly thereafter, the opposition candidate Senator John Neal (Craig T. Nelson) airs an ad showing images of the White House accompanied by Maurice Chevalier's song of romantic attraction from the film *Gigi*, "Thank Heaven for Little Girls." With eleven days to the election and the sitting President 17% ahead in polls, the breaking scandal demands a distraction so that the chief executive can appear "presidential." The "Thank Heaven" spot exemplifies how the reflexive and critical stances ground the spectator to further embrace an ironic one as s/he views *Wag the Dog*. Chevalier's song speaks from cinema's past, and it informs a political present that is worthy of critique. This perspective voiced by the benign, elderly gentleman Chevalier, as he gratefully looks back on amorous adventures of his past is now overlaid upon news footage of the President with inference of his sordid infidelity.

Manipulating the press through a series of leaks and manufactured events, political fixer Conrad Brean (Robert DeNiro), with the help of Motss, convinces the viewing public that war with Albania is necessary due to that country coddling terrorist cells and the possible transference of a "suitcase bomb" (an earlier manifestation of what has been termed WMDs or Weapons of Mass Destruction) to a location "near the Canadian border." Considering war no different from show business, Motss proceeds to produce what he calls "a pageant." Brean had asked presidential adviser Winifred Ames (Anne Heche) for $20,000 in cash to underwrite this production, off the books of course; he gets a neatly wrapped package containing $30,000. Motss enlists the support of the consultant Fad King (Denis Leary) whose specialty is concocting photo-ops, tie-ins, and publicity gimmicks that capture the zeitgeist of the media moment, like the real life yellow-ribbon campaign that accompanied Gulf War I. Motss calls upon country songwriter Johnny Green (Willie Nelson) to quickly compose a patriotic anthem that will soon be recorded in "We Are the World" fashion by several musical notables and then rush-released. The scenarists have been provided some time to develop these pranks, since the President is in Asia and delays his return to America. Political, corporate, and media forces join ranks to misinform the public in a way that will assure the President's re-election and *Wag the Dog* reveals these tactics in as straightforward and matter-of-fact manner as possible.

At a film production studio set, Motss boasts that the same digital process they shall employ was used in the last Arnold Schwarzenegger action movie. Here, his group creates phony news footage using a Hollywood actress running in front of a blue-screen with a bag of Tostitos in her arms! The image will be digitally manipulated until it becomes that of a young Albanian girl protectively cradling a kitten as she runs across a bridge in her village that is under attack. Motss orders flames, the sound of screaming, and what he calls "that Anne Frank siren sound." The footage is printed so it is visually distressed and delivered to the television networks as something smuggled out of the war zone; one news anchor dutifully reports that his network has just received information that the young Albanian national fleeing in this video is attempting to escape terrorist reprisals in her village. Meanwhile, stories about the Firefly girl incident have been buried late in the TV newscasts and deeper into the daily papers, or been trivialized as comic material for late-night television talk show hosts like Jay Leno.

Events in *Wag the Dog* both affirm and predict actual historical occurrences, sometimes directly and sometimes in conflated ways. For example, one of the real life deceptions as well as a major political success in media-age war making was mounted in October 1990. In *American Dynasty* (2004), Kevin Phillips describes the event.

> . . . a fifteen year-old Kuwaiti girl, named only as 'Nayirah,' testified before the Human Rights Caucus of the U.S. House of Representatives that the Iraqi

soldiers invading Kuwait tore hundreds of babies from hospital incubators and killed them. It turned out, after investigation by Amnesty International and others, that this was a lie.   There were just a few incubators in Kuwait, and hardly any babies in them; Nayirah hadn't been to any hospital—she was the daughter of Saud Nasir al-Sabah, Kuwait's ambassador to the United States and a relative of the ruling family.[4]

President George H.W. Bush quoted Nayirah on several occasions to solidify support for his military resolution for bombardment of Iraq, which indeed passed the Senate by six votes in November 1990. The continued demonizing of Saddam Hussein that this ploy affected had another benefit. It replaced front page and lead story highlights of son Neil Bush and his role in failed savings and loan bank scams. In the 1990s, sex scandals dominated and trumped several other political indiscretions. Investigations of Bush's various misdeeds—extending back to his role in the Iran hostage negotiations of 1980, the Iran-Contra dealings beginning in 1986, and the subsequent funding of Hussein's weapons build-up—were displaced in the media and the minds of many spectators by the misdeeds of Clinton, first involving the Whitewater real estate scandal in Arkansas, and then purported affairs with Paula Jones and later, Monica Lewinsky.

Stanley Motts (Dustin Hoffman), a Hollywood producer with vision but without credit in Wag the Dog.

During their strategy meetings at his Hollywood mansion, Motss and his associates have no compunction about creating fiction and presenting it as fact. They blur the line between fact and fiction and embody the cynicism and skepticism that grew in the 1990s when seeing was no longer believing, as media manipulation became more sinister with emerging digital technologies that could easily alter sound and image. At the same time in the film, significant activity such as the president mobilizing the 6th Fleet for deployment during the "world crisis" involving Albania is treated with the same level of interest and involvement by the chief executive as the kind of kitten the Tostitos bag-holding actress will have digitally superimposed in the fabricated news shot. Here, the momentous exists in parity with the trivial. For the record, a white kitten is eventually chosen over a calico cat.

Any concentration of power and influence is apt to breed discontent among those not nearest the core of power and decision-making. In *Wag the Dog* that is represented by the CIA and agent Mr. Young (William H. Macy). Trailing Brean and Ames, he taps into their cell phone calls and reroutes their limousine to a restaurant where Young demands to know more about their activities. The Agency's surveillance unmasks the war making as a fraud, and an action to which they were not privy. More importantly, their intelligence shows no evidence of terrorist threat or weaponry. But Brean adamantly insists there is a war, as he points to a TV set in the restaurant that is showcasing the phony coverage. At first, Young is not mollified, but Brean, ever the spin-meister, convinces him that covert terrorism has gone undetected by the means employed by the CIA which is prone to identify more overt nuclear and terror-related threats. Himself a bureaucratic player and a member of the PCM elite as well, Young seems to relent and lets them go on their way. But soon the "war" situation is resolved. Senator Neal announces on television that he has learned the troops are "standing down" and that there is cessation of hostilities. Brean sees this as just another political dogfight and that the CIA merely "cut a better deal." He is apparently ready to accept the "war story" as slightly rewritten and enacted, but an undeterred Motss angrily contests. Casting the situation in cinematic terms, Motss considers the event his picture and not one produced by the CIA.

Motss and Brean then create a "psuedo-event." According to Daniel Boorstin, psuedo-events are occurrences like news conferences and television debates which are staged to garner news coverage and shape public perceptions.[5] With the president returning from overseas, his airport landing will include the staged greeting of a young Albanian girl who presents him with the symbolic "first chaff of wheat" as part of her native harvest ritual. She speaks in Albanian, with translation conveniently provided on the spot by an interpreter. The girl's elderly mother stands in the drizzling rain just behind her as they greet the president, who accepts her humble gift. Then, he removes his overcoat and places it upon the old woman. All this action was scripted by Brean and Motss, including the diverting of Air Force One to Boca Raton, Florida, from its original landing site of Andrews Air Force Base to take advantage of the dreary weather necessary for the rainy payoff to the photo-op.

Boorstin notes the following characteristics of a pseudo-event. Consider how they have become the tail that wags the dog:

1. It is not spontaneous, but comes about because someone has planned, planted or incited it.
2. It is planted primarily for the immediate purpose of being reported or reproduced. Therefore, its occurrence is arranged for the convenience of the reporting media. Its success is measured by how widely it is reported. The question, "Is it real?" is less important than "Is it newsworthy?"
3. Its relation to the underlying reality of the situation it links with is ambiguous. Our interest in it arises largely from this ambiguity. Concerning a pseudo-event, the question "What does it mean?" has a new dimension.
4. Usually, the pseudo-event is intended to be a self-fulfilling prophecy. It *Accomplishes* because it *is*.

Certain characteristics of pseudo-events make them overshadow genuinely spontaneous ones:

1. Pseudo-events are more dramatic.
2. Pseudo-events, being planned for dissemination, are easier to disseminate and to make vivid.
3. Pseudo-events can be repeated at will, and thus their impressions can be reinforced.
4. Pseudo-events cost money to create. Somebody has an interest in disseminating, magnifying, advertising, and extolling them as events worth watching or worth believing. When possible, they are advertised in advance, and often rerun to get the most in return.
5. Pseudo-events, being planned for intelligibility, *are* more intelligible and hence more reassuring. Promoters of pseudo-events usually provide analysts and commentators to interpret for spectators.
6. Pseudo-events are more sociable, and more convenient to witness. Their occurrence is planned for our convenience.
7. Knowledge of pseudo-events—of what has been reported, or staged, and/ or how—becomes the test of being "informed."
8. Pseudo-events spawn other pseudo-events in geometric progression.

A spectator's willingness to accept pseudo-events as authentic representations transforms simulated reality into actual reality. The presence of a critical and ironic stance makes this difficult, however, and *Wag the Dog* illustrates this with its satiric impulse. Thus, one can appreciate Conrad Brean's acerbic reaction after watching Neal at a televised press conference announce a "cessation of hostilities"; the war is over because he saw it on television. The political fixer, a creator-purveyor of the fallacy, has himself accepted a new rendering of it. But Stanley Motss, the Hollywood producer of fictive moments, refuses to do likewise and instead frames the drama in the language of a screenplay. For him, it is nothing more than just the end of Act One.

The script of a pseudo-event must allow for the possible ruptures that are unplanned; these are, in effect, real life occurrences. In the example just referenced from *Wag the Dog*, inclement weather was necessary for the event to play as scripted and for the president to wrap the elderly mother with his cloak. When Virginia had sunny skies but Florida was under rain clouds, the president's landing site was rescheduled. These ruptures force what is akin to a rewrite on the set of a film production, a common circumstance in Hollywood moviemaking. Motss' Act Two will soon unfold with its own dramatic rupture causing a rewrite of the ending. Mindfully, the scenario constructed by Brean and Motss remains true to its intent—the president is reelected. But the developments in its wake are unexpected and fatal to some.

Faced with the end of their "war" and the potential resurrection of the Firefly girl story, Motss reminds his staff that every war needs a hero, perhaps someone left behind. He or she might even have been forgotten or discarded, like an old shoe. Motss instructs Ames to secure the name of a soldier in a Special Projects Unit who can be offered to the public as a fighting man captured in Albania behind enemy lines but who later is released and then transported back to the United States. All the better, Motts instructs, if his name is Shoemaker, Schubert, or some derivative of the word "shoe" because that connects to other planned attention-grabbing strategies (see #8 in the characteristics of pseudo-events). Sgt. William Schumann (Woody Harrelson) is located at a Special Projects Unit in Oklahoma where he will be picked up by Ames, Brean, and Motss.

Meanwhile, Johnny Green and a fellow blues singer concoct a song entitled "Good Old Shoe" and record it. Motss has the song pressed on 78 rpm shellac disc and instructs Ames to bury it in the Library of Congress where it will be "discovered" as a 1930s artifact by a reporter to whom its existence is leaked by his girlfriend who serves on Ames' staff. The "vintage" song receives media exposure, as does a ballad by Merle Haggard called "Courage Mom." That title comes from the translation of the Morse Code-like holes and slashes pictured on Schumann's shirt in his doctored "POW" photo, a secret communication concocted by the Motss-Brean team. A shoe-hurling fad is started and encouraged by Motss, which results in old footwear being tied together and thrown upward to hang on tree branches and telephone wires across the country. News services celebrate the fad. One TV news story covers "a moment of sheer patriotism"—hundreds of fans in the bleachers tossing pairs of shoes onto a gymnasium floor. T-shirts start to appear with imprints such as "Bring Him Home" and "Fuck Albania." Even midlevel Hollywood celebrities who happen to be Albanian—in this case, Jim Belushi—are given airtime to plead for the safe release of Sgt. Schumann.[6] The rapid assimilation of these pseudo-events prepares the public for the eventual return of the "war hero" and a continued diversion from the Firefly scandal. No tie-in is too absurd or trivial; Fad King even pitches a "happy meal"-like fast food product called "Schuburger" that comes in a container package with shoelaces as a ribbon! The ironic stance of *Wag the Dog* duly notes the transparent nature of these events, even as it straightforwardly presents the myth-making nature of them that is wholeheartedly endorsed by PCM forces.

When Sgt. Schumann is delivered to Brean and his cohorts at an airfield, they discover that he is a mentally unstable convict who was incarcerated as a wayward soldier in the appropriate Special Projects unit. Undeterred, Motss accepts the manacled "hero" and instructs their pilot to fly back to the reception site. A rupture transpires when their plane crashes in the heartland, but Motss keeps spinning and buying time as they work their way to Washington. Another unexpected twist occurs when Schumann is shot and killed by a farmer who discovers the soldier with his daughter! But Motss and Brean's rewrite of the unfolding story simply casts Shumann as a fighting man whose POW wounds were so critical that he did not survive the return trip, and is consequently delivered with full military honors in a flag-draped casket. A "Ballad of the Green Berets"-styled song plays on the soundtrack as a uniformed honor guard accompanies the coffin from the landing field to the reviewing stand. This mockery of a tribute plays well on television as an outpouring of grief and patriotism. The president's favorability rating ascends to 89% and he is assured re-election.

Motss and Brean watch the ceremony from a distance. The Hollywood producer marvels at this "complete fucking fraud" that looks 100% real. Brean is less impressed, as this is all in a day's work for him as a political fixer. Anonymity of his manipulative role and ultimate success in the staging of events are his rewards, and Brean's guarantee of future work assignments. It has been dawning on him that Motss is somewhat of a loose cannon, confirmed when film producer Stanley finally admits that he wants credit for this pageant. Of course, pseudo-events can never be revealed for what they are to the general public, especially one of this magnitude. The irony of reality as different from its masked appearance is made evident for the viewer of *Wag the Dog* and not, as noted, the electorate in the film. Motss is escorted back to his Hollywood mansion where he dies of a "massive heart attack." Director Barry Levinson considers Stanley Motss' recurring reaction to stupefying events—"This is nothing!"—representative of a man painfully dire and cynical, but alive with optimism.[7] The fact that Motss refuses to admit defeat, unto his death, insures his elimination and forces the audience of *Wag the Dog* to consider the stakes and consequences of pseudo-events that deftly masquerade as reality.

In a thought-provoking coda, there is a brief news story about an emerging resistance movement called "Albania Unite!" This can be read in one of two ways, both equally alarming: 1) There is some need to continue the distraction that a war brings to further complete the PCM agenda and attend to the demands of a misinformed or under informed electorate; 2) The pseudo-events that created this "war" have genuinely ignited a sense of revolutionary upheaval and resistance that will either conflict or conspire with the PCM agenda.

Wag the Dog illustrates Jean Baudrillard's concept of manipulating images to become simulacra. The successive phases of the manipulation of the image begin with (1) a reflection of a basic reality, but soon (2) mask and pervert that basic reality, and then (3) mask the absence of a basic reality, before finally bearing no relation to any reality whatever: it is its own pure simulacrum (*Selected Writings*, 1988). In fact, the simulation of reality is so perfect and intense that it usurps the very state itself and imposes its own set of perverse rules. Those new rules are simply about beguiling, seducing, and fascinating the spectator with further simulations. The difficulty in discerning the real from the unreal is a contentious state also maintained by media practitioners use of 'spin control,' a term that mostly implies interpretive analysis but, when conjoined with the creation of pseudo-events, becomes an important part of the follow-through and overall process. In *Wag the Dog*, an ironic stance is equipped to discern this strategy.

For Conrad Brean and Stanley Motss, their spinning never stops until the job is done. It is an aggressive game of spin that accommodates two aspects that define new media: speed and segmentation. Thanks to new technologies, information now travels at a quicker pace. That accelerated pace is insured by the burgeoning number of new media outlets that crave new stories all the time and are in competition with one another. Former Clinton Press Secretary Dee Dee Myers says:

> Things move so fast and impressions get imbedded in people's minds so quickly. . As time goes forward we see that media is going to become more

diverse, faster and, quite frankly, less accountable. The Internet is a great example. There's no accountability on the Internet. They can say anything they want. Even credible news agencies put things up on the Internet and then pull them down later. The long-term effect of that creates a difficult environment which will mean more spin, with the news business becoming more like a ping-pong match. Now, the good news in all this is that people become more skeptical. They don't believe everything they see on TV. They don't believe everything they read in the Internet or newspaper and that's pretty healthy given the reality. . . I think they'll become increasingly sophisticated as time goes on instead of becoming increasingly gullible.[8]

Wag the Dog is presented as a satire, a ridiculously clichéd satire at that. Sgt. Schumann, for instance, exits the story in an homage to farmer's daughter jokes! The "We Are the World"-style anthem, sung in melodic, over-the-top fashion, has a racially and sexually mixed chorus delivering the line-by-line lyrics that promote jingoism and militarism. Sometimes an unmasked misdeed or lie is only overcome by creating a bigger lie. This is evidenced in recent political memory with Nixon in 1973 (I am not a crook), Ford in 1976 (There is no Soviet domination in Eastern Europe), Reagan in 1987 (I didn't know about any diversion of funds to the Contras. No one kept proper records of meetings or decisions at the NSC), Bush I in 1991 (The specter of Vietnam has been buried forever in the desert sands of the Arabian peninsula), Clinton in 1996 (I did not have sex with that woman), and Bush II (By far the vast majority of my tax cuts go to the bottom end of the spectrum; Mission Accomplished!; Ken who?). Of course, U.S. presidents are not the only politicians capable of prevarication in the service of obfuscation. Two other recent false admissions: "We had no way of predicting that terrorists would hijack planes and crash them into buildings" (Condoleezza Rice, 2003), and "There is no doubt that Saddam Hussein has chemical weapons stocks" (Colin Powell, 2003).

As *Wag the Dog* interfaces with historical reality, it is clear that certain events have overtaken the satiric mindset of the film, and political reality may have moved beyond satire thanks to the explosion and acceptance of pseudo-events. In any case, the compliance of the media and many spectators' acceptance of such tactics that celebrate the simulacrum reverse the ideal that media is meant to convey information that communicates facts and reality to an audience. If the media creates and manipulates information and fabricates simulated reality in order to manipulate the audience for any other reason, then that is a reversal of the ideal. Acceptance of this results in a more jaded public, with the cost being disengagement and a failure to participate in the arenas of social, democratic process. The ironic stance is capable of discerning the mockery of this process and thus exposing it.

BOB ROBERTS (1992)

The pseudo-documentary is a unique cinematic form combining elements of fiction and nonfiction film. Distinguishable from *docudrama*, it is a term describing any dramatization that seeks to recreate, using performers, the activity of actual persons and events. The psuedo-documentary has the shape, content and formal components of pure documentary. Yet, it is revealed to be scripted and acted in the manner of a fictional film. While docudrama overtly acknowledges its mimicry of documentary content, pseudo-documentary strategies are more covert. At times, the phrases *documentary parody* or *mock documentary* are used interchangeably with pseudo-documentary. Parody mocks or ridicules its target—which is frequently a communicative form such as television commercials, sitcoms, newscasts, bumper stickers, or documentary films—and can address some conventions or codes emblematized by that form. Parody, like reflexivity, draws attention to the formal properties of the message-carrier or media.[9] Strategies of documentary/pseudo-documentary, parody, and reflexivity are all appropriated in *Bob Roberts*, which employs an ironic stance to skewer a variety of circumstances that surround a contemporary political campaign.

Reflexivity, as already noted, relates to self-awareness, for both the viewer and the filmmaker. Film historian Jay Ruby describes the reflexive state as being "sufficiently self-aware to know what aspects of self are necessary to reveal so than an audience is able to understand both the process employed and the resultant product and to know that the revelation itself is purposive, intentional, and not merely narcissistic or accidentally revealing."[10] The audience is constantly reminded that it is engaged in spectatorship every time the camera moves or a new setup is revealed. Indeed, the real-world images of documentaries are diminished in veracity when fiction film strategies are imposed. The need to capture a real event as it happens does not always allow for balanced lighting, hidden microphones, calculated camera movements, continuity editing procedures, and various other unobtrusive properties of the classical Hollywood style. It is especially important, then, to understand the production techniques of documentary film that are applied and then undermined by the narrative of pseudo-documentary when viewed through an ironic perspective. Both form and content are, ultimately, explored/exposed by this ironic stance.

As a pseudo-documentary, *Bob Roberts* can be said to present a false consciousness within a falsified form. Its insightfulness, however, is buried within this very rekeying of form.[11] Pseudo-documentray relies on the rekeying of narrative. *This is Spinal Tap* (Reiner, 1984) looks and sounds like a music documentary but it mocks much of that milieu; *Forgotten Silver*

(Jackson, 1995) uses the framework of homage and biography to honor an under-appreciated New Zealand filmmaker whose fictional story is told in a way both straight-faced and preposterous; *The Blair Witch Project* (Myrick, Sanchez, 1999) posits filmmakers exploring supernatural mysteries who eventually turn the cameras on themselves as they descend into (scripted) danger, fear, and anxiety. By rekeying, the pseudo-documentary demands an acknowledgment of the fabrication of filmmaking itself, blurring the lines between the parent genres of narrative and nonfiction.

The theme of *Bob Roberts* concerns the difficulty of really knowing what a political candidate stands for when that persona is seen in a carefully planned and staged media performance. This tendency, evident in some of the other films discussed such as *Network, Bamboozled,* and *Wag the Dog*, can lead to demagoguery through the compliant interlocking action of political, corporate, and media interests. *Bob Roberts* affords another example of this but also includes a direct warning about the lack of vigilance by the citizenry that allows demagogues to arise. At the end of the film, British reporter Terry Manchester (Brian Murray) who is assembling the documentary we are watching, visits the Jefferson Memorial in Washington, D.C. He confesses to one of Roberts' supporters that he doesn't know if he really likes the candidate, even wondering if Roberts is healthy America. *Bob Roberts* explores and critiques the image and the reality of leadership as it is pursued and practiced, and more importantly, projected, in mass mediated times. The film reaches what Jean Baudrillard calls "the hyperreal, a realm of simulated images and sounds constructed by powerful forces of marketing and media, as well as politics, so that the surest, quickest, broadest connections can be made to an otherwise disparate and diverse body of voters/consumers/viewers."[12]

Candidate Bob Roberts (Tim Robbins) is challenging a liberal incumbent senator named Brickley Paiste (Gore Vidal), whose lead in the voter polls is reduced, thanks largely to the innuendo of supposed sexual misconduct. Paiste represents old-style politics, and in a debate with Roberts they mouth phrases that seem lifted directly from the 1992 Presidential campaign (We need a strong America. I will bring the values of the common man to bear in Washington. We need to care about people. Let's cut taxes!).

The new politics of Roberts has an exciting, vibrant and visual appeal. In a country that casts ballots based on candidates' telegenic properties, the elderly, traditional, progressive Paiste will likely lose to the younger, slicker, and well-packaged candidate, substance notwithstanding. The cool and polished Roberts speaks in populist generalities, and while he has co-opted some rebel imagery in his persona, he remains true to conservative, Wall Street bedrock tendencies including the practice of insider stock-trading. He is religiously pious, standing for school prayer and creationism, and overly

The "rebel conservative" candidate for Senate, Bob Roberts (Tim Robbins), waves to supporters at a campaign stop under the watchful eye of manager Lukas Hart III (Alan Rickman).

aggressive in the war on drugs. At one campaign stop he makes an anti-drug speech that is pompous, condescending and somewhat false; the film later reveals Roberts as accused of using the humanitarian status of his Broken Dove organization to transport arms and supplies into South and Central America, and to funnel drugs out of them. His role in a failed savings and loan scheme is another historical referent that underlies the hypocrisy of the Roberts campaign. As Senator Paiste edges ahead in the polls, the Roberts campaign stages an assassination attempt on its candidate who survives, gains ground through public sympathy and concern, and wins the election while convalescing. At a Washington celebration in support of preparedness for the impending Gulf War I in January 1991, the wheelchair-bound senator is exposed by Manchester's camera to be tapping his foot to a musical number. It is a revelation that the senator is not paralyzed as the media has made the public believe, shown here through the probing camera of independent documentary film that is the pseudo-documentary *Bob Roberts*. Cinema reveals Roberts as an opportunist, skilled at the art of deception, and the mainstream mass media as his accomplice.

Manchester, the documentary journalist covering the 1990 Roberts campaign for a U.S. Senate seat in Pennsylvania, has no glitz or pretense of show business, nor does he appear allied with any PCM forces. His independent, outsider status as an objective, foreign-born observer, works to distance both himself and his viewers from readily empathizing with Roberts, especially when compared to Wayne Gayle's intensity and intrusion into the action of *Natural Born Killers*. In addition to utilizing an on-screen narrator in the person of Manchester, *Bob Roberts* contains several other devices associated with documentary film that accommodate the genre and the audience's information-processing habits. These include interviews, a biographical career recap, footage of news coverage and photo-ops, behind-the-scenes shots of the campaign, live event transmissions, and even performances and music videos created by the folksinger-candidate.[13] A reflexive and rhetorical device in pseudo-documentary is "testimony," the apparent truthful discourse invited upon a subject and delivered by one who has reason to evoke witness. Usually this takes the form of the head-on interview under controlled circumstances, edited into the film at the proper time for the desired effect.

The words of testimony, usually presented as answers to interview questions or direct address by an individual, are dispersed in the film at pertinent moments. The result is commentary on the PCM structures that makes *Bob Roberts* more than just a film about rekeying and reflexivity. Testimony becomes a type of dialogue (as opposed to monologue) working with other action and other testimony that engages critical and ironic sensibilities. Several times during *Bob Roberts*, there are scenes of Manchester's sit-down interview with an African-American investigative print journalist for *Troubled Times*, Bugs Raplin (Giancarlo Esposito), who doggedly asks difficult questions to which he receives lip service, at best, from the campaign. When the Roberts campaign fails to pin the charge of an assassination attempt on Raplin, he concedes that if people want the truth in America, they have to seek it out and be vigilant, unrelenting, uncompromising. The journalist announces his intention to get (i.e., expose) Bob Roberts, but not with a gun.

Testimony can also be revealing when caught on the run, as when Roberts campaign manager Lukas Hart III (Alan Rickman) speaks to waiting news people outside the hospital where his candidate lies in critical condition. He promises that his man will soon rise from his hospital bed and head "straight for Washington." Testimony can also exist in simple forms, such as the message on a T-shirt, billboard or political button. It emanates most dramatically and ironically, of course, from the mouth of the candidate in this film—in interviews, debate, speeches and in song.

While the voting public accepts the mass-mediated version of candidate Roberts, viewers of the film *Bob Roberts* are privy to the maneuvers and personalities that create what exists beneath the surface. Thus, by intuitively appreciating a film narrative in the challenging form of pseudo-documentary, cinema instructs us on our own gullibility and the forces that benefit from it. We are shown the seams and shortfalls in the electioneering structure that is maintained by the PCM state. We are given dissenting voices that are, regretfully, either silenced or merely worried. And most importantly, we are given the challenge and responsibility to maintain vigilance.

Bob Roberts does not spare the liberal media elite, either. When the candidate appears on a hip, late-night variety show called *Cutting Edge Live*, some members of its staff refuse to work with him. One goes so far as to disconnect audio and video cables during the telecast, causing feedback and chaos, as Roberts begins to sing his anthemic "Retake America." Behind the scenes at the show, monitors provide news coverage with images of George Bush, Saddam Hussein, and the impending crisis in Saudi Arabia. Characters on *Cutting Edge* dressed like bumpkins and lobsters rehearse their silly sketches and seem unaffected by the real news events in this network studio that panders to its corporate sponsors while presenting yet another version of controlled nonconformity. Roberts' presence is short-circuited, but he receives apologies from the TV show's producer and an invitation to return at a later date.

Bugs Raplin can never be part of mainstream TV or the newspaper medium. He and his ideas are too extreme, even though truth-filled. Raplin represents crusader-journalists, such as Danny Casolaro, who pursued the Iran-Contra controversy to its highest levels of influence as a freelance writer beginning in 1990. Casolaro's mysterious death in 1991 was deemed suicide.[14] When Manchester interviews Raplin after his release from custody, the shot begins on a television set in Bugs' apartment. The set is turned off, but on the dormant monitor we can see his reflection as he speaks to Manchester's camera. Before moving to a head-on angle, the dim and distorted form of Bugs that is reflected in the TV tube's glass front is at once an attempt to break through to the mainstream media as well as being representative of its very resistance to Bugs.

At several moments in *Bob Roberts* spectators are invited to view the reality of this candidate through various frames of reference. The apparatus of television or documentary film is acknowledged as part of the reflexive perspective, and then a critical stance engages as we discern just what Bob Roberts represents. Ultimately, the ironic is invoked through our new awareness that appearance differs from reality, and that this candidate signifies a shift toward theocracy and fascism that many voters unwittingly embrace. Sometimes, this is ratified by a literal representation of "framed" reality.

At the taping of the TV program "Good Morning, Philadelphia" spectators of *Bob Roberts* can be situated once, twice, or several times removed from the interview taking place on the set. We see the live interview and can observe it through the TV camera viewfinders and monitors in the studio where

Manchester's cameramen are photographing. Throughout *Bob Roberts*, the flickering images of the cathode ray tube remind us that this is television reality, different from the film that encases it, and different from lived reality. And observing these various frames of reference are people who regard Roberts with support, skepticism, or with neutrality. While Manchester remains neutral as he covers Roberts' campaign, two news people at the aforementioned taping—the interviewer Kelly Noble (Lynne Thigpen) and the news anchorman Dan Riley (Peter Gallagher)—represent what writer-director Tim Robbins calls examples of "the tough journalist and the whore journalist." [15] He continues, "Part of the problem with the press in this country is its cozy relationship with politicians. When you find these people mingling with each other at cocktail parties in Washington you realize there might be a problem here." Once Kelly Noble pegs Roberts a rebel conservative, deviant and brilliant, she will likely not be among those invited to the candidate's victory party in November. She tells Manchester that Bob Roberts is like Richard Nixon, only shrewder and more complicated. He has brilliantly adopted the persona and mindset of a free-thinking rebel and turned it on itself. This penchant for reinvention of self is a celebrated mark of the American character. Such transformations are gladly embraced in a mass-mediated environment where stories of change and makeover comprise the diversions of their comedic and dramatic bills of fare.

The seemingly paralyzed yet victorious candidate strikes a closing chord from his song "This World Turns" then segues into a salute to his well-wishers in Bob Roberts.

The apex of misconstruction, as in *Wag the Dog*, is unspoken to the general voting public in the film but made aware to the audience of *Bob Roberts* via the conventions of cinema storytelling that promote the ironic stance. The phony assassination story is parlayed by the media into a saga of the near-martyrdom of Roberts and then his eventual election. His supporters keep vigil outside the hospital where Roberts recovers. It is a pensive but volatile mob that erupts with cheers when it learns that Bugs Raplin—a suspect in the attempt on Roberts' life—has himself been killed when released from custody. As Terry Manchester's van drives past various D.C. sites toward the Jefferson Memorial, a news report of Raplin's death plays on the radio and, as in *Medium Cool*, informs him and the viewers of *Bob Roberts* of a character's fate. In *Bob Roberts*, however, the announcer situates this act of hostility—as opposed to the accidental deaths in *Medium Cool*—in its immediate historical context of larger violence.This includes the failure of diplomacy to avert conflict in Iraq and the rising poll numbers of American who support the use of force in the Middle East. The camera pans across the epitaph at the Jefferson Memorial. A quote from Thomas Jefferson etched in stone around the inner perimeter wall is readable: "I have sworn upon the altar of God eternal hostility against every form of tyranny over the mind of man."

In the nearly 25 years between the release of *Medium Cool* and the release of *Bob Roberts*, the whole world may have indeed been watching consequential events, but mass media's duplicity and complicity in obfuscating such events often goes largely unheralded. Tim Robbins said, "I set *Bob Roberts* in the fall of 1990 because I want to remember that time: it was an extremely significant time when we saw quite honestly how willing the news media is to go along with, and be the lap dog of, government. It is because of this corruption and complicity that Bob Roberts exists and is able to rise to power." Wishing to restore the responsibility for true agency—for eternal vigilance over *every* form of tyranny with the citizen-spectator where it belongs—Robbins concludes the film with a bold-type, four-letter word in the credits: VOTE. Perhaps fittingly, the final image is serious and forthright, devoid of any trace of irony.

BULWORTH (1998)

Bulworth displays an ironic stance as it examines the final stages in a campaign for political office, but not with a variance in narratology like *Bob Roberts*. Its storytelling technique is not pseudo-documentary but a straightforward narrative framework. *Bulworth,* with its hip-hop influenced white politician, like *Bob Roberts,* with its "rebel conservative," considers nontraditional characterology as the driving force for engagement and change in the film's players and the electorate. These apparent contradictions lend an aura of the surreal to the stories. Meanwhile, the writings of Kenneth Burke inform an interpretation of *Bulworth* in ways that make this surrealism better understood in service to the narrative.

Like *Bob Roberts, Bulworth* is mostly comic satire, but it, too, concludes in a fashion more akin to nightmare. Director-writer Warren Beatty would arguably agree with Tim Robbins who said *Bob Roberts* was designed to frighten people about the dangers of demagoguery when an image-controlled society does not question itself enough. Meanwhile, there exists a press that is not vigilant enough to expose or control errant elements of the government. The result is that people's lives are sacrificed because of ignorance and lack of vigilance.

Because *Bulworth* represents the most abrupt and radical transformation of a main character observed thus far in these films, and because this happens, for the most part, under the glare of the mass media spotlight, some insights from two social theorists are noteworthy. Kenneth Burke's dramatism, and Neil Gabler's thesis that life is enacted as a movie with the self as star known as a "lifie" (*Life: The Movie,* 2000), underpins much of what has already been discussed. As noted earlier, Burke's dramatism explores what is involved when we say what people are doing and why they are doing it. This method of sense-making finds contemporary application in the world of entertainment and information, which according to Gabler, has inspired a new way to look at and experience life itself as a movie or screen story.

Dramatism invites us to consider motivation in the symbolic action of others. Psychological and material patterns emerge that prompt action in such a way that certain desirable results are obtained. These patterns evoke a way of responding that can bring forth and build both culture and identity. The dramatistic model is "the most inclusive metaphor available to Burke for understanding and giving healthful direction to human action" (*The Dance of Language,* Robert Adams, 1983). Language, and by extension dramatism, is the keynote in the symphony of sense-making. And sense-making is the struggle for survival. We are compelled to embrace language—and the communication practices that later developed—as the building block of reality construction.

Other perspectives are acknowledged through language and action. Movies, especially, allow for the quick shifting of points-of-view; most films alter their *physical* point of view (i.e., the placement of the camera) hundreds of time in a feature-length movie, but the *philosophical* point of view (i.e., the moral posture of the narrative, or the theme) rarely shifts and usually has a

final consensus. Interpreting, then understanding other philosophical perspectives, is a process rife with ambiguity and difficulty. The potential for
uncertainty exists because of the varying, shifting perspectives in a system
of communication that invite states of disinformation and chaos.[16] This is a
vital part of the system's make-up. It invites free will to achieve a sense of
outcome. In the manipulation of images in some of the films observed, free
will is diminished *unless* viewers acknowledge the manipulations and accept
or reveal them for what they are.

Burke expresses a preference for the emotional, poetic process. He celebrates
the poetic metaphor over the neutral or mechanistic alternative, with the result
being ethical universe-building. His dramatistic approach is both well inten-
tioned and serviceable as it applies to these film texts, since it gives cinema spectators a clear window that incorporates the reflexive, critical and ironic stances
through which to view human motivation and the structures it creates.

Kenneth Burke's writings during the 1930's arrived at a time when the
modern world was expanding with postindustrial fury. The seeds of change
were being planted in political, economic, social and technological fields.
Burke qualified the strategies of art as especially adept at illuminating these
fields. His insistence that communication *is* perspective, a way of looking and
understanding, calls forth aesthetic truth.

Acceleration and change in the opportunities and attributes with which the
artist can engage are simultaneously a privilege and a challenge. The need for
an artist, in this case a filmmaker, to convey a sense of reality in his or her
art requires an intensity and spontaneity of purpose that arise out of the situations in life itself, according to Burke, until the artist "discovers himself not
only with a message, but also with a desire to produce effects upon his audience."[17] This is the approach, with varying degrees of risk-taking, assumed by
characters Mickey and Mallory (and Wayne Gayle), Stanley Motss, and Terry
Manchester, and by filmmakers Stone, Levinson and Robbins. What Burke
calls an "eloquence of profusion" is represented by the cinema artist who is
fully preoccupied by his subject, concerned with exceptional variety and/or
exceptional accuracy, functioning *in* the moment, as he is *of* the moment.

Much as Kenneth Burke would investigate the associational clusters of a
text, so *Bulworth* itself is an association of language and images that creates
patterns from where identity, values, and reality come forth. The film text is
presented as both social critique and entertainment positioned from an ironic
stance. With the subject matter or theme of *Bulworth* being the role of social
hierarchy and hegemonic control in a world where language and communication should bespeak qualified action but often don't, the film affords a
pragmatically humanistic approach that resonates with Burke.

Since the early 1990's, actor-director Warren Beatty had wanted to produce *Bulworth*. He co-wrote the screenplay with Jeremy Pikser and eventually was budgeted $30 million by Rupert Murdoch's 20th Century Fox Films for an unspecified directing project over which he would retain complete control. Its financing and distribution set, the resulting film carries a distinctly anti-Murdochian message of the need for limits and controls of media-ownership as it indicts the interlocking PCM power blocs that conspire to keep racial and economic barriers in place for the lower and middle-classes. Using rap music as another weapon in its language-based arsenal—even though a 60 year-old white man offers it up—*Bulworth* employs humor and perspective by incongruity to reclaim the ethical through the aesthetic. Hip-hop culture becomes the window from which Bulworth signifies. "Signifying" means using language to mean two or more things, applying parody, allusion, misdirection and code to make one word convey multiple meanings. For his part, Burke credits Oswald Spengler and his creation of historical perspectives:

> . . . by taking a word usually applied to one setting and transferring its use to another setting. It is a 'perspective by incongruity' since he established it by violating the 'properties' of the word in its previous linkages. . . . (Furthermore) Nietzsche knew that probably every linkage was open to destruction by the perspectives of a planned incongruity.[18]

Through situation and characterology, Beatty applies perspective by incongruity in *Bulworth*. Burke's "Lexicon Rhetoricae" in *Counter-Statement* deals with the appeal of form, its progression and repetitive value as well as other aspects—individuation, interrelation, rhythmic patterns, potential for conflict with other forms, and connection with ideology and experience. Rap and hip-hop music are vibrant representations of form as function, giving voice that is both radical and optimistic. Both the film and the music exist as vocabulary, or equipment, "for handling the complexities of living."[19]

Warren Beatty is a professed, old school liberal not unlike Senator Brickley Paiste in *Bob Roberts*. The photo of Robert Kennedy and Jay Bulworh (whom Beatty portrays in the film) in the opening scene is not computer generated, but a real image from Beatty's life of political activism. Though he has professionally benefited from some of the financially predatory PCM forces that Bulworth rails against, especially the movies and the media, Beatty's film uses language to advance ideas that are not often addressed in mainstream movies. He is, after all, a man whose previous directorial effort was *Reds* (1981), a celebration of American Communism produced as Ronald Reagan was moving into the White House. With the film character of Jay Bulworth and in 'biting the Hollywood hand that feeds him,' Beatty contends with what can be termed an occupational psychosis, prompting the performance style, or ingratiation, which incorporates signifying through political diatribe, melodrama, and rap music.

Senator Jay Billington Bulworth's epiphany comes early in the film with the rejection of the old language of political style. It is prompted by the repetition of pre-packaged television images of his reelection spots. As *Bulworth* opens, it is an evening in March 1996, and the last week of the California primary. Alone, incumbent Bulworth weeps in despair at his desk in Washington while a TV monitor plays variations of his recent campaign ads. The walls are filled with photos of a younger Bulworth next to Malcolm X, Bobby Kennedy, and Martin Luther King, Jr. The audio from the TV ads is a constant, slightly innocuous refrain spoken by Bulworth about "standing at the doorstep to a new millennium." Heard again and again, monotonic and without real feeling, it is not difficult to recognize the hollowness and hypocrisy of what passes for much of contemporary political rhetoric. And where he once was part of suggesting solutions to America's problems, Bulworth knows now that he is part of the problem. He is poised for what Burke would call a conversion downwards which will lead, ultimately, to a brand new realization of motives and accompanying rebirth.

Disgusted with himself and in the midst of a nervous breakdown, Bulworth arranges to increase his life insurance policy with the help of crooked lobbyist Graham Crockett (Paul Sorvino). The Senator, subsequently, puts out a contract on his own life without revealing himself as the intended victim to the contact, Vinnie (Richard Sarafian), nor wishing to know the identity of his hit man (who is yet to be revealed). Relieved that he will soon be out of his misery, Bulworth flies to Los Angeles for the last leg of his campaign. The first stop is an African-American church in South Central where, after beginning his canned speech, he cannot make himself speak its scripted banalities. The black congregation asks tough, pointed questions about the lack of federal funding for rebuilding their community following the urban riots of four years ago. After a long pause, the candidate answers to the surprise of all, including his advance men and handlers that he and other politicians (George Bush, Bill Clinton, Pete Wilson) paid visits to the neighborhood, got their pictures taken, told the people what they wanted to hear, and then "pretty much forgot about it." The crowd boos and gets more than a little hostile, but Bulworth is undaunted. When asked why politicians like himself ignore black and minority interests, especially in the areas of health insurance addressed by a pending Senate bill, he blithely responds that they have contributed very little money to his campaign especially when compared to large insurance companies. He admits their support encourages senators to stalemate legislation that would cause the entrenched interests financial loss and headaches.

What might be termed the "Bulworth moment" occurs when the unexpected emerges from a source not normally inclined to produce such an emanation, to the twin astonishment of the perpetrator and the witnesses. The epiphany is for both player and spectators, with the latter being both the audience in the frame—in this case, the church—and the film's spectators. Indeed, Bulworth even disparages his own party. He asks his constituents if they see any Democrat addressing their problems and then sarcastically challenges them to vote for a Republican! The average politician courting votes in the ghetto is hardly apt to utter Bulworth's warning and prophecy. He tells them they could have a *Billion* Man March, but if they don't "put down that malt liquor and chicken wings and stop backing somebody other than a running back who stabs his wife" then they will never get rid of ineffectual politicians.

Surprised at his candor, Bulworth begins to feel his own humanity and the provocative power of aesthetic truth on himself and his audience. *Bulworth* assumes a critical stance or consciousness (the critique of social structures and situations) and further explores its subjects with an ironic stance (an audacious and unexpected 'performance' by the senator). En route to the next appearance, Bulworth asks his limousine driver to pull into a Kentucky Fried Chicken stand. The distraught candidate hadn't eaten in three days, and appetites of all sorts are returning.

Bulworth's next campaign stop is a Beverly Hills gathering of high-rolling movie moguls. He asks them to admit candidly that most of their films are not very good, that they're likely motivated by profit only, and most bluntly, that they "turn everything to crap." Meanwhile, his campaign manager Murphy (Oliver Platt), a spin doctor in denial of these "Bulworth moments," also uses language to construct *his* version of reality, praising "the value of a frank exchange" and saying that everyone is "energized by this kind of give and take." At an all-night dance club, the senator smokes pot and tosses off some feeble rhymes to get the attention of Nina (Halle Berry), who has become part of his entourage. After closing, he toys with the DJ's turntables, feeling more and more comfortable in what Burke would call the "cracking" of language and action that supports perspective by incongruity. *Bulworth* appreciates the irony of this well-meaning white man who talks and acts like an undaunted "mack daddy," but is seemingly out of his league with unexpected words and deeds.

Bulworth's emergent style might be defined by Burke as a set of prescriptions and proscriptions for doing the right thing. It solidifies at a high-profile Wilshire Hotel fundraiser later that day. In attendance are the many well-heeled professionals and their operatives, including lobbyist Crockett, who support PCM establishment policies. The candidate shocks his audience by delivering a rap-style tirade. Strutting among the crowd seated at several

Nina (Halle Berry)—a woman both muse and political operative for Senator Jay Billington Bulworth (Warren Beatty).

round tables, Bulworth's mode of action is meant to arouse, educate and persuade. Bulworth has been moving, literally and figuratively, from the pulpit to the streets and back again, rediscovering his connection with the disenfranchised. Rap, like spoken language, is an "implement of action, a device which takes shape by the cooperative patterns in the group that uses it."[20] Bulworth adapts the rhythmic patterns and the outrage from rap and hip-hop culture, speaking with and to its inhabitants and to potential converts. In his rap—an extended Bulworth moment—he takes on hot-button issues most politicians avoid: campaign finance reform, the danger of catering to special interests, war for oil, savings and loan defaults, environmental decay and a crippled EPA, the need to create and focus on demonized targets such as Islam, the healthcare crisis and radical alternatives to it, and sex and sexism in politics.

Reborn, Bulworth begins to wonder who his potential assassin could be and when he will be struck down. The campaign takes on new life and Bulworth is personally reinvigorated in the process, even falling in love with

Nina. Now he wants to rescind his earlier request for the hit on himself, but its cancellation has to travel through a middleman who, as a plot contrivance to enhance the dramatic chase or "ticking clock" aspects of the storyline, has had a heart attack and is incommunicado. At a television interview later in the film, Bulworth is the very antithesis of his persona on the mind-numbing commercials seen at the beginning of the film. In a rapid free-association he broadsides institutions and individuals among the PCM elites that persist in dividing America. He now has his bully pulpit and is himself colorful media copy, gaining respect and support among his African-American constituents. He raps his political stances and they resonate with aesthetic *and* reflexive truth. We know, in other words, that this is a white guy trying on black cultural idioms for utilitarian purposes. However idiosyncratic it appears, it *feels* right. Bulworth engineers a campaign victory and the start of a romance with Nina, but is unable to short-circuit the real shooter in the shadows that deems him and his ideas threatening to entrenched political, corporate and media powers.

The farcical tone in Bulworth is inviting to Burkian analysis and its penchant for wordplay. Even the senator's name, as if to ask "is the bull worth it all?" is a playful meditation on style and substance. The conceit of a character reveling in his honesty is at odds with most people who, ultimately, are often appalled by sudden honesty. In fact, the ironic stance is evident in other Hollywood movies that have made the convention of absolute truth-telling a time-honored plot and character twist, in films featuring Bob Hope such as *Nothing But the Truth* (Nugent, 1941) and Jim Carrey in *Liar, Liar* (Shadyac, 1997).

The most extreme example of perspective by incongruity in Bulworth involves a 60 year-old white establishment politician—the ultimate lame duck, or "gargoyle" in Burke's lexicon—in full hip-hop regalia cruising South Central L.A. with a street gang. But even here, the film is able to educate and persuade, making points about drug dealers using children to sell their product since they are too young to legally prosecute (and can make more money than whatever career the under-funded public schools prepare them for), the inefficiency of media coverage of substantial issues (Bulworth tells reporters he leases his legislative agenda to the same communications companies that pay their salary, and then funnel more money back to them in the form of campaign ads; it is no surprise that anything ever gets done to improve the material aspects of ordinary citizens), and the alliance of the medical and insurance industries (He reminds voters the reason the health care industry is so profitable is that they get 24 cents of every dollar). Truth is revealed through direct, honest address not normally vocalized in these situations. In *Bulworth*, perspective by incongruity violates notions of propriety as established

Another "Bulworth moment" as the Senator debates his opponent on live TV and exposes waste in the health care and insurance industries.

by PCM forces. The farcical approach to serious subject matter is certainly evident in this film and many of the others explored. At once both tragic and purposeful, it sustains the poetic metaphor in which, according to Burke, the participant action of character attains its maximum expression.

Bulworth, released within a year of two other politically oriented films (*Wag the Dog, Primary Colors*), resonates with them as well as two other movies also mentioned that address the PCM state. Like *Bob Roberts*, it suggests that those who dare to tell the truth in America shall be quickly silenced. Like *Network*, it challenges the spectator-citizen to maintain vigilance on the connection between corporate power and the political process. *Bulworth* illuminates social problems and creates uncertainties in the mind of audiences, utilizing the eloquence of poetic metaphor to seek out aesthetic and reflexive truth that is illuminated by the ironic stance.

The assassination attempt on Senator Bulworth is the climax of the story. It occurs outside a South Central home where he had taken refuge, and as he emerges to greet his constituents. The sequence is given dramatic resonance in a challenge delivered earlier by the poet-activist Amiri Baraka, playing a homeless man who has appeared in crowd scenes throughout the film. He represents the voice or conscience of well-intentioned America. In one early scene Baraka admonishes Bulworth, saying "You got to sing!" and later, when the senator is in the throes of his own rebirth hollers, "You got the life!" Now outside the hospital where Bulworth lays dying from the assassin's gunfire, in a direct address to the audience he exhorts *us* to be a spirit and not a ghost. The film admonishes audiences to find/create the new spirit that must envelop the land. It is a radical outlook, indeed, if Senator Bulworth's advice given in an earlier television interview is taken to heart. He preached that rich people have always stayed on top by dividing "white people from colored people." But, he contends that white people have more in common with blacks than they do with rich people. Bulworth simply advises that all colors be eliminated in a "voluntary, free-spirited, open-ended program of procreative racial deconstruction." The audacious answer to racism is to mingle all races and bloodlines, obliterating color distinctions. If the color lines ultimately fade, then we are left with the very real division or distinction in society. Race is a superficial, even accidental distinction; the real issue is the disparity of wealth in America. Class, not race, matters.

The fate of the movie *Bulworth* seems ironically tied to the fate of Bulworth the man in the movie. Fox Films and its owner, Rupert Murdoch, minimized Bulworth's advertising and distribution upon its release. As a conservative media practitioner with significant corporate holdings in several media, Murdoch exists in the tradition of William Randolph Hearst. Warren Beatty, in some ways, is akin to writer-director Orson Welles whose film *Citizen Kane* ran afoul of Hearst in 1941. Hearst tried to buy the negative of *Kane* so he could destroy it, and his newspapers refused to accept advertisements for the film, which only began to turn a profit in 1950s re-releases. *Bulworth* grossed just below $27 million in its U.S. theatrical run, not enough to cover its costs.[21] Fox also scheduled its national release simultaneously with the opening day of 1998's most anticipated and hyped film, Columbia TriStar Pictures' *Godzilla*.

Still, considering this film in the company of others that illuminate personalities and the political process, one can appreciate how they have enraged and engaged spectators who can re-ethicize an outlook on reality. By the late 1990s, film and the Internet represented two places where such interrogations of political, corporate and media forces could be undertaken without rampant concern regarding sponsorship and censorship. Television and mainstream media grew more homogenized, existing primarily to deliver audiences to advertisers. Cinema, meanwhile, remains a more singular and risk-worthy sense-making activity, and as such it endures firmly within Kenneth Burke's dramatistic framework of language as an instrument that has the ability to both illuminate and solve problems.

THE TRUMAN SHOW (1998)

Film Exhibition, Voyeurism and Exhibitionism

Before exploring *The Truman Show* as an example of the ironic stance in a film that situates itself within a reality TV show and an admittedly surreal environment, some consideration of a media landscape in the late 1900s that has served the causes of voyeurs and exhibitionists is in order.

By the last century's end, the culture of cinema had become more pervasive and inviting, more inhabitable and habit-forming, and more personal and private. Despite a proliferation of movie screens and multiplexes that signaled some return to the communitarian past, there was a vast deepening of the relationship between the individual and a singularly consumed or customized programming/participation in the cinematic process. The shapes and procedures that inform this relationship in the first decade of the 21st century deserve some mention. In a simplified and general notion, they represent a return to the peepshow past.

The first commercial exhibitions of moving pictures were by Kinetoscope, developed by William K.L. Dickson in Edison's laboratory. They provided scenes of motion for the price of a penny to persons who peered into the slot opening of an upright machine. Films lasted about one minute. Patrons could move from machine to machine and view several "flickers," a term which became more firmly rooted in language during the years that followed. The control of the action's speed could be hand-crank or motorized, and some machines offered the short-lived experiment of a phonograph that played music in accompaniment through a primitive, headphone-like apparatus. Called kinetoscopes, these were found in some drug stores, hotel lobbies, department stores and, primarily, penny arcades. It was the last setting that attracted mostly men and boys who peeped at frequently sexually suggestive or action-laden films. The Kinetoscope fad was brief, lasting only about five years from 1895 to 1900, when projection systems and screens replaced it as the dominant form of movie watching. Consider, however, that almost 100 years later the singular, privatized and smaller-scaled representations of movies came to dominate the act of film spectatorship, especially as television encouraged the private home consumption of the moving image.

The rise and influence of, first television as the dominant forum for presenting and consuming films, and then home video (the VCR, cable TV, DVD) as a preferred mode of spectatorship, insured that the movie watching habit would be increasingly choice-filled. This involved both means and methods of consumption as well as program selection. The option of gathering on a Friday night with hundreds of other like-intentioned spectators at a theater still existed in the late 1900s, but several alternative filmic experiences did, too.

More than likely, a person or persons known to one another consume a movie today in a home or homelike environment, and the spectator controls the presentation of that narrative to a large degree. The dominating factor of new technologies—DVD, video on demand, TiVo, and others innovations—has inarguably altered the manner in which we consume motion picture narratives. Should the viewing experience be less than expected, the person watching can change channels, retrieve another movie, fast-forward to a more compelling scene, or seek other diversions from a DVD menu. In many ways—not just relative to the size of a screen—the act of spectatorship has conventions akin to the pre-Nickelodeon days of the Kinetoscope. The single consumer, controlling the flow of action/replay and moving to other programs when finished or discontented with the one being watched, is not concerned with the communal, shared appreciation of the narrative while viewing something on a screen as small as two inches. Indeed, the portability of DVD players with LCD screens, laptop computers and iPods on which movies can be viewed has increased the options for playback sites and made more ubiquitous the moving image as part of the social landscape.

One other connective to the slightly seedy penny arcade experience of the Kinetoscope era is the role that home video has played in rearticulating the film and video pornography market beginning in the 1970s. The VCR made private, home consumption of adult films an option for viewers perhaps too timid to venture into XXX-rated theaters and, in turn, forced those establishments to modify their own structures. The Kinetoscope-like playing of "peepers" (a term, when used as a noun, referring to those who enjoy seeing the sexual acts or sex organs of others) had an ongoing presence in sex film presentations, especially in sex shops and establishments where peep-show booths presenting 8mm or 16mm loops were part of the overall offerings. Eventually, some adult theaters that embraced the large-screen experience underwent an odd multiplexing of sorts in the 1960s and 1970s when several were reconfigured and repartitioned with viewing rooms or booths. Finally, the easy availability of pornography for playback on home or hotel video doomed the cinema-going experience for the spectator of that specialty niche; now the spectator was quite content to be one with himself or herself.

It is not indelicate to consider ourselves voyeurs when we are spectators at the movies. Indeed, the aforementioned example of adult films and peep shows is an appropriate place to explain the connection that leads to an exploration of *The Truman Show*. According to PsychNet-UK, a website on psychological disorders, *voyeurism* is a disorder of sexual arousal that:

> involves the act of observing unsuspecting individuals, usually strangers, who may be naked or in the process of disrobing or even engaging in sexual activity . . . in current society, a certain amount of voyeurism is considered normal. . . However, the key factor here is that unless you seek out these experiences, you are not a true voyeur.[22]

Voyeurism may occur with another paraphilia known as *exhibitionism*. This is the willingness of an individual to allow himself or herself to be subject to the voyeur's gaze.

Much has been written on the psychoanalytical applications of voyeurism and exhibitionism in cinema ("Visual Pleasure and Narrative Cinema," Laura Mulvey, 1973; *From Reverence to Rape*, Molly Haskell, 1973; *The Imaginary Signifier*, Christian Metz, 1974). While the clinical manifestations give rise to further discourse most specifically in the areas of feminist study and ideological framings, there is the purely physical composition of roles to consider. A voyeur is, by extrapolation, a movie spectator; an exhibitionist is, by extrapolation, a willing actor in a movie. And the film lover is the "supreme voyeur," because according to Raymond Lefevre:

> Hidden in darkness, he watches. . . There is no shame in this, because the screen is not a keyhole and, above all, he is not watching alone. A totally sane complicity joins him to the other spectators. He is far removed from the guilty conscience of those who leer alone.[23]

We may taint the terms voyeur and exhibitionist with moral judgment, but that is not the preference here. A voyeur likes to watch, just as did Chauncey Gardner in *Being There* and also anyone who regularly views film and television shows. An exhibitionist enjoys (or at least is compelled to pretend to enjoy) the act of being watched, which any actor needs to achieve recognition and a successful career. Indeed, the concepts of a voyeur and exhibitionist can specifically apply to the roles of spectator and actor-player in the audience and the performers featured in *The Truman Show*.

Media and Real Life

The Truman Show explores the blurring of life as lived and its representation in the arts, specifically in the framework of 24-hour television programming. The artificial world of that program—the home, neighborhood, the island town of Seahaven, and accompanying environments as studio/performance space—has been constructed especially for Truman Burbank (Jim Carrey). At the start of the film, a title card reads: Day 10,909. Therefore, as he emerges from his front door on that day, Truman has been in this incubative environment for nearly 30 years. He knows no other milieu. Actors surround him, although he relates to them as fellow human beings rather than performers in roles. Some 5000 cameras monitor his life and actions, with his every move and word broadcast live to the world. "The Truman Show" is the creation of erstwhile TV producer Cristof (Ed Harris) who humbly announces at the beginning of the film that many viewers leave the show on all night for comfort.

The Truman Show was released in 1998. One obvious tendency in contemporary media that must be acknowledged is the proliferation of reality shows on television since the early 1990s. Many media critics trace the acceleration of the trend from that era but it has deeper roots. Television's ongoing presence at the Army-McCarthy hearings in the early 1950s, as well as its coverage of presidential funerals since John Kennedy's assassination, are precedents; regularly scheduled network programming was interrupted for these unfolding news stories. The Watergate hearings in 1973 represent another example of the electronic media's round-the-clock vigil of an intriguing subject. But in 1994, for 251 days, the O.J. Simpson trial created what Frank Rich called "an addictive brand of marathon diversion.' Rich notes:

> It was during the O.J. soap opera that we first learned we could spend not just hours and days but weeks watching a drama even when it was unfolding in slo-mo (under Lance Ito's Warholesque direction) and even when nothing was happening beyond the idle, frequently erroneous speculation of camera-hogging experts.[24]

By 2008, media practitioners had co-opted the Simpson trial playbook from Court TV. Now, sponsors, networks and presenters of events susceptible to constant, uninterrupted (or regularly-interrupting) coverage furtively construct these news stories and packages as worthy investments for audiences to extend their viewing times. These mechanics were applied to the Reagan calliope when the former president's orchestrated funeral in Southern California was produced for mass consumption via television. The trappings of ritual, politics, history, and homage, converged with Hollywood and Washington glamour. Media coverage of the death and funeral of Princess Diana of Wales in 1997, and the flood of stories following attacks on the World Trade Center and the Pentagon in 2001, also encouraged lengthy relationships between viewers and the mass media that focused on singular, inspired events. Indeed, they became "televents." Surely, this represents for the spectator, a kind of numbing or comforting application of voyeurism mixed with exhibitionist tendencies of the television medium at large.

The Truman Show contends that we have had enough of this construct, that a surreal or hyper-real media landscape disallows individuation. The frame-breaking in *The Truman Show*—indeed, he will ultimately puncture his way out of the TV show—is exercised due to the transformation of Truman. He will move from an indifferent and unaware participant in a world, a life, and a TV program where he is the main cogwheel and simultaneously ignorant of the controls and manipulations enacted upon him, to a character compelled to break free and make choices, exercising free will in a non-scripted fashion much like the players in the reconstructed "Pleasantville" and unlike those in the restored world of "The Purple Rose of Cairo." Truman's outright rejection of the scripted environment is liberating to both his character and to the audiences of the film. Initially, however, both the voyeur-viewers of "The Truman Show" and the spectators of *The Truman Show* through most of its running time are complicit in enjoying Truman's non-consenting exhibitionism, perhaps revealing their own celebration of innocence and embrace of the ordinary.

Meeting Truman: The Routine and Unexamined Life

The Truman Show begins with a close shot of television producer Christof in a direct address to the camera. He contends that audiences have become bored with watching actors give them phony emotions, and tired of pyrotechnics and special effects. Admitting that Truman's world is counterfeit, there is nothing fake about Truman himself. With no scripts or cue cards, it may not be Shakespeare, but it is genuine. It is, indeed, a life to examine.

Then a pixilated Truman is seen, as if viewed very close to a TV screen. The camera pulls back to reveal that this is a shot from inside his bathroom medicine cabinet as Truman Burbank prepares himself to meet the day—another day of life and of shooting "The Truman Show." He seems to be "talking" himself into a performance, mirroring internal conflict even as he boosts his self-confidence. Like an actor in his dressing room, Truman wavers between fear and doubt about his role to a determined embrace of his character and duty to perform. He will eventually get a stage call from off screen, actually an alert from his wife that he is running late. It signifies that for *The Truman Show*—as well as "The Truman Show"-within-the-show—it's showtime. As seen in *Bamboozled*, a performer steels himself for a performance.

This segment acts as a promotional clip for "The Truman Show" and an introduction to *The Truman Show*. It intersperses interviews with the show's actors—including Hannah Gil (Laura Linney) as Truman's wife Meryl, and

Louis Coltrane (Noah Emmerich) as his best friend Marlon—along with producer Christof, and serves as a lead-in to the programmed day. Day 10,909 in the life of Truman Burbank begins like any other. He emerges from his house with a cheery "Good morning!" and waves to the neighbors, a light-skinned African-American couple with their young daughter, and to Spencer (Ted Raymond), a retiree who is taking out his trash accompanied by his Dalmatian that excitedly jumps to greet a wary Truman. Most of the shots in this opening are brightly lit with a prefabricated set design and captured by a variety of static cameras, some at unusual angles. Director Peter Weir conditions viewers with a calculated tone—one that exudes a feeling of benign surveillance—evoking the promotional tagline for the film: "On the air. Unaware." This artifice is affirmed and revealed when suddenly a large studio light fixture comes crashing to the ground near Truman's driveway, just as he is entering his car. He approaches what, to him, is a curiosity. He cautiously touches and taps the big canister-like fixture that seems to have dropped from outer space. The fallen equipment even has a label—Sirus (9 Canis Major)—that implies starlight. Truman looks up to the picture-perfect blue sky with a quizzical expression and seems to wonder if there is a world beyond what hovers above. "The Truman Show" places its subjects under the surveillance of many cameras and labels the spectacle that develops forthwith *reality*.

Driving to work, Truman listens to a radio newscast. The announcer reports with a news flash that an aircraft in trouble began shedding parts as it flew over Seahaven just a few minutes ago and that, luckily, no one was hurt. This explanation seems to satisfy Truman as he moves through the town, taking for granted the perfectly manicured lawns and orderly nature of the city streets and Town Square. Characters weave in and out of the bustling early morning activity, like extras on a film shoot. The setting mixes all the synchronized, soothing qualities of suburbia and small town life. Indeed, this could be Pleasantville forty years later! Truman's day in the city continues with a visit to the corner news stand, followed by a cheery and cliché-filled chat with its vendor, then a stroll across the street with his briefcase in hand, and many "Good morning" greetings with other commuters on their way to work. Two men stop Truman and somewhat unceremoniously glad-hand him backwards against a poster advertisement for Free Range Kaiser Chickens. They really have nothing to say and it is a puzzling moment for both Truman and the film's viewer. The presence and repetition of brand-name commodities within the reality TV program are eventually revealed to be a production strategy that underwrites the show. At first encounter, it merely seems quizzical. Like *The Purple Rose of Cairo*, *The Truman Show* begins with a defenses-down glimpse of the routine, unexamined life that is supported and/or

The picture-perfect world of Seahaven in The Truman Show has extras on the set to validate the unexamined life of television star Truman Burbank.

programmed by the media. Later, however, there will be rupture, realignment and rejection of this routine.

Truman works at an insurance company, an ironic choice for a character in a program about scripted life. Insurance nominally serves as a hedge against the indefinite or unforeseen. Unbeknownst to Truman, the policies he sells are always assured by plot machinations that are foreseen as the policies are written. Therefore, his real purpose in life is moot since Christof and the program writers control the future. Truman has no agency—even though he works in an "agency"— and can affect no change in his life or in others.

In his cubicle at work, his co-workers watch Truman. They, like other players in "The Truman Show," serve as Truman's handlers of sorts. Handlers, in the world of politics for example, function as guide persons for candidates and smooth the way of campaigning; they deflect issues and circumstances that would be time-consuming or embarrassing for the candidate to confront and attempt to keep a campaign "on message." Truman seems to be growing concerned that he does not know the "message" of his life. He makes secretive calls to find the identity of someone named Garland and flips through the pages of a fashion magazine only to notice that the faces of the all the models resemble one another. Still, he is intrigued enough to rip some images of those faces and file them for later consideration. Truman's boss instructs him to visit a client in Wells Park, a harbor community outside of Seahaven, and at first Truman is reluctant. But since he is an unwitting pawn in this managed narrative, he concedes in order to be considered a team player.

Truman attempts to board a ferry off Harbor Island and we watch him through several fisheye lenses in images that resemble the contoured screens of electronic observation posts. He confronts a primal fear of water (aquaphobia) not uncommon among small children or the uninitiated. This phobia forces Truman to cancel his visit to Wells Park, and return to Seahaven where he goes to work in his garden. Meryl returns from grocery shopping, and there is a second opportunity for product placement. At this point, it becomes clear to the viewers of *The Truman Show* that the scripted life portrayed in "The Truman Show" needs sponsorship to tell its story. Product placement is the common practice in scripted narrative that directly or indirectly evokes a commercial product or service, incorporating it into the characters' lives in subtle or unsubtle ways. This is usually done with some compensation due the production company—monetary payment, goods in trade-out, cooperative advertising campaigns in other media for the film and product, and other arrangements.[25] Since *The Truman Show* is a satire on, among other things, the device of product integration in modern media, its uses are, to the critical media eye, abuses; they allow the purely commercial moment to dominate the narrative, artistic one. Meryl rides her bicycle into the frame and removes a bag of groceries. She is in an objective viewpoint at first, speaking to Truman who is on his hands and knees in the garden, his posterior dominating the reverse-shot angle. Weir likely imposes this purposefully, unflattering shot to alert the spectator to the satiric impulse. The ironic stance implies that those who willfully submit to the domination of the commercial over the creative (scripted product integration over natural life) are asses! A medium close shot has Meryl in a shifted point of view, with a wide-eyed gaze directed at the subjective camera (the recorder/receiver that stands in most intimately for the spectator here), enthusiastically performing just like any seasoned TV pitchman who wants viewers to know the attributes of the product s/he is selling. But the vacuous nature of Meryl's "performance" seems to somewhat unsettle Truman.

The Doubting Truman

That night, Truman and his friend Marlon practice golfing drives. Truman declares that he is thinking of quitting the insurance business. Marlon, who works as a stocker of vending machines, reminds Truman that a desk job is a good job and one with which he should be satisfied. But doubt has begun to invade Truman's life in little ways that promise larger changes. In fact, Truman confesses a desire to go to Fiji which, he demonstrates on a golf ball that substitutes for a world globe, is about as far away from Seahaven as you can get before getting closer again. Truman longs for a primitive beginning that he was denied, an alternative far from the super-civilized and overly controlled present. This wistful moment of yearning for another world, articulated in the moonlight, directly imparts a tone of nostalgia-fantasy. Ironically, this instance of spontaneous, dream-like intensity rests in the flow of very calculated TV play, offering the possibility for resistance to the lifie that is Truman in "The Truman Show." Marlon offers casual support, but seems to fathom this outburst as merely a character quirk that can and will be dealt with before restoring Truman to his proper scripted mindset.

Sitting at the waterside, Truman remembers a childhood episode with his TV father (Brian Delate) and himself on a small boat. They get caught in a storm at sea, and the father disappears overboard despite the brave effort of young Truman to save him. Truman wrestles with this memory, albeit a scripted one, and it validates the source of his aquaphobia that has, indeed, ensured he remains landlocked and incapable of reaching the Fiji Islands. But he is fixating too deeply on these concerns—the water, the father, the possible escape—and a force of nature is deployed by Cristof and his scenarists, engaging the phobia to roust Truman from his thoughts. A drenching rainstorm is called down upon Truman and the small patch of sand where he sits; oddly, no other area of the land is getting rainfall. The little cloudburst follows Truman as he tries to elude it. When it continues to drench him, and he finds it not all that unpleasant, he raises his hands in a "Hallelujah" manner and the entire beach receives the rain. This moment seems to convince Truman that he has the ability and the need to claim control of his destiny.

Soaked and excited, he returns home to Meryl, but when he tells her his dream of departure and adventure, she readily deflates him and accuses him of talking like a teenaged fantasist. Meryl reminds him of their responsibilities to home and their hope to have children, in short, the conformities and values of middle class life celebrated by television narratives like "The Truman Show" and "Pleasantville." She approaches Truman, dressed in her nightgown and ready for bed, now playing the role of the comforting wife. She kisses him gently.

At this point spectators of *The Truman Show* receive their first glimpse of the audience within the film watching "The Truman Show." While the notion of a televised program was revealed at the outset with the promo-intro segment, that merely identified the players in the show; now, its viewers are revealed. In this case it is a brief, 10-second shot of two security guards at work who likely are used to watching monitors connected to observation cameras. Here, however, they are tuned to "The Truman Show" and anticipate the turns that the program will make. A little jaded, one of the guards assures his friend that you "never see anything anyway" and that the producers just pan away from the action and play music. While this may have been true in the earlier days of 1990s reality TV programming, there has been a relaxation in censorship related to sex and propriety starting with cable telecasts such as MTV's *Real World* and moving into network fare such as CBS's *Survivor* and FOX's *A Simple Life*. Internet web cams and subscription video feeds have all but erased the boundaries of censorship, with adult sites offering any imaginable, or unimaginable, sexual situations. Today, you *can* see everything anyway, including video of the torture and beheading of human beings. In the above scene, Weir is reminding the spectator of the impenetrable nature of scripted reality where controls are in place. The real world, permeable and without boundary, is a more volatile and expansive place. Reality television after 2000 was reflecting that world, especially in unflinching shows on premium cable and on the Internet.

Weir provides an overhead view of Seahaven at this point. It is an island community just off the mainland, shaped like a half-circle that has been cut from the land mass. Its diameter is a picaresque shoreline and houses in the neighborhoods extend from the hub of the town, with greenery fanning out from them to the water's edge. While everyone else is an actor filling a role, Truman remains the "true man" of Seahaven and soon will impose that premise—a natural man reinventing himself through free will—on the outside world when he rejects and breaks the frame of "The Truman Show." He is, at this point, like the residents of Pleasantville—soon to be discontented with his existence within boundaries.

Memory

Another workday begins with another visit to the magazine stand. Walking down the main street, Truman passes a disheveled looking older man. He pauses, moves toward the man and tentatively recognizes his as his father. Immediately, the music on the soundtrack shifts to a brisk tempo associated with action and espionage films as a few extras adjust their earphone-radios, alerted to this rupture in the scripted play. Two of them abruptly usher the old man away just as a gang of joggers runs toward Truman to block his pursuit. Other obstacles persist to insure that Truman fails to connect with his father. Finally, the man's abduction is complete and Truman is left standing in the middle of what is now a not-so-busy street. Calm and order have been restored to Seahaven and to "The Truman Show," at least externally. Inside Truman Burbank, however, there is increased confusion.

The role of "memory" in *The Truman Show* is significant. Events that transpire in "The Truman Show"—as reality or serial television—provide memories for the viewers *about* the show, but Truman himself develops as a character prone to question these very memories in which the viewers are invested. As this rejection of memory becomes part of Truman's character, it serves to both challenge and redraw the program's storyline.

Memory is a human function that was, at least in the 1950s and 1960s, usually denied to players in many serial television comedy and drama shows. References to past shows or to past characters and situations were rare, with producers and audiences preferring the interchangeable nature of most formula television and the shuffled manner of the shows' presentations which included reruns and reprises of certain episodes, and later, syndicated runs on various other channels. An episode of *Bonanza*, *The Andy Griffith Show* or *The Brady Bunch* was relatively self-contained. One could watch an installment of *The Dick Van Dyke Show* from 1964 and then a program from its second season in 1962 without much concern for the production timeline, and likely no acknowledgment of the activity that constitutes overall character development, with the obvious exception of the maturing of adolescent characters. What screenwriters call the character's arc—his or her growth as a person given the circumstances of the narrative—was minimized and somewhat contained in each 30 or 60 minute program. Beginning in the early 1970s with shows like *All in the Family*, network television began building into their prime-time storylines some of the tenets of soap opera drama seen in their afternoon programs. These included delayed gratifications, the planting of plot points for later payoff, intermittent character development, or mini-climaxes per episode that included the promise of further address in the next installment. This is best epitomized by the season-long storyline that reaches a final payoff, or provides a season-ending cliffhanger to entice viewers to tune in again in the fall season; *Dallas* became the most prominent example of the nighttime soap opera formula in the late 1970s and 1980s that was later practiced in shows such as *The Sopranos*, *Sex and the City*, and *Deadwood*. Today, the serial narrative is a mainstay of television with shows such as *30 Rock, Mad Men, Californication, The Tudors, Desperate Housewives,* and many others.

The concept of memory is also acknowledged in the spinning off of characters into other narratives. During the 1970s, *Rhoda* emerges from *The Mary Tyler Moore Show, The Jeffersons* springs from *All in the Family*, and viewers could observe the cross-presence of former co-stars on subsequent installments. By the 1990s, this became a promotional tool in network prime time that needed no shared backstory, just the sharing of network affiliation. Thus, stars from NBC's *Mad About You* and *Friends* (Helen Hunt, Lisa Kudrow) would perform on one another's shows, or *Friends* would feature George Clooney and Noah Wylie as doctors, recognized as doctors from their roles in *ER*. Today, a spectator's loyalty is measured by an awareness of both the arcane and profound elements in a program to which they are dedicated, just like David in *Pleasantville*. Extending beyond the standalone segments of the sitcom "Pleasantville" are today's program trajectories that incorporate memory in their characters and a season-by-season regimen—albeit subject to revalidation and rearrangement by the program fan—that ultimately informs the narrative character play as a life lived.[26]

In "The Truman Show," Truman visits his mother (Holland Taylor) and questions his own memory of a relationship with his father and that man's disappearance. She tries to allay his concerns but ends up affirming some sense of guilt in her son for wanting to sail out with his father on that fateful day. Doubt, then, begins to inspire memory even as memory inspires doubt. It is an ironic double back that will move Truman forward in his self-discoveries. In his basement, Truman unlocks a trunk of toys and paraphernalia, including a cigar box with photos of a young boy and an older man at a birthday party, some maps of faraway islands and an old red sweater. Truman studies them carefully. The image blurs to retrieve what passes for scripted memory in "The Truman Show," and there is a shot of two waitresses watching the program on TV at an establishment called Truman Bar. Remembering Truman's infatuation with another character who was the owner of the red sweater, one woman reminds the other that the producers got rid of her but they couldn't erase Truman's memory of her.

What follows is a flashback montage of college life that includes Truman, Meryl, Marlon and a pretty young woman named Lauren (Natascha McElhone) who has caught the eye of Truman during a football pep rally. She will, in fact, turn out to be the red sweater-wearing object of Truman's affection. This seemingly natural, romantic moment is interrupted when the youthful cheerleader Meryl "accidentally" trips and falls into Truman, affecting a cliché of the "meet cute" moment so popular in formula romantic comedies. Once Truman and Meryl have introduced themselves and recovered their bearings, Lauren is gone from sight, much to Truman's dismay. At a party later, Truman spots Lauren while he dances a carefree step with Meryl. Even though the shots are close up and the dance floor crowded, it is obvious that Meryl has noticed Truman's glances of interest toward Lauren. Others have as well. In a scene reminiscent of the ushering away of Truman's father, several tuxedo-clad young men ease Lauren out of the dance hall. Later, in the school library, Marlon and Meryl leave Truman to his studies that are interrupted by Lauren who is studying in a nearby cubicle. She informs Truman that she is not allowed to talk to him. As Truman struggles with the awkward naturalism of this moment—getting a girl to accept a date despite her reservations—Lauren struggles to stay "on script." A button she wears intrigues Truman. It reads: "How's It Going to End?" He points to it and wonders aloud the same question.

"How's It Going to End?"

"How's it going to end?" is the most direct questioning of the scripted life and an invitation to reject it thus far in the film. The query and opportunity come from a character, Lauren, who exists in two worlds—the real (where she is an actress named Sylvia) and the televised. Lauren accepts a date with Truman on the condition that it is immediate, so the pair flees with some abandon to a sandbar near the water. Lauren begin to reveal the actual nature of scripted life in Seahaven, but the moment of romance and truth is interrupted by the headlights of an approaching black sedan. A man gets out of the car and identifies himself as Lauren's father, but she denies even knowing him. Lauren struggles as the man forces her into the car but not before she reiterates the falseness of Seahaven. Picking up sand from the beach, Lauren/Sylvia calls it "fake, and all for you." She points to the sky and the sea declaring them part of set construction on the show. Finally, Sylvia warns Truman that her abductor will lie to them. And indeed, he speaks to her like an exhausted parent who has frequently dealt with a wayward daughter. She pleads for Truman to leave quickly, but to come back and find her. Sylvia's alleged father tells Truman they are moving to Fiji. As the taillights dim in the distance, Truman is left holding the red sweater that Sylvia dropped on the sand, the one that triggered this entire memory and flashback to begin with. The waitresses, still glued to the set in the Truman Bar, update viewers of *The Truman Show* on what has happened in "The Truman Show." Truman did not follow Lauren/Sylvia to Fiji because his mother became ill, and then he married Meryl on the rebound. Back in his basement, Truman holds the sweater close. The "How's It Going to End?" button is still there. Marie-Laure Ryan, observing this prop as evidence of a significant subtext, says:

> Through its eschatological overtones, the message "How will it end" is also the
> first intimation of a religious theme that becomes more and more explicit as the
> movie nears, precisely, its climax and its end. Truman, the ordinary man whose
> life is scripted from above, becomes the sacrificial lamb of a media religion that
> redeems the tedium of everyday life by making its banality into the object of a
> TV show. Through the mediation of Truman, everybody is vicariously raised to
> the highest glory that humanity can hope to attain in a media-dominated culture,

namely the status of TV celebrity. In the religion masterminded by Christof, Hamlet's dilemma, "to be or not to be" is reinterpreted as "TV or not to be." According to a standard mythical pattern, the fulfillment of the redemptive scheme requires the sacrifice of the redeemer's life. In keeping with the preoccupations of contemporary culture, this sacrifice does not mean the loss of life, but simply the loss of privacy. Truman's life is indeed offered to mankind by being put on public display.[27]

Truman observes the button, as well as other beloved objects in his scripted life by contrasting the studio-like head shot of Meryl with the images he had torn from the fashion magazines—a pastiche of eyes, nose, forehead, hair and other facial features—that strive to compile a picture of Sylvia. There is then a brief shot of the interior of an apartment where we see the blue-green eyes of Sylvia watching "The Truman Show," now no longer employed as an actor in the show.   Truman, meanwhile, his collection of eyes clipped from magazines and, like a detective working on an Identi-kit picture, he tries to match his memory of Sylvia.

The motif of a puzzle-picture that is slowly and meticulously composed in order to force reality into focus is a common trope in storytelling, especially cinema. It is the essence of detective fiction where the problem solver is himself a kind of "picture maker." Film directors work closely with their editors in piecing together the disparate parts of film, tape or digital information to construct a coherent whole. *Citizen Kane* is, perhaps, the best example of this motif at several levels—a detective story that aspires to discover the meaning of Rosebud utilizing a variety of sources and narrators in order to understand the meaning of a man's life. Literally within that film, a character (Susan Alexander Kane) puts together jigsaw puzzles as a hobby and distraction. *Kane* is, arguably it should be noted, the exception that this strategy always provides answers. At its conclusion, the meaning of Rosebud is multifaceted for the spectator who interprets the narrative, and unclear for the questing reporter on the trail of Rosebud in the film. The meaning of a life fully lived—or even one unfulfilled—demands explanations and excursions too far-reaching to be contained in a single word or an epitaph. In the end, seemingly, we may only have the jigsaw puzzles and their fragments-into-wholes that can allude to the mysteries of living. The nostalgia fantasy films under study, however, consider the ramifications of characters rupturing the jigsaw puzzle of the picture maker (TV Land, Raoul Hirsch, Christof) as they become frame breakers of "Pleasantville," "The Purple Rose of Cairo," and "The Truman Show." They give film spectators evidence that realignment strategies—reconstructive, restorative, and rejective—can exist with the movies that their namesakes evoke.

The next morning while driving to work, Truman hears static and interference on his car radio. He bangs on the console and eventually receives an odd signal of chatter that seems to be tracking his movement on streets and past town landmarks. Truman almost runs over an old lady on a crosswalk and suddenly, there is a blast of feedback on the radio. Every pedestrian, motorist and shopkeeper along the street winces in pain and hold his or her right ears at exactly the same moment. They are all receiving, and reacting to, the radio frequency broadcast. Then a moment later, transmission and life on "The Truman Show" set appears to return to normal. We sense that technology, however advanced, is subject to breakdown or dissonance of some degree. These cracks in the system, like poorly secured studio grid lights, can interconnect to disastrous effect for those who want to keep the super-structure in place. This disruption is the direction in which *The Truman Show* is headed, a movement toward a rejective tendency in the lead character and of the mass mediated world in which he lives.

Indeed, when Truman enters the revolving door to his office he continues full circle and reenters the outside world, a man no longer part of the scripted crowd. He looks but does not feel the part. Walking more slowly and ostensibly more observant of his surroundings, he also appears especially aware of those watching him. When a bus miraculously misses running him over, Truman stops traffic with a mere extension of his hand. He is, after all, the star of the show and a valuable property that must be coddled, connived and controlled. The supporting players seem preoccupied in their roles as extras and do not react until Truman abruptly walks into another office building and strides confidently past the security desk as if he belonged there. A security guard tries to block Truman's path to the elevators and directs Truman to a crafts and services area where actors mill about consuming coffee and doughnuts. These, of course, are the actors and technicians working on "The Truman Show." A grip quickly closes the access door, and Truman is even more befuddled as he is roughly escorted out of the building by the guards. He passes a construction worker standing on a ladder and slaps the man on his rear with his briefcase. This anarchic impulse does not register a response with anyone, because unlike in the office building, they have not been instructed to respond. With his confusion compounded, Truman turns to his best friend for counsel. He suggests to Marlon that he thinks much of the strangeness that surrounds him is related to his father's disappearance. Truman has even become paranoid about the townspeople/extras who appear to be watching him.

Marlon's "friendship" is utilitarian and meant to keep Truman in his place as the star of "The Truman Show." As they ponder the beauty of a sunset, Marlon thanks "the big guy" for creating it but, despite this reverie, Truman confesses that he will be "going away for awhile." This is a gesture, acknowledged as such by all except Truman, of a performer on a successful TV show deciding to pull its plug by withdrawing his services. In series television, this frequently emerges when essential creative personnel have contract disputes for salary demands and time commitments. The loss of a major participant to whom much of the show is anchored will force disruptions among all who watch and witness, engage and participate. This includes viewers, program producers, advertisers, actors, and the non-actor Truman Burbank. It is now necessary to set countermeasures in motion to prevent such a frame-breaking so that "The Truman Show" will continue as a viable program. Truman's desire to rupture the scripted narrative of his life must be dampened, his free will denied or inhibited, and the punctured society of Seahaven—which began with the fallen studio light fixture—made whole again.

Road-blocking Truman

Meryl, Truman, and his mother leaf through the pages of a family photo album, looking at a collection of manufactured memories and "Kodak moments." The pictures have a slightly cut-and-paste, PhotoShop-like construction, with some perspectives a bit off-kilter such as one of the Burbank family in front of Mount Rushmore. These are reminders and reconstructions of a falsified past, the mediated memory. To firmly drive home that surrounding aura, the television in the background plays a teaser for a movie soon to air. It is a much-loved classic entitled "Show Me the Way to Go Home," full of "laughter and love, pain and sadness, but ultimately redemption." This mythical film is a hymn of praise to small-town life and the announcer continues regaling viewers with highlights from the film, reminiscent of the promotional spiel for "Pleasantville" heard in the teaser for its marathon. While the film about to begin evokes memories of the perennial holiday classic *It's a Wonderful Life* (Capra, 1947) and the celebration of small town Americana, it represents one more commoditization of that ethos, recycled here within "The Truman Show." As Truman flips the pages of the family photo album, he sees flat images of himself encased in clear plastic sheets, affixed with black or white arrowheads at each corner, and trapped in the white perimeter of the individual photos. To anyone else, these pictures would seem idyllic. They aim to lull Truman into a state of acquiescence, until he looks closely at one of himself and Meryl on their wedding day and sees that she has her fingers crossed! This is, of course, the code for a visual admission that the action or words being performed or spoken should be considered invalid. Thus, the "ideal" life for Truman Burbank—mediated and scripted—is a lie.

Nostalgia and fantasy impulses invite the longed-for perfection of the sensibilities championed in *It's a Wonderful Life*. Like George Bailey in that film, Truman is an unenlightened co-conspirator in his own imprisonment. But instead of reconstructing his world in a new configuration after his own frame-breaking experience—with Clarence the Angel, George is allowed to envision the sordid nature of his town minus his personal impact—George restores Bedford Falls to its natural state. Like *The Purple Rose of Cairo*, *It's a Wonderful Life* exhibits the restorative tendencies of a conservative, closed film. The discontent that is initially present in David in *Pleasantville* and Cecilia in *The Purple Rose of Cairo* ferment in Truman's character until he commits to a reconstructive or rejective strategy. His discontent is a byproduct of a consumer society that seeks predictable, calculable, and efficient results for every discourse epitomized by his programmed life. David and Cecilia find comfort, at first, in the predictability of the shows they watch; like Truman, they later come to acknowledge the false groundings of their mediated world, with Cecilia retreating into its safety and David restructuring it with his lived experience.

Truman attempts to book a flight to Fiji, but the travel agent informs him that no seats are available for a month. He decides to take a bus out of town, but the driver is an actor who has never piloted one before. The producers of "The Truman Show" are trying desperately to roll with the punches and incorporate the improvised, narrative curves that Truman sends their way. Viewers watching the show in the bar discuss the turmoil in Truman's life as if he were a real part of their own lives and as if the outcome actually mattered and affected them.

Weary of his predictable, calculable and efficient (at least for others) existence, Truman coaxes Meryl into his car and drives off to be "spontaneous." More than a little recklessly, he at first careens the car with wild abandon around Seahaven, but soon runs into synchronized and scripted traffic jams. Truman maneuvers away from them, ending up at a causeway. He appears paralyzed at the wheel, unable to accelerate. Suddenly, he musters confidence. The car speeds off and together they navigate over the bridge. A portable highway sign warns of extreme danger and a forest fire ahead but Truman dismisses is as exaggeration. Indeed, they drive through a firewall that is a hastily created special effect and roadblock meant to fence in Truman and his newly exercised impulses. The couple is headed for New Orleans, but the practical-minded Meryl reminds Truman that they have no travel money and will have to inform his mother of their absence as well. Those obstacles prove irrelevant, however, when a more devastating scripted one surfaces. The Seahaven Nuclear Power Station has conveniently experienced a radiation leak and all roads are now closed. Truman relents and is ready to turn back, but when the law officer calls him by name, Truman leaps from his car and runs toward the supposedly contaminated area. Workers in silver safety-suits with protective gloves and helmets chase him into the woods. They subdue Truman, and return him to his home where Meryl tries to convince him he is having a nervous breakdown. In their kitchen, she fends off his rapprochement with The Chef's Pal, nervously waving the utensil that "slices and dices" at her TV husband. When Truman finally gets her in a choke hold, Meryl breaks from her character's persona, looks up at one of the many omniscient cameras that capture "The Truman Show," and cries for intervention. The couple continues their brawl, moving into the living room when the doorbell rings and Marlon enters with a six-pack of beer. Relieved, Meryl runs to him for protection and fully reveals herself as an actress in the televised show. She is flustered at trying to remain professional under these unsettling conditions.

Marlon and Truman have another talk in the moonlight, with Truman more confused than before and Marlon more certain, at least as an actor whose confidence must reassure his fellow player that their lives are ones of contentment and fulfillment. While Truman is confounded because he "feels like the whole world revolves around me somehow," most people in a consumer society are invited to feel just that way. Mass media affirms the consumer's position of alleged control of their choices and principles but, like Truman's situation, it is part of the orchestration of life itself. Marlon, played by an actor, must be utterly convincing to Truman who needs assurances that his own life is not a role with preordained patterns and outcomes. We discover that Marlon is being fed lines from Christof, who monitors and manages (i.e., produces) "The Truman Show."[28] Christof speaks the words just seconds before they are imbued with greater emotion when delivered by the actor playing Marlon.

Then, as a topper to this scene, Marlon is allowed to present Truman with a man who is presumed to be his father. Music swells on the soundtrack and Christof directs the reunion of father and son that is captured by cameras from several locations. The scene crosscuts from the studio control room where Christof works with his technical crew to shots of spectators around the world watching "The Truman Show" to the feed that is the programmed reintegration of parent and child. Here is an appropriated meditation on a basic storyline—that of the Prodigal Son and reunification with the father figure. Christof, a producer par excellence now surrounded by members of the production crew who wear shirts lettered "Love Him, Protect Him," is congratulated by program executives for this manipulation of his actors' capabilities and the emotional reaction of his unwitting star.

Incursions into Truman's World

Christof orchestrates a persistent flow of images in a style that Martha P. Nochimson calls *televisuality*.[29] This refers to the aesthetic potential of television
and can be applied to contemporary TV's unprecedented ability to produce
virtually endless visual, serial narratives. Cinema narratives deliver a resolution or a satisfactory conclusion to the spectator within a roughly two-hour
time period, but television has added the quality of seriality, postponing narrative closure almost indefinitely. Although Nochimson explores televisuality within the multi-plot, episodic narrative of *The Sopranos* and praises its
cinematic tendencies as part of her overall thesis, televisuality's application
in "The Truman Show" affirms both the tedium and the occasional surprise
of a lengthy, ongoing narrative.

A promotional spot for "The Truman Show" is the lead-in to an interview
program called "Tru Talk," a forum where guests and callers discuss and
analyze recent events on the show. After images of Truman's life pass in
chronological order, the spot shows a mammoth, domed structure at the base
of a mountain along with the dishes that are part of the apparatus of satellite
television transmission. The announcer enthusiastically informs us that 1.7
billion viewers tuned in for Truman's birth, 227 countries watched him take
his first steps, and the drama of life continues broadcast live and unedited 24
hours a day. With excitement cresting in his voice, he announces that this is
the 30th year of the show originating from the larges studio ever constructed
and along with the Great Wall of China, one of only two man-made structures
visible from space. In shared fashion with the *March of Time*-like newsreel
that opens *Citizen Kane*, this represents the world's view of Truman Burbank.
It is neatly organized and compartmentalized to both affirm the myth of
celebrity and connect audiences with those that are so unlike themselves by
highlighting the universal rites of passage that spectators have, indeed, probably experienced. Truman is Everyman, except that he is on TV.[30]

Mike Michaelson (Harry Shearer), the host of "Tru Talk," interviews
Christof, the creator and director of "The Truman Show." The interview,
live from the Lunar Room on the 221st story of the OmniCam Ecosphere, is
enacted in the manner of Edward R. Murrow's *Person-to-Person* CBS television program of the mid-1950s, where his camera was present at the guest's
site (home, studio, office) but Murrow was in a New York City studio. Part
of the thrill for early TV audiences in that era was seeing firsthand the often
closed-off environment where noted personalities lived or operated.

Michaelson has Christof discuss the intrusion of outsiders into the show,
with Truman's father (named Kirk) as the latest incursion, and how the production staff incorporates or diminishes their presence. The father, however,
is the first intruder to be a former cast member, a dead one at that. The actor

playing Kirk, it seems, was disappointed to be written out of the script as part of the "storm at sea" segment necessary to instill a fear of water in Truman, and thus impede his desire to leave the island setting and help contain any fantasies of escape. This effectively ensured the unwitting star's self-imprisonment and the steamrolling success of the show. When asked by Michaelson what would explain Kirk's disappearance and return after 22 years of absence, Christof gives the cliché answer so popular in soap operas when a popular or former character suddenly resurfaces: Amnesia. We also learn that Truman was among five babies considered near the time of their births for this show. He arrived on cue and became the first child to have been legally adopted by a corporation, representing one more manipulation of human existence in the name of enterprises that make up the Political-Corporate-Media state.

Audiences, nevertheless, are likely pleased that "The Truman Show" is an uninterrupted broadcast. Christof admits that the show has no commercial interruptions because of product placement revenues. He adds that viewers can also buy into the Truman ethos through purchases of various merchandise and accessories from "The Truman Catalog."

Sylvia calls in to "Tru Talk" when Michaelson opens phone lines to viewers of the show. She lambastes Christof as a liar and manipulator who has turned a human life into a mockery. He allows her air time, inviting the audience to recall her voice and then identifying her as a former cast member whose few moments with Truman hardly qualify her to judge what is right for him whereas Christof, who sees himself as the creator/father of Truman Burbank, claims he has given Truman a chance to lead a normal life. Ironically, while this is being said—indeed, while the whole interview is progressing—a small window of "The Truman Show" transmission feed can be seen in the upper corner of the frame. A scene from his "normal life" is occurring, as Truman sits in his nightclothes drinking coffee, eating a bowl of cereal, blowing his nose, and scratching himself nonchalantly. He looks like an oblivious prisoner whose late-night opportunity for privacy—the chance to serve the bodily need of sleep or hunger—is being well observed. Sylvia persists and becomes contentious, and we see from the decor of her apartment that she belongs to a "Free Truman" movement, part of a phenomenon known as culture jamming. Henry Jenkins notes how the culture jammer builds upon long-standing assumptions:

> . . . the dominant media operate as institutions of control that dupe consumers into buying into a corrupt consumer economy and blind them to meaningful political alternatives. . . Culture jammers define themselves as cultural outsiders who seek 'liberation' from the intrusion of mass media into their lives. The culture jammers embrace a politics of disruption and destabilization, defacing billboards, developing 'anti-commercials', spoofing ads, all with the goal of encouraging us to opt out of media consumption.[31]

Those not among the passive voyeurs who watch "The Truman Show" might try to disrupt its world, free Truman, and liberate the audience from the power of deceptive images. In *The Truman Show*, Sylvia wishes to assist Truman in his escape from mass mediated reality into a truly authentic life. Christof, however, champions the programmed life. He defends the model of Seahaven as the way the world should be, and concedes that perhaps Truman prefers that world to any alternative.

The fawning Michaelson concludes the interview, chides the heated comments "from a very vocal minority," and congratulates Christof on an overwhelming experience for Truman and the viewing public. The two men spin Sylvia's crisis call into a thing of the past and Christof hints at future plot points, such as Meryl leaving Truman and the introduction of a new romantic partner, that will further dramatically disorient Truman and ensure high ratings. Finally, Christof reveals his determination to present television's first on-air conception. Here, he speaks both as a television entrepreneur and a video pornographer about to invade one of the two most private moments in a human being's life. Arguably, most persons cherish the opportunity to render nonpublic the chance to create life (sex) and the instant of its extinguishing (death). The ease of videotaping—and, by extension, the proliferation of reality TV—can disrespect the privacy of certain moments or at least reveal them with unintentional results, although as a culture we are becoming more and more accustomed to surveillance by camera. Meanwhile, pornography usually entails a willing and complicit participation between camera and subject; for one or more subjects *not* to be aware or consenting in this instance might be considered video rape.

An enigmatic moment follows. With simple and plaintive piano underscore on the soundtrack, Christof approaches a huge video screen that displays Truman's face on a pillow. He sleeps peacefully as the director, a rolled towel around his neck after an exhausting day, gets closer to the screen. The pixilated Truman has a green tint due to the night filter on the video camera capturing his slumber. Christof, looking so small in front of his creation's face, gently caresses the area between Truman's closed eyes. Peter Weir pulls back his camera to reveal only Christof, the Lunar Room's technical director (Paul Giamatti), and the music engineer working a piano keyboard in the control room. The tenderness that Christof displays towards Truman's image recalls the human interaction with another unwitting, larger than life character in *King Kong* (Cooper and Schoedsack, 1933; Guillermin, 1976; Jackson, 2005); at times during the life, and after the death of that great ape, human characters are allowed to approach its reposed body, console and minister to it in like fashion. Christof, like Kirk, is a father figure to Truman, and he seems conflicted with a desire for what he thinks is best for his boy and the show, and the indeterminate future that all freethinking individuals deserve—a life that parents undergird as they nurture and condition their offspring to move somewhere beyond the frame of adolescent confinement.

Truman Reborn

Truman awakes and seems to tease the production technicians, and by extension the TV spectators of the show, monitoring his morning ritual. He draws an outline of a television set with a bar of soap on his bathroom mirror, positioning himself in the tube's center. Truman wipes off his artwork and then stares directly at a camera that is behind the mirror and winks at it. Now we see the re-introductions of other characters who were first observed in the film's opening—the couple next door with their daughter, Spencer taking out the garbage with his Dalmatian dog, passers-by in Seahaven as Truman goes to his job. Truman interacts with them cheerily, as if part of ad-libbed action that is well within his character. But Truman has acknowledged the creation of a TV media frame and the cameras that capture it, has indeed drawn one and winked at it in his bathroom. Where to take this new awareness? Has he

Trapped in the frame, Truman Burbank (Jim Carrey) acknowledges one of the cameras located behind his bathroom mirror that monitors his life. He uses a bar of soap to draw another enclosure for himself, resembling both a space helmet and a television screen with antenna.

been made comfortable to proceed with the show, now reunited with Kirk? Or is Truman just playing along and waiting for the right moment to break free?

In his office, Truman is introduced to Vivian (Heidi Schanz) whom, we sense from the coded and coy manner of her presentation, is the new romantic interest that Christof has scripted. The distraught Meryl has been written out of the series, and Truman himself has moved into his basement where he has placed some obstructions in the way of a few observation cameras and allowed others a clear view. Truman appears to be sleeping, but from the control room Christof is suspicious. He instructs that a phone call be placed to Truman's house, and when Truman does not answer, Christof suspects Truman is not in the basement and dispatches Marlon to roust him. Marlon arrives and finds an inflated snowman under the bed covers and a tape recorder that plays snoring sound effects. When Marlon discovers part of the roof sawed away, he looks at the lawn cam lens and tells Christof and all who watch that Truman is gone! At this, Christof, acting like a scared parent who has lost his child but is trying to remain calm, orders that transmission cease. TV spectators at locations around the world on Day 10,913 of "The Truman Show" gasp when their screens showcase this interruption in the transmission with a "Please Stand By" placard.

There is chaos at the Lunar Room production headquarters, which resembles a military or police operation in full alert mode. Christof is informed that all available extras and support personnel are looking for Truman. In addition, if Truman did escape from the studio of Seahaven, he would be noticed. Truman can't disappear, reasons the technical director, because he has the world's most recognizable face. Streets in Seahaven slowly fill with a well-organized mob of vigilantes searching for their very reason for existence and employment. The scene of a massive, all-white community marching on its pristine streets, mobilized to realign a distressed situation, recalls the mob in *Pleasantville* angrily denouncing the art mural. The night's darkness works against this search, however, and Christof paces impatiently. After a moment in thought, he orders his production assistant Chloe (Una Damon) to cue the sunrise.

Suddenly, Seahaven is awash in daylight, much to the confusion of the extras who quickly look at their watches to consider this earlier-than-usual sunrise. The god-like Christof is exercising the film storyteller's prerogative and playing with time, thereby violating the "real time" imperative of "The Truman Show." Indeed, movies rest on the manipulation of space and time with the director as one who orchestrates action assisted by the editor as his accomplice. In *The Truman Show*, the metaphor signifies the ultra-reality state of this type of frame-making, causing a resistance to it all the more difficult. The well-crafted programs—"Pleasantville," "The Purple Rose of Cairo," and especially "The Truman Show"—are strong signifiers of assurance and control. They comfort and assuage some spectators but are suspect by those embracing an ironic stance. Since they are also TV shows that signify commercial properties containing and representing values (monetary and ideological), sustaining them is purposeful for many. While the frame-breaking witnessed in two other films—*Pleasantville* and *The Purple Rose of Cairo*—has been a round-trip experience for David and Cecilia, Truman's trajectory of character is pulling him out of the frame with no regard for return. Thus, the stirring of rejective impulses rightfully comprises most of *The Truman Show*'s remaining narrative.

One of the cameras spots Truman in a small sailboat, facing his phobia of the water in an attempt to escape the island of Seahaven. Director Peter Weir provides shots of viewers who, oddly, seem to be rooting for Truman to break free of his environment and from the scripted narrative itself. Perhaps they feel the show would continue in an unsealed setting, but more importantly, "The Truman Show" viewers likely embrace the idea of breaking free from this frame of containment, the next logical, liberating step that Truman should take. They have, after all, witnessed Truman's discontent and his new

Christof (Ed Harris) is creator and director of the life of Truman Burbank in The Truman Show. *He orchestrates 24 hour-a-day reality programming for the television cameras from the Lunar Room Studio, assisted by his technical director (Paul Giamatti).*

perspective. An attentive Truman mindfully steers the boat, itself containing small cameras that now transmit the action. At sea, Truman appears happier than he has ever been. Christof, ever-hoping to maneuver his creation back into the plotline, calls the moment "our 'hero' shot." Truman reaches into his pocket and unfolds not a map, but the composite photo he had been constructing from bits and pieces of magazine art. It turns out to be the face of Sylvia. While Christof cannot control her actions or the depth of her inspiration to Truman, he can order a ferryboat to impede Truman's progress out of Seahaven. But, just as Tom Baxter could not drive a car in *The Purple Rose of Cairo*, the ferryboat captain (the same actor who could not get a bus started earlier) and his crew cannot maneuver this vessel as sailors because they are merely actors.

Christof resorts to manipulating nature once again, ordering a localized thunderstorm with great intensity. He believes Truman will turn back out of fear, and assures the others in the control room. But there seems to be a hint of doubt in his self-assurance. Rough seas, high winds, and lightning strikes force Truman to fall overboard, and he struggles to get back on the small boat. A network executive (Philip Baker Hall) is angered at Christof's hubris. He worries that because the whole world is watching, to let this character die in front of a live audience would be wrong. But Christof counters by reminding the boss that Truman was *born* in front of a live audience.

Perhaps Christof sees this as a logical conclusion for his artistic creation. The executive, meanwhile, echoes the chanted line from *Medium Cool* when protesters *wanted* the world to watch a violation of human rights—"The whole world is watching." When a resolute Truman finally succeeds in making it back on board the boat, he defiantly yells to the heavens. Christof absorbs the taunts of Truman and increases the wind and wave forces so that the boat will capsize. The conflict plays between the emerging free will of Truman and the technology of Christof, the latter's force tempered by an emotional investment in an artistic creation. The technical director observes that Truman is going down and doesn't even care, but the fact is that Truman *does* care. He has been battling a state of passive subjugation despite the self-pity and terror he feels.

To inform *The Truman Show* with Oedipal tensions invites consideration as to the identity of the good father and that of the bad father. Truman was the result of an unwanted pregnancy, it is noted, and so the identity of the natural father is unknown. Since this would likely represent the "good" father, we are left with variations on "bad." Kirk is a figurehead in this analytical sense, a bad, archaic father who disrupts the civilized world of rationality and order that is "The Truman Show." Freud terms the bad father the "primal" father and maintains that, embedded deeply in the masculine psyche, is a fear of the primal father who acts as an obstacle that prevents his son from obtaining power and independence, as well as access to the bodies of women who represent an alternative reality and lifestyle to the one they are providing.[32] Surely, Truman is embroiled in this relationship with Christof as the primal father who even negotiates the sexual partnerships of his "son." Tanya Krzywinska identifies the adversarial nature of the primal father, even to the point of his demonic nature, in horror films. But applications to other genres persist.

> The battle with the primal father is evident in many popular films in which the young male hero has to do battle with an older and more cunning oppressor or villain. Often this is enacted by the villain's abduction of the hero's female love interest.[33]

We have seen Alfredo in *Cinema Paradiso* and Mallory's father in *Natural Born Killers* provide, respectively, benign and vociferous representations of Freud's bad, primal father. Christof is maneuvering himself as a bad father at this point but could reposition himself to represent the good in the absence of the natural father. Christof may, at times, wear the mask of the good father, but his ultimate function is as the adversarial force who constructs frames around his son and proves unwilling to endorse the breaking and rejection of them in order to attain individuation and maturation.

Rejecting Seahaven

A mammoth wave overturns the sailboat, but Truman has lashed himself to its deck. When it rights itself, he is lying sprawled over the side and appears to be unconscious. He coughs, sputters, and stumbles back to the steering wheel as Christof orders the storm to cease and the sun to emerge. Truman musters the strength to raise the sail once more. The sun's rays dry him, and he seems set on a course towards the horizon. Weir provides a picaresque shot of the boat entering the frame from the right and moving slowly across the water that meets the cloud-spotted, blue sky in the deep background. Truman steers his wrecked sailboat towards the infinite and receding horizon. Suddenly, the bow of the boat strikes a huge, blue wall, knocking Truman off his feet. He recovers and looks out at the sea, which is a colossal cyclorama. The sky is revealed as a painted backdrop. Truman tries to penetrate the backdrop by poking, then punching, and finally throwing his body weight against it to no avail. He is agitated and mournful at the blockade, finally collapsing against the blue backdrop while keeping one hand on the masthead. The frame of containment, at least literally, cannot be broken. He seems unable to release himself from the prison that is the mediated, narrative life in Seahaven.

The boat has run aground near the polymer fabric backdrop, so Truman can get out and appears to walk on the water that is only an inch or so deep at this point. He approaches a stairway that leads to a platform that seems cut into the sky, stepping upward from the ocean that Truman had feared for most of his life, which is really a tank containing 650 million gallons of temperature-controlled, synthetic salt water. He spots the recessed door handle that reads "Exit." Pushing on the door, it reveals a dark opening, an abyss awaiting Truman. Just as he takes in this visage, Christof, who has been monitoring Truman's defiance, speaks with confidence and omnipotence as the creator of a television show that gives hope, joy and inspiration to millions. He attempts one final, fatherly overture to convince Truman to stay in a world without fear. Truman's hesitation signifies fear of the unknown and, indeed, he seems to be weakening in the face of what appears to be genuine paternal affection. But when Christof-the-director becomes impatient and demands a dialogue line in response, Truman reverts to his TV character and delivers a line that allows him to "break" character as a means of escape from Seahaven. He reprises the opening line of each show: "In case I don't see you—good afternoon, good evening and good night."

Truman takes a stage bow with the black background of the doorway behind him, and steps into the abyss. Sylvia, who has been watching the broadcast along with the rest of the world, runs down a stairway in the direction, assumedly, of the "true man" she has helped liberate. Viewers in offices, bars, and homes who have tuned in the show are surprised and elated at Truman's frame-breaking, spontaneously signifying empathy despite the conclusion of their beloved series. The network executive in the Lunar Room orders that transmission be ended. The TV monitors in the studio and the TV screens carrying "The Truman Show" around the world go blank with static. Christof sits slumped, staring at the monitor that last showed the open door in the sky. In the final shot of the film, the two parking lot guards are eating pizza and, noticing the satisfactory conclusion to their program, merely wonder what else is on TV. Unlike the closing moments of Italian Neorealist films such as *The Bicycle Thief* (De Sica, 1947) or *Umberto D* (De Sica, 1952) where the hero is integrated into the crowd, or even American films that championed conformity and ideological complacency such as *The Crowd* (Vidor, 1928) and *The Man in the Grey Flannel Suit* (Johnson, 1956), Truman disavows the invitation to fit and fill a niche. He has stepped into the darkness, and faced with an opportunity to create a new world has outright rejected his old one. The viewers of "The Truman Show" have rooted for their hero's escape and apparently welcome it. Truman no longer aspires to live in a mass mediated world, nor does his audience wish to endlessly consume this particular version of life as mandated by the mass media. *The Truman Show* thus represents cinema's adeptness at detailing the falseness of a life monitored and mandated by television.

NOTES

1. Louis Althusser. "Ideology and Ideological State Apparatuses" from *Lenin and Philosophy and Other Essays*. New York and London: Monthly Review Press, 1971. p. 162

2. Ebert, Roger. *Chicago Sun-Times*. May 25, 1997.

3. Another recent historical referent for *Wag the Dog*'s war of distraction in Albania was the 1983 invasion of Grenada during Ronald Reagan's first administration. Two events occurred in the weeks prior to the foray into that tiny island where inferior Cuban troops were easily overtaken by U.S. forces. First, there was a sense of anger and impotence over the shooting down of a Korean airliner by the Soviet missiles when the plane evidently veered off course into restricted airspace; among the 269 passengers and crew killed were 61 Americans. Second, a terrorist bombing of the U.S. Marines Headquarters in Beirut, Lebanon, killed 241 soldiers; earlier in the year the American Embassy in Lebanon was also the target of a deadly bombing. The victory in Grenada was seen by some as a vainglorious attempt to reclaim some international resolve in the face of these tragedies, or at least banish their newsworthiness from Page One for the moment.

4. Phillips, Kevin. 2004. *American Dynasty: Aristocracy, Fortune, and the Politics of Deceit in the House of Bush*. New York: Viking Press. 309.

5. Boorstin, Daniel J. 1962, rev. 1987. *The Image: A Guide to Pseudo-Events in America*. New York: Antheneum.

6. Again, art imitates life. When domestic reprisals against persons of Middle Eastern and Iraqi heritage recently occurred, noted radio personality Casey Kasem became a spokesperson for tolerance. In a case from Gulf War II, the rescue of Pfc. Jessica Lynch and the publicity in its aftermath was managed as a media event for maximum, positive exposure.

7. Barry Levinson in public forum at the Austin Film Festival, October 16, 2004.

8. Myers in the documentary film *From Washington to Hollywood and Back*, New Line Home Video, Inc. 1998.

9. For more on the satiric and parodic impulses of pseudo-documentary, see *Revisioning Film Traditions: The Pseudo-Documentary and the NeoWestern* by Del Jacobs, Lewiston: Mellen Press, 2000.

10. Ruby, Jay. 1977. "The Image Mirrored: Reflexivity and the Documentary Film" from *New Challenges for Documentary* ed. by Alan Rosenthal (1988), Berkeley: University of California Press. 65.

11. Erving Goffman defines a *key* as the set of conventions by which a given activity, already meaningful in terms of some primary framework, is transformed into something patterned on this activity but seen by the participants to be something else.

Playfulness, daydreaming and dramatic scriptings are keys employed in society to foster make-believe—wherein reality is imitated or transformed. The result is a pastime or entertainment. Keyings are vulnerable to *rekeying* when the established frame of reality is ruptured. This can occur through actual (real life) or scripted play (filmed reality). An inexperienced bank robber, for example, who merely wishes to threaten and intimidate the cashier, may accidentally fire a shot that wounds him; a robbery has now been unexpectedly rekeyed into a more serious crime that reroutes the outcome of reality, resulting in a graver punishment for the robber when he is captured. In some nostalgia-fantasy films, a character moves across a threshold and into another place or time, with her removal from one story and intrusion on another affecting two levels of scripted play—the narrative she escaped and the narrative she invaded. A dramatic scripting is a transformation of reality, and its rupture through rekeying—a process of "frame-breaking"—is a retransformation. A presupposed style of filmmaking like the documentary film can have its thematic intent and spectatorship reaction ruptured through the rekeying of pseudo-documentary. Goffman suggests "a rekeying does its work not simply on something defined in terms of a primary framework, but rather on the keying of these definitions. The primary framework must still be there, else there would be no content to the rekeying; but it is the keying of that framework that is the material that is transposed." (from *Frame Analysis*. 1974. Boston: Northeastern University Press. 81.)

12. From *Hauntings: Popular Film and American Culture 1990-1992* by Joseph Natoli. 1994. Albany: SUNY Press. 201.

13. The music and lyrics in *Bob Roberts* were written by Tim Robbins and his brother David Robbins. The lyrics are integral to the candidate's philosophy and advance the story line at certain points. A testament to their effectiveness as both politics and drama was Tim Robbins' refusal to sanction a soundtrack album release of the songs, for fear that the ballads and anthems ("I'm a Bleeding Heart," "Drugs Stink," "Wall Street Rap," "What Did the Teacher Tell You," "Pride," "Complain," and "Times are Changin' Back") would be wholeheartedly embraced by right-wing factions and not used or appreciated for their satiric intent. Similarly, the soundtrack to *Wag the Dog* only includes the themes and instrumental music by Mark Knopfler and not the various parodies of songs that satirize commercial and ersatz patriotic tendencies.

14. Joseph Daniel Casolaro was a 44 year-old freelance investigative reporter who wrote for publications including the *Washington Star* and the *National Enquirer*. At the time of his death he was working on a book aimed at exposing what he called "The Octopus," a group of less than a dozen shadowy figures whose machinations figured heavily, he claimed, in the Inslaw case, Iran-Contra, BCCI, and the October Surprise—controversial events surrounding the exchange of weapons for American hostages in Iran during the early 1980s. In August 1991, Casolaro was found dead at a West Virginia motel where he was to meet a source that would provide a key piece of evidence he needed to complete his investigation. For more information, see *The Mysterious Death of Danny Casolaro* by David MacMichael (http://www.american-buddha.com/mystery.death.htm) and "The Last Days of Danny Casolaro" by James Ridgeway and Doug Vaughan (*The Village Voice*, October 15, 1991).

15. Tim Robbins' statements from *Bob Roberts* DVD audio commentary track. Polygram Film Productions GmbH., Artisan Home Entertainment Inc. 2000.

16. The "assassination" of Bob Roberts is a cinematic case in point. News footage of the shooting is reviewed and it reveals—from select vantage points—the distraction created in the crowd that allows the Roberts team to plant the gun in Bugs Raplin's hand. Were a spectator to ignore or reframe this physical perspective, then the philosophical one—Roberts as an innocent victim— withstands. Because the news footage is not widely disseminated by the media, Roberts emerges as martyr-hero.

17. Burke, Kenneth. 1931, rev 1953, 1968. *Counter-Statement*. Berkeley: University of California Press. 54.

18. Burke, Kenneth. 1935, rev. 1954, 1984. *Permanence and Change*. Berkeley: University of California Press, 3rd ed. 90-91.

19. *Counter-Statement*. 183.

20. *Permanence and Change*. 173.

21. Source: Box Office Mojo. http://www.boxofficemojo.com/movies/?id=bulworth.htm

22. www.psychnet-uk.com/dsm_iv/voyeurism

23. Lefevre, Raymond. (1968). "Du Voyeurisme a l'Infini" from *Midi-Minuit Fantastique*. Reprinted in *Horror Film Reader* New York: Proscenium, 2000. 87.

24. Rich, Frank. (2004). "What O.J. Passed to the Gipper" *The New York Times*, June 20, 2004. The Warhol reference is to the avant-garde's proclivity for commissioning films that celebrate the gaze and the "direct cinema" strategies of observation with a fixed camera. To film the Empire State Building or a sleeping person for eight hours provides Warhol with an unmitigated window on the real world is a component of underground or experimental cinema in the 1960s but wholly embraced by the reality cinema/TV motif of the post-2000 times.

25. Perhaps the ultimate in product placement—also referred to as "product integration"—is the 2008 CBS network reality show, *Jingles*. Here, contestants write songs and lyrics to promote real products. While product sponsorship of television shows dates back to the late 1940s and *The Milton Berle Show: Texaco Star Theater* as well as soap operas underwritten by detergent companies, the practice diminished somewhat in the 1990s in favor of 30-second commercial spots. Fourth and fifth generation audiences that are prone to multitasking while watching television during commercials or worse, ad-zapping by incorporating TiVo, are now being reached by advertisers within the programming. An *Entertainment Weekly* survey noted that 66 percent of respondents did not care about or mind product integration, and 16 percent claimed they did not even notice it ("Ad Nauseam," *Entertainment Weekly*, July 25, 2008. 39-40).

26. In *Everything Bad Is Good for You*, author Steven Johnson acknowledges the complexity of today's serial television, beginning with the multiple threading seen in shows such as *Hill Street Blues* beginning in 1981. The simple, stand alone storylines of *Dragnet* in the 1950s and 1960s and of *Starsky and Hutch* in the 1970s have been displaced by the challenges that multithreaded episodic dramas from *thirtysomething to Six Feet Under* have given spectators. Johnson embraces the ability of audiences to manage several storylines and characters across time and at varied depths in each episode as part of the cognitive changes in the popular mind.

27. Ryan, Marie-Laure. (2002). "From *The Truman Show* to *Survivor*: Narrative versus Reality in Fake and Real Reality TV" from *Intensities, The Journal of Cult Media.* www.cult-media.com/issue2/Aryan.htm. 6.

28. The use of a radio frequency transmitter that links to an earpiece on the "player" is applied to this relay from Christof to Marlon, just as it is used in *Wag the Dog* to facilitate a scripted response by the White House Press Secretary in a relay from Stanley Motss. Beyond cinematic examples, it was during the third presidential debate between George W. Bush and challenger John Kerry in 2004 that there was conjecture that Bush had an earpiece fitted to receive response lines from his handlers.

29. Nochimson, Martha P. (2003). "Tony's Options: *The Sopranos* and the Televisuality of the Gangster Genre" from *Senses of Cinema*, Vol. 29. www.sensesofcinema.com/contents/03/29/sopranos_televisuality. html

30. Fittingly, Truman's last name is also that of a city in Los Angeles County where several film and television studios are located.

31. Jenkins, Henry. "The Poachers and the Stormtroopers: Cultural Convergence in the Digital Age"; http://web.mit.edu/21fms/www/faculty/henry3/pub/stormtroopers.htm

32. Freud, Sigmund. (1939). "Moses and Monotheism" from *The Origins of Religion*, Harmondsworth: Penguin, 1990.

33. Krzywinska, Tanya. (1999). "Demon Daddies: Gender, Ecstasy and Terror in the Possession Film" from *Horror Film Reader*, Silver, Alain and Ursini, James, eds. New York: Proscenium. 255.

Chapter Five

Life as Movie

BURKE MEETS GABLER IN *THE PURPLE ROSE OF CAIRO, PLEASANTVILLE,* AND *THE TRUMAN SHOW*

In exploring various films that interrogate the moving image, we come to a clearer understanding of how cinema perceives itself and its audiences. During the course of these explorations, films that spotlight the role of television and other applications of the moving image in our lives have also been examined. These texts, for better and for worse, have facilitated a social construction of reality. It is a construction that, when ruptured in dramatic play as these stories suggest, can be restored, reconstructed or rejected.

Literary theorist Kenneth Burke's theories in the areas of rhetoric and aesthetics, beginning in the 1930s, interlace with the writings of journalist and political commentator Neal Gabler some 50 years later. Burke's dramatistic method, which views the relationship between life and theater, offers wisdom and guidance for the way people can live their lives. If all the world's a stage to Burke, then all the world is akin to the movie screen for Gabler since he inserts cinema as a way of selecting, reflecting and deflecting reality. The capstone films in each of the last three chapters are vivid illustrations of the power of symbols, language and ideology working together to inform interpretive strategies.

While American culture was transforming itself in the early 1900s, the movies reinforced the preoccupation of transforming oneself into one's dreams. Early film genres frequently spotlighted morality plays, rags-to-riches tales, and wish-fulfillment fantasies. These aspects of the escapist musical are evident in *The Purple Rose of Cairo*. Neal Gabler notes that, during the early decades of the 20th century, "at the movies, and under the affect of the movies, reality for the first time seemed to be truly malleable."[1]

During this same period, news stories began to be stage-managed and created. As early as the 1890s, William Randolph Hearst considered the newspaper reporter the star or protagonist of any story he covered. A culture of celebrity and the celebration of cultural forms nurtured one another in the shadow of the powerful American dream that it is everyone's right to reinvent themselves. With the coming of television and the rise of network programming as exemplified in *Pleasantville*, perpetual exposure to dramatic play of the two-dimensional variety was a democratizing principle. In the age of home video and surveillance cameras–the period of *The Truman Show*–if all moments are subject to video capture, then all moments hold the possibility of performance. Erving Goffman bridges the gap between Kenneth Burke and Neal Gabler, considering life itself "a dramatically enacted thing." He posits "life itself is a dramatically enacted thing." Everyone is involved in a series of roles in a series of plays, an "exchange of dramatically inflated actions, counteractions, and terminating replies."[2] Although, it was a few centuries earlier that Shakespeare wrote these words in *As You Like It* that marked his own time and anticipated ours: "All the world's a stage and all the men and women merely players."

Television and the movies have recently, to a large extent, usurped the place of myth and oratory as both the repository and carrier of ideals, and have come to define cultural values in contemporary society. Marie-Laure Ryan situates older media forms as, likewise, having an effect but in a less provocative way.

> The prospect of an absolute and complete truth about a human being is more disturbing to the contemporary mind than the lies and fabulation for which media have traditionally been blamed. *The Truman Show* inscribes itself in a long tradition of fear of new media, but it also demonstrates the displacement that the object of this fear has undergone since the early age of print and the birth of the novel. The main threat to our ability to relate to the world and to its members no longer comes from escapes into the fictional, as seemed to be the case in the days of *Don Quixote* and *Madame Bovary*, but from the transformation of life itself into a spectacle. Whereas Don Quixote and Emma Bovary innocently lived fiction as if it were life, we are now so jaded that we watch the representation of life as an entertaining fiction, mindless both of the violence done to the individual whose privacy is being invaded and of the life we sacrifice when we live vicariously through televised hyper-reality. We are more alienated from the real by its supposedly exact copy than by the worlds openly made up by narrative imagination.[3]

Gabler sees life itself as "gradually becoming a medium all its own." An entertainment-driven, celebrity-oriented society may not necessarily destroy all moral value; it merely establishes the standard of value as whether or not something can fix and hold the public's attention. And truth, for Gabler, becomes more fascinating than fiction, with an ongoing tension between the movies and lived reality.

> Reality is ultimately more entertaining than conventional entertainment because everything you see is actually there. And then, there is this kind of cross-fertilization, because real life, of course, gets pollinated by conventional entertainment. So you have this constant process in which our lives become more cinematic and our movies become more real.[4]

How can cinema, then, through its own interrogation of the moving image and all the implications, presume to both inform and form character? As viewers watch and identify with film characters, what new "injections" are received from these "projections"? Cecilia in *The Purple Rose of Cairo*, David in *Pleasantville*, and Truman on *The Truman Show* exemplify those who have literally broken through the frame of film or TV, while most spectators, admittedly, accept the limitations of the film medium while suspending disbelief during viewing. By exploring how the aforementioned characters negotiate within a contrived movie or TV story, these films help us understand the media's influence and guide us to create adaptive strategies. Psychologist Shelley Taylor suggests the presence of "positive illusions" as embellishments or exaggerations that are the preferred spin that spectators put on the plots in which they play.[5] She defines these as distinct from delusions, and not a form of denial or repression. The "movies" we create for ourselves give us the same kinds of pleasure that conventional movies do, the former through direct identification with character (the self as player) and the latter through vicarious identification (with performer-player). Should the cinema spectator of *The Purple Rose of Cairo, Pleasantville, The Truman Show* and all the other films discussed at length–now alerted to the reflexive/reflective, critical and ironic stances–consider their perspectives a liberation by dramatism or a limitation of it? Two points must be considered, and it is important to re-invoke some concepts advanced by Kenneth Burke.

The first consideration is the commercial nature of mass media and its reliance on calculable consumer response to ensure dramatic capture, replay and revision. As noted, genre programming in media tends to reinforce predictability and repetition more than unique ruptures in their strategies that force a stronger evolutionary turn in the genre development. The frame-breaking actions of Cecilia, David, and Truman in the films discussed represent an extreme modification of the clichés in the romantic musical film, the TV sitcom, and the television reality show. Usually, media producers are representatives of the dominant ideologies and, at least in capitalist cultures, rarely veer from centrist positions, keeping audiences engaged in minimally challenging ways before delivering a satisfactory conclusion to their narratives.

The bar that measures transcendence, then, is noticeably low. It can be raised when human purpose is made necessary and present by invoking a teleological model, according to Burke. Teleology–the fact or quality of being purposeful–holds that mechanism or scientism alone cannot explain the facts of nature. A teleological argument makes the case for existence of a Creator who wills circumstances into existence. While there is great technical prowess in the mechanistic, there is likewise poetic power in the teleological. Pieties are restored. Perspectives by incongruity emerge as the language is "cracked." Things are renamed. Critical and interpretive positions are manifest. A new scheme of orientation reigns. This is an effect, or affirmation, of Burke's dramatism in spite of, or maybe beyond, Gabler. Both *Pleasantville* and *The Truman Show*, in fact, also use Gabler's thesis that our lives have become more cinematic to instigate their narrative, and then subvert it by celebrating the redemptive capacities of film and identification. What Burke calls the "revolt of the poetic" is displayed in their reconstructive and rejective finales. Dramatism functions as a purposeful tool here.

Effective symbols and signs that encourage spectators to make meaning from them are produced by the god-like guides such as Christof in *The Truman Show* and the TV repairman in *Pleasantville*. They are made further effective by Truman Burbank, the ensemble of characters in *Pleasantville*, the films' writers/directors, critics and the spectators. Both Christof and the repairman are ultimately false god-guides, necessarily masked as such so that Truman and David can develop a higher human potential that a true god-guide would inspire. We sense that, ultimately, all correctives to maintain the mechanistic, or false-teleological order, will fail. From a TV set in the showroom, the repairman screams his demand that to David come home, but David turns off the set and rejects the order. Likewise, Truman is adrift at sea trying to escape when Christof calls in the violent rainstorm. Truman survives and yells in challenge if this is "the best you've got?" David and Truman will make their own way, not unlike Mickey and Mallory in *Natural Born Killers*, without the manipulators of mass media. Dramatism serves as a purposeful and liberating tool, then.

The second consideration is posed as dialectic. It is the great cultural debate of our time between the realists and the post realists, between humanness and happiness. Gabler condenses the argument as between "the realists who believed that a clear-eyed appreciation of the human condition was necessary to *be* human, and the post realists who believed that glossing reality and even transforming it into a movie were perfectly acceptable strategies if these films made us happier."[6]

The technological advancements of recent years have made the temptations towards happiness far greater than the desire for humanness. Despite the well-oiled technologies that support "The Truman Show," *The Truman Show* exposes the hollowness at the core of what is, apparently, a well-adjusted life. Ironically, these three films of the nostalgia fantasy genre that provide spectators with coping strategies all contain production and narrative techniques that are the result of scientific and technological breakthroughs in both moviemaking (*Pleasantville* and its black-and-white world rendered in gradually emerging color; *The Purple Rose of Cairo* and its use of special effects to incorporate a character into action already filmed, as well as the doubling of Jeff Daniels' character that is Tom/Gil in the same shot) and storytelling (*The Truman Show* and its familiar life-as-it-is aura, made believable and engaging due to technology's omnipresence). So the movies' ability to make us understand the limitations of living a life dictated by media are, in these examples, assisted by the very technologies that make the movies more life-like. It remains for the conflicted individuals in these films to challenge the structures of control.

The closed societies of Pleasantville and Seahaven are created or "talked" into existence by media operatives, but are soon refashioned by personal and individual voices. Society, like the self, is malleable and changeable, created moment-by-moment and filled with the tensions of uncertainty and ambiguity. *Pleasantville* and *The Truman Show* deal with knowledge–its acquisition, the consequences of its attainment, and its liberating nature. At the same time, their characters contend with passions such as love and violence. Ambiguities abound in these stories as well as in *The Purple Rose of Cairo*. Speaking of the actor Gil and the character Tom, Cecilia marvels at how she was formerly unloved, but that now two people love her, and it's the same two people! Ultimately, she chooses her restorative option after a frame-breaking experience that positioned Cecilia to possibly reconstruct or reject the world from which she comes. Cecilia makes her decision within the vacuum of abject personal relationships. The inhibitions she might express regarding the breaking of the frame seem less a concern in the other narratives set in the 1950s and 1990s. Nevertheless, the restorative tendency exists as an alternative recuperative or therapeutic strategy as exemplified in *The Purple Rose of Cairo*.

Truman Burbank, significantly, is not really a "true man" but a media construct of one. He has difficulty dealing with the ultimate manifestation of ego and tells his best friend Marlon that he sometimes feels like the whole world revolves around him Truman is Neal Gabler's prime example of a "lifie" wherein one's life *is* a movie. Truman's life is not *like* a movie. It *is* a movie/TV show. And when the unplanned elements invade Seahaven–the reappearance of Truman's father, Truman's continued infatuation with Lauren/

Sylvia–they represent ruptured moments outside of the planned causality, true precipitating events that motivate Truman to literally and metaphorically cross bridges.

It has been noted that three precipitating events in *Pleasantville* served to realign that narrative: David's acceptance of cookies from Margaret (which angers her TV boyfriend Whitey and culminates in the fight with David), Jennifer's date with Skip (which ultimately brings notions of sex to the town), and Mr. Johnson's cessation of his routine wiping of the soda fountain counter (which starts his journey toward genuine self-expression and culminates in a passionate connection with Betty Parker and the civil disobedience of painting murals on Main Street). Small surprises and seemingly insignificant acts compose our life as a movie, too; their eventual impacts can be magnanimous, however. While dramatism employs normal transitions–such as intermissions and act breaks–and chains of causal events to engage the audience, it also utilizes messy surprises and reversals. These are part of the ambiguities of life. The revolt of the poetic is about this ambiguity and the rules that life may or may not follow. Surely, the violence that is introduced into Pleasantville is an example of such an ambiguity, having positive and negative effects.

Another ambiguity is sex. Sex is the powerful, transformative event in *Pleasantville* and love is its counterpart in *The Truman Show*. In *The Purple Rose of Cairo*, it is an unrealized notion of both and the attraction/distraction of idealized models that Cecilia prefers to release to their rightful place on the movie screen. Love ultimately drives Truman to face his greatest fears (water, the ire of Christof, the unscripted life where he is no longer a star) when he leaves the illusionary, human-made paradise of Seahaven in search of the banished, former co-star Lauren/Sylvia.

The ambiguity of sex as a tool in driving away pluralism has both amoral and moralistic overtones. This dichotomy speaks to the clash of values between today and the time of "Pleasantville." From a critical or ironic stance, it can force an anti-nostalgia mindset, a desanctifying of memory that is not an altogether bad circumstance. For some, memory is the last place of hope about the "good old days." But hope belongs in the present, which is where David eventually returns to bring the lessons he learned in Pleasantville, and it is to the present of the real world where, we hope, Truman Burbank escapes. The sexual awakenings in *Pleasantville* and the promise of genuine sexual contact in *The Truman Show* (remember, Truman's TV wife Meryl kept her fingers crossed in their wedding photo) are the launch points in learning to confront the many other things that trouble society–such as racism, ageism, class divisions, runaway technology, and revolutions of all sorts. There are two extreme poles of disengagement from those potentially discomforting things: develop a cynical and pessimistic worldview; or long for the supposed harmony of a world of organization and order like Pleasantville or Seahaven. In all likelihood, it is the middle ground where we should find ourselves. Cinema invites reflective/reflexive, critical and ironic stances and allows us to consider these positions as byproducts of the nostalgia fantasy film as it also interrogates the place and purpose of the moving image, acknowledging the movies' viability as equipment for living.

NOTES

1. Gabler, Neal. (1998). *Life the Movie: How Entertainment Conquered Reality.* New York: Knopf. 51.

2. Goffman, *The Presentation of Self in Everyday Life.* 72.

3. Ryan. ibid. 14-15.

4. Gabler interviewed by Steven Heller. www.typotheque.com/articles/neal_gabler.html

5. Taylor, Shelley E. (1989). *Positive Illusions: Creative Self-Deception and the Healthy Mind.* New York: Basic Books.

6. Gabler. *Life the Movie.* 243.

Epilogue

The Sixth Generation Audience

In the introduction, five generations of audiences were identified and some new demands of the contemporary spectator were noted. The sixth generation–coming to terms with the role of the moving image in their lives during the early 21st century and beyond–likewise welcomes the stances and the therapeutic possibilities of contemporary films, and not just in movies about media. Recent films such as *Good Night and Good Luck* (Clooney, 2005) and *Jarhead* (Mendes, 2005) invite reflexive/reflective, critical and ironic perspectives. Contemporary spectators of *Good Night and Good Luck* may connect the circumstances surrounding Edward R. Murrow's confrontation with Senator Joseph McCarthy in 1953 with the kind of demagoguery challenged (or celebrated) by journalists in politics today; in a critique of parallel face-offs, they might even perceive the William Paley of CBS in the 1950s, Murrow's boss, as a more heroic representation of the reconstructive tendency than media moguls Rupert Murdoch or Sumner Redstone represent today. Viewers of *Jarhead*, a film that follows a group of young Marines during Operations Desert Shield and Desert Storm during Gulf War I, may by disappointed by the lack of war action that they expect in a film such as this; the reflexive notions apply directly, however, to the current Gulf War aftermath as *Jarhead* displays undersupplied American troops in defense of Middle East oil supplies, and it critiques the plight of the soldier who is worn down by fear in a combat zone where, ironically, a four-day war does not give him a chance to truly engage and fulfill his agency. Both of these recent films seem to invite a reconstructive tendency, for both their major characters and their spectators.

Another contemporary popular genre is the coming-of-age film. It is especially geared for the emerging generations of spectators, namely, the fourth through sixth. Two recent examples are *Wedding Crashers* (Dobkin, 2005)

and *The 40-Year-Old Virgin* (Apatow, 2005). These films are critical observations of their characters flaws–in the former the "crashers" are unabashedly
extroverted and selfish, and in the latter a character's introversion is an im-
pediment to his maturity–and they afford formulaic opportunities and resolu-
tions that point toward a reconstruction of their characters' personalities and
outlooks. Even in modern melodrama, the spectator stances are invoked. *The
Constant Gardener* (Meirelles, 2005) weaves the story of the mysterious
disappearance of an activist in Kenya with the plight of her husband, a British diplomat, as he connects her death to a pharmaceutical company and its
deployment of a new drug in Africa. Here, the critical and ironic perspectives
are strongest, and a rejective tendency dominates in conclusion.

So as these narrative stances persist in viewers and filmmakers today,
what of the actual viewing process will be different as the sixth generation
emerges? More than any other generation, the sixth confronts a mediated
world with several opportunities for interaction with moving images–in film
and in other media using moving pictures–that dwarf the choices of previous
generations that were faced with cinema and television as the major means of
spectatorship. As a species, we still manage sense-making by applying and
understanding techniques of storytelling, and narrative film has provided the
model and the grounding for an understanding of much of what will follow.
Building upon some observations in the Introduction, the sixth generation of
spectators—whether going to the movies, using the Internet, or sitting before
high definition video screens large and small–will be marked by these attributes.[1]

A Comfortability and Compatibility with New and Emerging Technologies.
While the Internet is certainly a participatory medium for all generations of
spectators, it has been a matter in everyday life for many fifth generation
spectators and most sixth generation ones. Today's Net Generation has already incorporated e-mail, hyper links and surfing for audio/video clips into
their media habits, and is fast making other uses just as vital.[2] The online
broadband capturing and streaming of video has made the Internet a forum
for hosting feature films, with the sixth generation spectator able to create,
as well as call up, moving images at will and consume them in new ways
(desktop, projection, laptop, iPod). Many believed the Web would be a medium dominated by professional writers and artists, but the sixth generation
filmmakers, social and media critics, and bloggers have commandeered the
technology and have refashioned the media landscape with popular personal
journal sites on the Web such as myspace.com.

Just as technology changes the spectators' ways of experiencing the moving image, it also changes their means of responding to it. Recall that Neal
Gabler envisioned life as a movie, and the nostalgia fantasy films of frame-

breaking such as *The Purple Rose of Cairo* and *Pleasantville* allowed viewers to project themselves into the filmed narratives. Today, the online diary is a dominant form of discourse on the Internet, incorporating text, color, graphics, sounds and moving pictures and it is composed and managed by spectators themselves.[3] Steven Johnson seems to echo Gabler, except now the projections of self are online:

> A decade ago Douglas Rushkoff coined the phrase 'screenagers' to describe the first generation that grew up with the assumption that the images on a television screen were supposed to be manipulated; that they weren't just there for passive consumption. The next generation is carrying that logic to a new extreme: the screen is not just something you manipulate, but something you project your identity onto, a place to work through the story of your life as it unfolds.[4]

Once the concept of a virtual community is in place and the ease of initiation in uses of new technologies is habitual, the sixth generation of spectators will gladly accept screens and cameras everywhere. As in *The Truman Show*, surveillance and exhibitionism will be drained of their negative connotation and made acceptable in the new media landscape. Scenarios from recent science fiction films might frighten spectators as to the ultimate melding of body/mind and machine (*Terminator 2, Westworld, Robocop, Tetsuo: The Iron Man*), but the mitigating stories that celebrate pleasure and utopian–as opposed to the dystopian visions of the aforementioned films–are also in circulation. Steven Spielberg's *AI: Artificial Intelligence* (2001) and *Minority Report* (2002) both embrace the promises of new technologies. In the latter, characters walk through a modern shopping center and are confronted with personalized commercials on multiple screens, geared to their own consuming patterns as detected by an implanted chip-transmitter when they enter the media space. If sixth generation spectators take their cues from various cinematic representations of this new interplay with technology, they will likely be armed with a conflicted sense of purpose.

Portability. Sixth generation audiences will experience entertainment and information content "on demand," that is, when they want it, where they want it, and how they want it. Portability further insures that desire will be fulfilled. Emerging audiences are more comfortable with the concept of nomadicity than any previous set of consumers. By the mid-20th century, America was evolving into a suburbanized nation and the post World War II-era saw an acceleration in changes rooted first in the Industrial Revolution, and then followed by the affordable automobile, planned communities such as Levittown, the interstate highway system, shopping malls and their franchised tenants that began to de-center the town square from Main Street to the outlying lands, and television as a dominant mass media forum for the moving image.

In the late 1950s, the transistor radio revolutionized teenage culture, freeing young audiences to listen to what they wanted away from the home. At drive-in theaters, they could also escape to the compartmentalized experience of the automobile while watching movies. By the 1970s, battery-operated, affordable portable television sets were in use by nomadic viewers who wanted their news, sports and entertainment that the over-the-air broadcasters were usually prone to deliver to Nielsen homes throughout the country. As the last century ended, Walkmans and Watchmans, wireless phones and personal computers were reduced to hand held devices so that the spectator-consumer-communicator was now akin to a sending and receiving station. A member of the sixth generation of audiences may elect to never be out of touch, to remain in a constant state of alert to new sounds and images, indeed, may feel disenfranchised if he or she is unable to maintain what would earlier have been considered sporadic, remote access to communication structures. The sixth generation spectator is really a structure in himself or herself. They send and receive transmissions wherever they wish.

In *The Future of Music: Manifesto for a Digital Revolution*, David Kusek and Gerd Leonhard describe what may be a component of the structure that is the spectator in the year 2015.

> Our Universal Mobile Devices (UMD) are 'always on' at 8 MB/second, and we have anytime-anywhere access to music, films, games, books, news, streaming video, online banking, stock market transactions, instant messaging, e-mail and chats. It's a global telephone, a digital communication and data transfer device, a Global Positioning Device (GPS), a personal digital assistant, a music/images/film storage device, a recorder, a personal computer, a gaming platform, and much more. . . . Our UMD can project a fairly large and sharp image onto any white surface, it can set up instant secure wireless connections to other computers, beamers, monitors, screens, and printers, and it can connect to other UMDs to exchange data and files, instantly and securely.[5]

One hundred years before the UMD surfaces, a first generation spectator may have sat transfixed at the grandeur of a moving image such as *The Birth of a Nation* at a cinema palace. As sensational as that experience may have been–accompanied by a symphony orchestra, in shared viewing with hundreds of others, a Civil War melodrama that Woodrow Wilson remarked was like writing history with lightning–the UMD's wizardry promises the sixth generation spectator greater control over content and consumption. Now, s/he can not only make their own history felt through interactive personal expression and make sense of the world surrounding them through instant connectivity, but can, should they choose, create their own screening space with the projection of images from their UMD.

Interruptivity. A new sensitivity to management of the sixth generation's time and its apparent focus or concentration on new media forms is demanded by both viewers and producers of moving images. The ability to be connected or disconnected at will is a hallmark of most portable devices, as well as a component of everyday use of hard-wired computer and video technology. Earlier generations of film spectators had little or no control over the flow of information displayed on cinema or network TV screens. Interactivity–a term not used during the first three generations, to be sure–could be assumed in responses such as attendance figures at the box office, amount of fan mail received by a celebrity or due to an issue explored by a TV show, or the Nielsen ratings. High figures or scores in these areas insured those programs were well received by audiences. Narratives unfolded at the pace and in the locations prescribed by the structures of media (in cinemas or over the air or on cable, for the most part) and at preordained lengths or in calculable blocks (feature films lasting about two hours, and TV shows in half-hour increments or multiples thereof). Until the advent of the VCR and video-tapes, the spectator surrendered to the time schedules of the media providers. After home video erupts, the spectator begins to have more control the over the viewing environment, the start/stop time of programming, the moments of interruption, and the overall ambiance of spectatorship regardless of the program content. DVDs chop films into chapters with subtitled headings that allow spectators to skip to segments for re-viewing, unimpaired by the need to watch what the filmmaker created as orientation to those scenes in prior sequences. The recomposition, remixing, or "mashing" of the moving image experience is in the hands of the new spectator who becomes akin to co-author of the text with the media providers.

Other social concerns associated with accelerated lifestyles certainly enter the discussion, but shortened attention spans, information overload, fast food diets that alter the body's metabolism, the rise in ADD and prescribed drugs to address it, and other components of modernity are subjects for another text about living in the 21st century. The general tendency has been to become comfortable with interruptivity in all walks of life, more so now than ever. There is the cell phone conversation that interrupts a personal chat, the audible signal that an email has been received while reviewing an unrelated written document, or the pop-up message that comes on a desktop computer screen and catches the eye of the person facing the screen, diverting his attention from the interviewee across his desk. And if a spectator can segment a narra-tive program to suit personal whims, the filmmaker must be canny enough to acknowledge that capability, and perhaps welcome the opportunity and build a narrative that encourages pause, reflection, rerouting and an eventual return to the flow. The obvious danger is that another media experience diverts the spectator's attention from a primary one. By discouraging any interruptions through an intense concentration on storytelling form, character and spectacle, the filmmaker resorts to strategies that served the earlier generations of cinema practitioners successfully. The two outlooks coexist today, however the sixth generation spectator is in the catbird seat and dictates the patterns of consumption relative to interruptivity more than the media makers.

Driven by Multiple Activity. The sixth generation of spectators is quite comfortable with the concept of multitasking, the performance of two or more activities that simultaneously or alternatingly occupy attention. Multitasking demands both an intellectual as well as physical or physiological comportment. The mind processes what the senses are receiving. Multitasking may have components traditionally unrelated to one another; initially at least, the concept of listening to music and jogging were disparate things, until the promotion of the Sony Walkman and other portable devices to accompany runners on their routes. Multitasking can encompass a singular media experience with several data streams—such as viewing a television program while stock market results or weather updates are delivered in a banner across the bottom of the frame, to which can be added a voice-over during the closing credits that promotes the upcoming program and perhaps a picture-in-picture display at the corner of the screen, a miniature frame showing what is on another channel.

The portabilization and segmentation of media space has increased the opportunities for multitasking to envelop a variety of media and communication tasks. For example, at an office desk a worker may be using the telephone (a first generation spectator novelty), listening to recorded playback of background music with some appreciable fidelity (arguably, a dominant second generation experience), keep one eye on the CNN monitor in the background that is silent but delivers closed-captioned text to accompany its moving images (television as a third generation experience), utilize his desktop computer to compose a document related to the work he is getting paid for (word-processing as a fourth generation experience), but also keep an eye on another window that hosts an online video game where he awaits his competitor's next move (fifth generation at play), and lastly, downloading video and music files to be stored on his iPod (sixth generation).

The ability to follow and engage multiple story threads is an attribute to be expected of sixth generation spectators. Earlier generations weaned on simple video experiences such as Pong, Pac-Man or Tetris, have moved onward to Zelda, SimCity, Second Life and Grand Theft Auto (which allows participants to create their own narratives while exploring urban space). The activity that gaming enthusiasts know as probing and telescoping—the movement into and through the world of a video game—is really an actualization of the scientific method that is nestled like a collapsible telescope in the framework of levels in a video game. Put scientifically, a player probes the virtual world and, based on reflection while probing and afterward, forms a hypothesis about what something (a text, an artifact, object, event or action) might mean in a usefully situated way. Then, the player probes the world with that hypothesis in mind, and witnesses whatever effect emerges. The effect is feedback from the world, and then the player can accept or rethink his original hypothesis.[6] The virtual gaming worlds, like the worlds of many filmed narratives, offer spectators multiple story threads that also demand a strategy of probing and telescoping. Steven Johnson considers multithreading "the most celebrated structural feature of the modern television drama" and he charts the growing complexity of narratives beginning with *Hill Street Blues* in 1981 (a fourth generational experience).[7] Third generation experiences such as *Dragnet* and *Starsky and Hutch* afford simple, linear narratives that conclude with each episode and rarely, if ever, reflect on previously exposed narrative turns. Fifth and sixth generation audiences tolerate complicated narratives in TV shows like *ER, 24, The Sopranos, Deadwood* and *Rome*. These programs–along with recent films such as *Being John Malkovich* (Jonze, 1999), *Magnolia* (Anderson, 1999), *Memento* (Nolan, 2001), *Eternal Sunshine of the Spotless Mind* (Gondry, 2004), and *2046* (Wong Kar-Wai, 2004) to name just a few–challenge spectators in ways quite distinct from the first four generations. They create:

> . . . a thick network of intersecting plotlines; some challenge by withholding crucial information from the audience; some by inventing temporal schemes that invert traditional relationships of cause and effect; some by deliberately blurring the line between fact and fiction. (All of these are classic techniques of the old cinematic avant-garde, by the way.) There are antecedents in the film canon, of course: some of the seventies conspiracy films, some of Hitchcock's psychological thrillers. But the mind-benders have truly flowered as a genre in the past ten years–and done remarkably well at the box office, too.[8]

The ability to engage in multiple activities and confront multiple threads in spectatorship energizes both the media viewer and media producer to consume and create in novel ways that simultaneously build upon and make obsolete the old structures in this relationship.

Customization and Selectivity. With the multitude of program and platform choices now available, it becomes necessary for some filtering of the consumer options amidst the media torrent. Fifth generation spectators became comfortable with "artificial intelligence" inclusions in software or affixed to user-profiles that both disallowed certain messages to come through and gave preference to others based on past uses/purchases or stated interests. This is a step beyond the RIYL–Recommended If You Like–strategies employed by clothing salespersons in brick-and-mortar stores to amazon.com suggestions of other videos, books or CDs to compliment your initial purchase. In the film *Minority Report* (Spielberg, 2002), set in the near-future, characters stroll through a shopping venue and as they pass various video screens a customized message is flashed before them; the sensors in the video apparatus receive impulses from a chip implanted in the passerby, and then provide a selected, customized moving image based on data received about buying habits and interests. Sixth generation spectators will need to manage the apparent freedom of choice unleashed by new technologies, along with the tension created by those same technologies which can also foist a control or containment of those choices.

How these attributes express both gains and losses for the spectator regarding the overall emotional and tactile experience of watching the moving image can be contrasted in the bill of fare at a cinema in the era of the second generation–or in the living room of a third generation spectator–with that of a fifth or sixth generation viewer of the moving image today.

A family of viewers in 1937 attends the Strand Theater, a downtown cinema showing a double-feature. The new film is *In Old Chicago*, a major 20th Century-Fox production. The second film is *Stowaway*, released the year before but still popular in reprise showings on the bottom half of a double bill. *In Old Chicago* centers on the O'Leary family, pioneer settlers of a bustling big city. Two brothers (played by Tyrone Power and Don Ameche) battle over the future of Chicago's slums, until a massive fire wipes out much of the town and changes their lives forever. *Stowaway*, a shorter film, features Shirley Temple as an incurably curious child in a shipboard story with music and romance. The films are run continuously, and sandwiched before or between them are previews of coming attractions (such as an upcoming Shirley Temple vehicle, *Heidi*, or Tyrone Power's next film, *Alexander's Ragtime Band*); a color cartoon, perhaps from RKO Radio Studios which released the Walt Disney shorts such as *The Old Mill*; a Fox Movietone newsreel, this one concentrating on the Civil War in Spain; and a short subject leased from MGM entitled *Romance of Radium*. The unified, mass audience consumed entertainment and information as what can be described as a democratic unit–all equal in the dark and all getting the same images at the same time. Those images were certainly diverse in their content–escapist fare laced with some historical context (*In Old Chicago*); Depression-era comedy/drama as seen through the eyes of a child (*Stowaway*); commercials to engage and inform future attendance; lively animation, in color; real-world events in the newsreel that supplemented the radio and print accounts of the world between the wars; and the MGM Pete Smith Specialty short that made, in this case, the science of particles more approachable to the average spectator. The viewing experience was linear, controlled, and communitarian.

Flash forward nearly 30 years to a living room in America on a Sunday evening. A rather nondescript gentleman in a suit is introducing acts as if he were the master of ceremonies at a vaudeville theater. Indeed, Ed Sullivan updated that performance ethos for the television age, showcasing a variety of acts in his weekly, hour-long program on the CBS network. Classical and popular musical performers, comedians and monologists, impressionists, specialty acts, excerpts from Broadway plays, oratory and spoken word, circus and animal acts, acrobats, opera singers, dancers, jugglers and clowns were some of the show business types revealed on Sullivan's show. Imagine a family (Mom, Dad, Grandma, children from ages 4 to 16, maybe a cousin or neighbor as well) gathered to watch these acts in succession, with no opportunity to fast-forward and little inclination to leave the room, since one's favorite could be on next: Maria Callas from the Metropolitan Opera performing a selection from *Aida*, the Marquis Chimps dressed as humans trying to negotiate a tricycle track, Richard Pryor or Flip Wilson delivering their brand of racial humor into white living rooms, actor Richard Burton doing a soliloquy from *Hamlet*, Cassius Clay taking a bow from the audience, The Rolling Stones singing "Let's Spend the Night Together," Gordon MacRae and Shirley Jones reminiscing with a number from their stage musical *Oklahoma!*, Alan King or Myron Cohen doing Jewish jokes, Johnny Rivers from California debuting his version of the Motown hit "Baby, I Need Your Lovin'," Frank Gorshin pretending to be Kirk Douglas, Cab Calloway leading his band in "St. James Infirmary," some circus performers from Yugoslavia who spin plates on sticks, Topo Gigo (a stereotyped, overly gracious Italian mouse who played to Ed's straight-man sensibilities), and the parents of comic Ben Stiller–Jerry Stiller and Anne Merra–whose act turned on the trauma of harried couples in love. The point is that this was a rich and varied contingent of performance traditions, captured and presented via the moving images on television, to a third generation (or earlier) audience that was receptive to alternative impulses of mediaplay. Grandma may not have understood the phenomenon of Mick Jaggar, but she observed and consumed the message from The Stones' song alongside her granddaughter. Dad's appreciation of Pryor or The Doors might be different from his son's, but both are evocative of their political/generational perspectives. A child might even become intrigued with opera or gymnastics through the Sullivan show. The niches of programming were evident; in this case, they were just revealed to spectators one after the other. It is quite different for the fifth and sixth generations of television spectators today.

Beginning in the 1970s with an explosion in the number of broadcast and cable channels, accompanied by the increasing number of television sets in use, spectators of the moving image at home grew comfortably apart as they sought out programs and time-slots convenient to their own interests and lifestyles. The community of viewers was linked by the common program or broadcast, not by the fact that they gathered in the same location to watch one. In fact, skepticism of group viewing of the moving image was evident as far back as the time of Thomas Edison who initially embraced the peepshow parlor viewing style because he was fearful that watching films en masse would use up audiences quicker. Although this mindset was quickly displaced by the seats in front of Nickelodeon screens, a testament to Edison's thinking is the home video viewing environment of the 1970s when the VCR further segmented spectators into niches both physical (living room, bedroom, den, kitchen) and program-selective (multiple channels and formats). Indeed, it was as if the audience for moving pictures had come full circle and now returned to the single viewer, singularized space and away from the previous arenas of hundreds in a cinema or a handful gathered in a living room.

The sixth generation spectator is free to fashion his or her own type of program flow and construct it through channel-surfing (a kind of amped-up, ad hoc Sullivan experience, if you consider the diversity of images across the spectrum that can be sampled), through file-sharing, or compilations of various sorts. The third and fourth generations' cinema multiplex experience of six or eight screen has grown to 24 or more in a single location, and the ability to select and sequence images on the computer screen or personal display devices affords the sixth generation a combination of portability and niche-segmentation. Indeed, the sixth generation can be considered "platform agnostic," a designation that infers it will view movies on any screen, large or small, under a variety of circumstances.

Perhaps the innovation that best incorporates the sixth generation's predilection for these attributes is YouTube, an Internet site that is a virtual video village where people post their own videos, watch other contributors, and search, rate and comment on them as well. YouTube was created in 2005 and acquired by Google, Inc., the following year. The site airs over 100 million videos a day.[9] It has been enabled by three revolutions: a video revolution, where cheap recorders and production software holds sway; a social revolution where–along with web sites such as MySpace, Facebook, Wikipedia, and Flickr–virtual communities come together, thrive, and share information; a cultural revolution, where consumers are impatient with mainstream media and its spoon-feeding to passive audiences, preferring unfiltered sounds and images. The ramifications of these revolutions remain to be seen, but at its root is our preoccupation in communicating with moving pictures.

In comparing these generational experiences we can see that much has been lost and much has been gained for both media makers and spectators during the past century or more. Whatever the era or the dominant technologies, by energizing reflexive, critical and ironic stances we can insure an active engagement with film narrative and recognize its transformative potential, especially when its stories comment on other media. Viewing a moving image now demands an understanding of both the text of the narrative and the apparatus that carries it. It has been discussed how films that directly incorporate mediaplay into their narrative and character development point to alternate routes in the socialization process. Spectators are reminded that the invitations to reconstruct, to restore, or to reject are privileged ones. They are offered here as a means of reading and making meaning from films where the spectatorship process is positioned front-and-center in the movies themselves. The second, third and fourth generation spectator-characters in *The Purple Rose of Cairo*, *Pleasantville* and *The Truman Show* witness a projection of self that mirrors both the hope and the fear of what they, and we, can be.

NOTES

1. In *Media Unlimited* (2001), Todd Gitlin details how attributes and aspects such as these define the next emerging generation of media consumers.

2. The 'Net Generation consists of spectators born between 1976 and 1998 and represents over 30 percent of the U.S. population. They have more information available to them than any other group of people have ever had. The opportunities for them to consume media content are also increasing on a daily basis.

3. Technorati, a blog-tracking service, estimates 275,000 blog entries are published every day. In two years, the number of active bloggers in the U.S. reached the size of the prime-time television network audience.

4. Johnson, Steven. (2005). *Everything Bad Is Good For You: How Today's Popular Culture is Actually Making Us Smarter.* New York: Riverhead Books. 229.

5. Kusek, David and Leonhard, Gerd. (2005). *The Future of Music: Manifesto for a Digital Revolution.* Boston: Berklee Press. 16.

6. James Paul Gee as quoted in *Everything Bad Is Good For You.* 45.

7. Ibid. 72.

8. Ibid. 130.

9. While few statistics are publicly available regarding the number of videos on YouTube, the company revealed that 2.5 billion videos were watched in June 2006. 50,000 videos were being added per day in May 2006, and this increased to 65,000 by July ("YouTube Serves Up 100 Million Videos a Day Online." *USA Today.* July 16, 2006). In January 2008 alone, nearly 79 million users had made over 3 billion video views ("YouTube Looks for the Money Clip" by Yi-Wyn Yen. *Fortune Magazine.* March 25, 2008).

Bibliography

Adams, Robert M. "The Dance of Language." London Times Literary Supplement, July 8, 1983.

Armstrong, Jennifer. "Ad Nauseam." *Entertainment Weekly*. July 25, 2008.

Attebery, Brian. *Strategies of Fantasy*. Bloomington and Indianapolis: Indiana University Press, 1992.

Allen, Woody, dir. *The Purple Rose of Cairo*. Screenplay by Woody Allen. Orion Pictures, 1985.

Allen, Woody. *Three Films of Woody Allen*. New York: Random House, 1987.

Anderson, Christopher. *Hollywood TV: The Studio System in the Fifties*. Austin: University of Texas Press, 1994.

Ashby, Hal, dir. *Being There*. Screenplay by Jerzy Kosinski, based on his novel. United Artists Productions, 1979.

Auster, Albert. "Television as Seen by Hollywood" from *The Political Companion to American Film* (Gary Crowdus, ed.). Chicago: Lake View Press, 1994.

Bagdikian, Ben H. *The New Media Monopoly*. Boston: Beacon Press, 2004.

Baldick, Chris. *In Frankenstein's Shadow*. Oxford: Oxford University Press, 1990.

Baudrillard, John. *Selected Writings*. ed. Mark Poster. Stanford; Stanford University Press, 1988.

Baudry, Jean-Louis. "Ideological Effects of the Basic Cinematographic Apparatus." *Film Quarterly,* Volume 28, Number 2 (Winter 1974-75), translated by Alan Williams.

Bazin, Andre. "The Evolution of the Language of Cinema" from *What is Cinema?* Berkeley: University of California Press, 1967.

Beatty, Warren, dir. *Bulworth*. Screenplay by Warren Beatty and Jeremy Pikser. Story by Warren Beatty. Twentieth Century-Fox Film Corporation, 1998.

Belton, John. *Widescreen Cinema*. Cambridge: Harvard University Press, 1992.

Bogdanovich, Peter. "Adapting and Directing *The Last Picture Show*"; *Scenario*, Vol. 4, No. 4, Winter 1998-99. Interviewed by Annie Nocenti.

Bogle, Donald. *Toms, Coons, Mulattos, Mammies & Bucks: An Interpretive History of Blacks in American Films.* New York: Continuum, 1973, rev. 1989, 2003

Boorstin, Daniel J. *The Image: A Guide to Pseudo-Events in America.* New York: Antheneum, 1962, rev. 1987.

Braudy, Leo. *The World in a Frame: What We See in Films.* Chicago: University of Chicago Press, 1976.

Briggs, Joe Bob. *Profoundly Disturbing: Shocking Movies That Changed History!* New York: Universe Publishing, 2003.

Browne, Nick. "The Spectator in the Text: The Rhetoric of *Stagecoach*" from *Film Quarterly*, Volume 34, Number 2, Winter 1975-76.

Burke, Kenneth. *Attitudes Toward History.* Berkeley: University of California Press, 1937.

———. *Counter-Statement.* Berkeley: University of California Press, 1931, rev 1953, 1968.

———. *Permanence and Change: An Anatomy of Purpose.* Berkeley: University of California Press, 1935, rev. 1954, 1984.

Campbell, James. *Talking at the Gates: A Life of James Baldwin.* Berkeley: University ofCalifornia Press, 2002

Chayefsky, Paddy. *Network* screenplay, from *The Collected Works of Paddy Chayefsky—the Screenplays: The Hospital, Network, Altered States,* New York: Applause, 1994.

Christensen, Terry. *Reel Politics: American Political Movies from Birth of a Nation to Platoon.* New York: Blackwell, 1987.

Corliss, Richard. "Can This Man Save the Movies?" *Time.* Vol. 167, No. 12. March 20, 2006.

Cowie, Peter. *A Ribbon of Dreams: The Cinema of Orson Welles.* S. Brunswick/NY/ London: Barnes/Nativity Press, 1973.

Dante, Joe, dir. *Matinee.* Screenplay by Charlie Haas. Story by Charlie Haas and Jerico. Universal Pictures, 1993.

Darabont, Frank, dir. *The Majestic.* Screenplay by Michael Sloane. Castle Rock Entertainment and Warner Brothers Pictures, 2001.

Dika, Vera. *Recycled Culture in Contemporary Art and Film: The Uses of Nostalgia.* New York: Cambridge Press., 2003.

Encyclopedia Britannica, Vol. 28. "Theatrical Production." Chicago: Encyclopedia Britannica, 1998.

Ferrero-Regis, Tiziana. "Cinema On Cinema: Self-Reflexive Memories in Recent Italian History Films" from *Transformations*, No. 3, 2002.

Freud, Sigmund. "Moses and Monotheism" from *The Origins of Religion*, Harmondsworth: Penguin, 1990. Original essay published 1939.

Frye, Northrop. *Anatomy of Criticism: Four Essays by Northrop Frye.* New Jersey: Princeton University Press, 1957.

Gabler, Neal. *Life, The Movie: How Entertainment Conquered Reality.* New York: Knopf, 1998.

Gert, Hans and Mills, C. Wright, eds. *From Max Weber.* New York: Oxford University Press, 1958.

Girgus, Sam B. *The Films of Woody Allen*. Cambridge: Cambridge University Press, 2002.

Gitlin, Todd. *Media Unlimited: How the Torrent of Images and Sounds Overwhelms Our Lives*. New York: Metropolitan Books, 2001.

Goffman, Erving. *Frame Analysis*. Boston: Northeastern University Press, 1974.

———. *The Presentation of Self in Everyday Life*. New York: Knopft, 1959, reprint 1972.

Grossberg, Lawrence. "Teaching the Popular." in *Theory in the Classroom*,ed. Cary Nelson. Urbana: University of Illinois Press, 1986.

Hamsher, Jane. *Killer Instinct: How Two Young Producers Took on Hollywood and Made the Most Controversial Film of the Decade*. New York: Broadway, 1998.

Harman, Gilbert. "Semiotics and the Cinema: Metz and Wollen" from *Film Theory and Criticism* (Braudy and Cohen, eds.). Oxford: Oxford University Press, 1999.

Heath, Stephen. "Narrative Space," from *Narrative, Apparatus, Ideology*, Ed. Philip Rosen (New York: Columbia University Press, 1986). Originally published in *Screen*, Autumn 1976.

Hebdige, Dick. "From Culture to Hegemony." In *Subculture: The Meaning of Style*. New York: Methuen, 1979.

Himmelstein, Hal. *Television Myth and the American Mind*. Westport, Connecticut: Praeger, 1994.

Jameson, Frederic. "Postmodernism or, the Culture of Late Capitalism." *New Left Review* No. 146, July/August 1984.

Jenkins, Henry. "The Poachers and the Stormtroopers: Cultural Convergence in the Digital Age"; http://web.mit.edu/21fms/www/faculty/henry3/pub/stormtroopers.htm

Jensen, Joli. *Redeeming Modernity: Contradictions in Media Criticism*. Newbury Park: Sage Publications, Inc. 1990.

Jensen, Rikke Bjerg. "Do We Learn to Read Television and Film and Do Televisual and Filmic Codes Constitute a 'Language'?" www.aber.ac.uk/media

Johnson, Steven. *Everything Bad Is Good For You: How Today's Popular Culture Is Actually Making Us Smarter*. New York: Riverhead Books, 2005.

Knight, Arthur. *The Liveliest Art: A Panoramic History of the Movies*. New York: MacMillan Publishing Co., 1957.

Konigsberg, Ira. *The Complete Film Dictionary*, Second Edition. New York: Penguin Reference, 1987.

Krzywinska, Tanya. "Demon Daddies: Gender, Ecstasy and Terror in the Possession Film" from *Horror Film Reader*, Silver, Alain and Ursini, James, eds. New York: Proscenium, 2000.

Lee, Spike, dir. *Bamboozled*. Screenplay by Spike Lee. New Line Cinema, 2000.

Lee, Spike. *Bamboozled* audio commentary track. New Line Home Video Productions, Inc. 2001.

Lefevre, Raymond. "Du Voyeurisme a l'Infini" ("From Voyeurism to Infinity") from *Midi-Minuit Fantastique* (October). Translation by Alain Silver. Reprinted in *Horror Film Reader*, Silver, Alain and Ursini, James, eds. New York: Proscenium, 2000. Original essay published in 1968.

Levinson, Barry, dir. *Wag the Dog*. Screenplay by Hilary Henkin and David Mamet, based on the book *American Hero* by Larry Beinhart. New Line Cinema, 1997.

Lumet, Sidney, dir. *Network*. Screenplay by Paddy Chayefsky. Metro-Goldwyn-Mayer and United Artists Pictures, 1976.

Malcolm X. "We Have Risen From the Dead." *Pittsburgh Courier* magazine section.. December 22, 1956.

Metz, Christian. *Film Language: A Semiotics of the Cinema*. New York: Oxford University Press, 1974.

———. "Identification, Mirror" from *The Imaginary Signifier*. Screen, Vol. 16,No. 2, 1975.

Morissette, Isabelle. "Reflexivity in Spectatorship: The Didactic Nature of Early Silent Films." *Off Screen*. July, 2002.

Myerhoff, Barbara and Kaminsky, Marc. eds. *Remembered Lives: The Work of Ritual, Storytelling and Growing Older*. Ann Arbor: University of Michigan Press.

Nachman, Gerald. *Seriously Funny: The Rebel Comedians of the 1950s and 1960s*. New York: Pantheon Books, 2003.

Navasky, Victor. *Naming Names: The Social Cost of McCarthyism*. New York: Viking Press, 1980.

Niccol, Andrew. *The Truman Show: The Shooting Script*. New York: Newmarket Press, 1998.

Nochimson, Martha P. "Tony's Options: *The Sporanos* and the Televisuality of the Gangster Genre" from *Senses of Cinema*, Vol. 29, 2003.

Palmer, William J. *The Films of the Seventies: A Social History*. New York: Scarecrow Press, 1987.

Pietrass, Manuela. "Means of Structuring as Interpretive Indications: A Frame Analysis Look at Infotainment in Accordance with E. Goffman" from *Media and Communication Research*, Winter 2002.

Powers, Stephen and Rothman, David J. and Rothman, Stanley. *Hollywood's America: Social and Political Themes in Motion Pictures*. Boulder: Westview Press, 1996.

Rich, Frank. "What O.J. Passed to the Gipper" *The New York Times*, June 20, 2004.

Robbins, Tim, dir. *Bob Roberts*. Screenplay by Tim Robbins. Paramount Pictures, 1992.

Robbins, Tim. *Bob Roberts* DVD audio commentary track. Polygram Film Productions GmbH., Artisan Home Entertainment Inc. 2000.

Rodowick, D.N. *The Crisis of Political Modernism: Criticism and Ideology in Contemporary Film Theory*. Berkeley: Univ. of California Press, 1994.

Ross, Gary, dir. *Pleasantville*. Screenplay by Gary Ross. New Line Cinema, 1998.

Ross, Gary. *Pleasantville* audio commentary track. New Line Home Video Productions, Inc. 1999.

Ruby, Jay. "The Image Mirrored: Reflexivity and the Documentary Film" in *New Challenges for Documentary*. Berkeley: University of California Press, 1998.

Ryan, Marie-Laure. "From *The Truman Show* to *Survivor*: Narrative versus Reality in Fake and Real Reality TV" from *Intensities: The Journal of Cult Media*, 2002. (www.cult-media.com/issue2/Aryan.htm)

Schatz, Thomas. *The Genius of the System: Hollywood Filmmaking in the Studio Era.* Austin: University of Texas Press, 1988.

Schickel, Richard. *Woody Allen: A Life in Film.* Chicago: Ivan B. Dee, 2003.

Shambu, Girish. "Cinema Elegy: Peter Bogdanovich and *The Last Picture Show*" from *Senses of Cinema.* March, 2001.

Stamm, Robert. Burgoyne, Robert. Lewis-Flitterman, S. *New Vocabularies in Film Semiotics: Structuralism, Poststructuralism and Beyond.* London: Routeledge, 1992.

Stone, Oliver, dir. *Natural Born Killers.* Screenplay by Oliver Stone, David Veloz and Richard Rutkowski. Story by Quentin Tarantino. Warner Brothers Pictures, 1994.

Stone, Oliver. *Natural Born Killers* DVD audio commentary track. Warner Bros. Productions Ltd., Monarchy Enterprises B.V. and Regency Entertainment Inc. 1994.

Sturken, Marita and Cartwright, Lisa. *Practices of Looking: An Introduction to Visual Culture.* Oxford: Oxford University Press, 2001.

Taylor, Shelley E. *Positive Illusions: Creative Self-Deception and the Healthy Mind.* New York: Basic Books, 1989.

Thomson, David. *The Whole Equation: A History of Hollywood.* New York: Knopf, 2005.

Toplin, Robert Brent ed. *Oliver Stone's USA: Film, History, and Controversy.* Lawrence: University of Kansas Press, 2000.

Tornatore, Giuseppe, dir. *Cinema Paradiso (Nuevo Cinema Paradiso).* Screenplay by Giuseppe Tornatore and Vanna Paoli. Christaldifilm, 1988.

Volger, Chris. *The Writer's Journey: Mythic Structure for Writers.* Studio City, California: Michael Weise Productions, 1998.

Weir, Peter, dir. *The Truman Show.* Screenplay by Andrew Niccol. Paramount Pictures, 1998.

Wenders, Wim. http://www.brainyquote.com/quotes/authors/w/wim_wenders.html

Wexler, Haskell, dir. *Medium Cool.* Screenplay by Haskell Wexler. Paramount Pictures, 1969.

Wollen, Peter. "Godard and Counter Cinema: *Vent d'Est.*" from *Afterimage*, Fall 1972.

Glossary

characterology - A method of character reading developed in the 1920's that attempted to combine revised notions in Physiognomy (the study and judgment of a person's outer appearance, primarily the face, to gain insights into character or personality), Phrenology (from the early 1800s and discredited as pseudoscience, it reads character, personality traits, and criminal tendencies on the basis of the shape of the head), and Pathognomy (the study of passions and emotions, including the expression of emotions that are indicated in the voice, gestures, and by features) with ethnology, sociology, and anthropology. *Bulworth* with its hip-hop influenced white politician, and *Bob Roberts* with its "rebel conservative," considers non-traditional characterology as the driving force for engagement and change in the film's players and the electorate.

cineliteracy - The critical understanding of the moving image developed through the processes of reading and writing the screen. This results in a state of understanding and being comfortable with the language of the moving image, along with its use and application in everyday life.

Classical Hollywood Cinema - This designates both a visual and sound style for making motion pictures and a mode of production that arose in the American film industry of the 1910s and 1920s. The Classical era begins around 1915 with the release of D.W. Griffith's *The Birth of a Nation*. The end of the classical period is considered to be the 1960s, after which the movie industry changed dramatically and a new era (the post-classical or the New Hollywood era) can be said to have begun. Classical style is fundamentally built on the principle of continuity editing or "invisible" style. That is, the camera and the sound recording should never call attention to themselves, as they might in a modernist or postmodernist work. The mode of production came to be known as the Hollywood studio system and the star system, which standardized the way movies were produced. Most film workers (actors, writers, directors, etc.) were employees of a particular film studio. This resulted in certain uniformity to film style. The end of Hollywood classicism came with the collapse of the studio system in the wake of The Paramount Decision, the growing popularity of auteurism (the director as the central figure in film construction), and the increasing influence of foreign films and independent filmmaking, which brought greater variety to the movies.

defamiliarization - The artistic technique of forcing the audience to see common things in an unfamiliar or strange way, in order to enhance perception of the familiar. A basic satirical tactic, it is a central concept of 20th century art, ranging over movements including Dada, postmodernism, epic theatre, and even science fiction. Viktor Shklovsky, who was associated with Russian Formalism, initially used the term defamiliarization in the mid-20th century.

diagetic - Elements of a film can be diagetic or non-diagetic. These terms are most commonly used in reference to sound in a film—diagetic music emanating from within the world of the film (such as a jukebox or a singer in a scene) and non-diagetic (the score latter added on a soundtrack)–but can apply to other elements. Diagetic typically refers to the internal world created by the story that the characters themselves experience and encounter. This is the narrative "space" that includes all the parts of the story, both those that are and those that are not actually shown on the screen (such as events that have led up to the present action; people who are being talked about; or events that are presumed to have happened elsewhere).

dramatism – A critical technique and theory of language developed by Kenneth Burke. The foundation of dramatism is the concept of motive: the reasons why people do the things they do. Burke believed that all of life was drama (in the sense of fiction), and we discover the motives of actors (people) by looking for their particular type of motivation in action and discourse. He set up a pentad, which are five questions to ask of any discourse to begin uncovering the motive: (1) Act: What happened? What is the action? What is going on? What action; what thoughts? (2) Scene: Where is the act happening? What is the background situation? (3) Agent: Who is involved in the action? What are their roles? (4) Agency: How do the agents act? By what means do they act? (5) Purpose: Why do the agents act? What do they want?

dystopian – A condition or location where everything is as bad as it possibly can be. This includes the vision or description of such a state. The opposite is utopian.

French New Wave – Also known as *Nouvelle Vague*, a movement in French cinema beginning in the late 1950s that sought innovation in subject matter and technique. It was a response to the moribund French movie industry at the time, arguing for highly individual approaches and sensibilities with the director situated as *auteur* whose indelible stamp was marked on the films themselves. New Wave films took advantage of the new, lightweight portable sound and film recording equipment and were often shot on location rather than in studios. They had loose and realistic plot structures, elliptical cutting, and were generally unsentimental in their treatment of character. Significant New Wave films include *The 400 Blows* (Truffaut, 1959), *Hiroshima Mon Amour* (Resnais, 1959), *Breathless* (Godard, 1959), and *Jules and Jim* (Truffaut, 1961).

hyper-capitalism - A term credited to author and economist Jeremy Rifkin in 2000, it refers to a recent form of capitalism gaining ground in a unipolar world without a major ideological challenger to capitalism. As a comprehensive ideology, it is notably interlinked with a network society and a pro-business political philosophy. Rifkin points out that the world of hyper-capitalism will be one based on access, where every experience will be paid for, and where ownership will be dissolved into economic relations of access to data.

Italian Neorealism – A movement that was primarily a response to the artistic limitations of the Italian film industry under the fascist government and to the social conditions of Italy during and immediately after the Second World War. Central to the films in this movement were realistic, authentic settings; ordinary people played by both professional and nonprofessional actors, everyday social problems explored through episodic plots in scenes with clear, linear cause-and-effect relationships; and unobtrusive camera and editing techniques. Important neorealist films include *Open City* (Rossellini, 1945), *The Bicycle Thief* (De Sica, 1948), *The Earth Trembles* (Visconti, 1948), and *Umberto D* (De Sica, 1952).

inculturation - A theological term that defines the ongoing dialogue between faith and culture. In Christian missiology, it refers to the adaptations of the Gospels and the manner in which they are presented for the specific cultures being evangelized. In cinema studies, inculturation can express a similar, sustained relationship between film and society. The more secular term, enculturation, refers to the process whereby an established culture teaches an individual its accepted norms and values, so that the individual can become an accepted member of the society and find his or her suitable role. This is accomplished through speech, words and gestures as well as the unique images, objects, places and experiences that define a culture.

Most importantly, it establishes a context of boundaries and correctness that dictates what is and is not permissible within that society's framework. The moving picture is a tool of enculturation.

interpellation - A concept first coined by Marxist philosopher Louis Althusser to describe the process by which ideology addresses the individual subject, thus effectively producing him as an effect. Interpellation specifically involves the moment and process of recognition of interaction with the ideology at hand.

intertextuality – A term first credited to poststructuralist Julia Kristeva in 1966, this is the process of shaping texts' meanings by other texts. It can refer to an author's borrowing and transformation of a prior text or to a reader's referencing of one text in reading another. This is often invoked through allusion to another text, discourse, or media representation, and can include a parodic or satiric turns as well as serious homage.

keying (rekeying) – According to social theorist Erving Goffman, keying emerges from the concept of "framing" that allows individuals or groups to locate, perceive, identify, and label" events and occurrences, thus rendering meaning, organizing experiences, and guiding actions. Frame transformation is required when the proposed frames may not resonate with, and on occasion may even appear antithetical to, conventional lifestyles or rituals and existing interpretive frames. When this happens, new values, new meanings and understandings are required in order to secure participants and support. Goffman calls this "keying" where activities, events, and narratives that are already meaningful from the standpoint of some primary framework, are seen differently in terms of another framework. Pseudo-documentary film, for example, allows for the rekeying of traditional documentary in its frame transformation.

narratology - From the French, *narratologie*, used by Tzvetan Todorov in his 1969 *Grammaire du Décaméron*. Narratology is the study of all kinds of narrated texts, both fiction (literature, poetry, etc.) and non-fiction (historiography, academic publishing, etc.). It also considers the dramatic structures, plot devices, characterization, settings, genres, and literary techniques. Usually, narratology is used in connection with fictional texts, but this does not imply that non-fictional texts or other forms of fiction (theater, films, electronic entertainment, etc.) are not included in the studies' field.

Paramount Decision – This 1948 Supreme Court ruling United States v. Paramount Pictures, Inc., 334 US 131 is also known as the Hollywood Antitrust Case of 1948, the Paramount Case, or the Paramount Decision. The Court held in this landmark case that the existing distribution scheme wherein the major studios owned theater chain and gave favorable consideration to their networks was in violation of the antitrust laws of the United States, which prohibit certain exclusive dealing arrangements. It changed the way Hollywood movies were produced, distributed, and exhibited. Among the consequences of the decision were the end of the old Hollywood studio system and, effectively, The Golden Age of Hollywood; the rise of more independent producers and studios to produce their films free of major studio interference; a weakening of the Production Code, due largely to the rise of independent "art house" theaters that featured foreign films; a catalyst for some studios selling their backlog of films to others–for example, most of Paramount's classic films ended up with EMKA, Ltd./Universal Studios, Warner Bros.' library to Associated Artists Productions (later United Artists Television and Turner Entertainment), as well as an incentive to sell older titles to the new medium of television–in an effort to refashion studio cash-flow after having lost the guaranteed outlet of studio-owned theaters to play their product.

PCM – An acronym standing for the collusive forces that are Political, Corporate and Media. These institutions and structures intertwine networks, operations and personnel in the 21st century in service to the prevailing ideology, maintaining rationalized controls over the populace and the economic underpinning.

perspective by incongruity – Kenneth Burke builds upon Oswald Spengler definition of this phrase as "taking a word usually applied to one setting and transferring its use to another setting." Perspective by incongruity is established by violating the properties of the word in its previous linkages, as it is applied in other texts and contexts. The application of perspective by incongruity creates a new reality as it has forced reorientations and reconfigurations of communication patterns. In *Bulworth*, perspective by incongruity is achieved when a 60-year old white politician decides to "rap" his message to constituents.

Production Code of 1934 – In 1930, the Motion Picture Producers and Distributors of America (MPPDA) created guidelines for filmmakers in response to public criticism of the "immorality" of the film industry. This code, initially voluntary, spelled out how certain subjects were to be treated in movies. By 1934, the actions of several pressure groups—including the newly formed Catholic Legion of Decency, which advocated the boycotting of films it did not approve—motivated the MPPDA to strengthen its enforcement of the Code. After July 1, 1934, any film released without a Seal of Approval from the newly created Production Administration (PCA) would result in the production company being fined. No film could play on the screens of the studio-owned theaters throughout the United States unless it had a Seal of Approval. The PCA office would approve both the screenplay before shooting and the completed film affecting a form of self-censorship that dominated American film for twenty years, especially in the areas of sex, crime, violence, domestic life, and religion.

pseudo-documentary - The pseudo-documentary is a unique cinematic form combining elements of fiction and nonfiction film. Distinguishable from *docudrama*, it is a term employed for any dramatization that seeks to recreate, using performers, the activity of actual persons and events. The psuedo-documentary has the shape, content and formal components of pure documentary. Yet, it is revealed to be scripted and acted in the manner of a fictional film. While docudrama overtly acknowledges its mimicry of documentary content, pseudo-documentary strategies are more covert. At times, the phrases *documentary parody* or *mock documentary* are used interchangeably with pseudo-documentary.

pseudo-event - Daniel Boorstin defines a psuedo-evens as an occurrence staged in order to get news coverage and shape public perceptions. News conferences and television debates are some examples. A pseudo-event is a self-fulfilling prophecy and not spontaneous, but comes about because someone has planned, planted or incited it.

reflexivity – According to Jay Ruby, this is the capacity of any system of signification to turn back upon itself, to make itself its own object by referring to itself. In a social theory context, reflexivity is an act of self-reference where examination or action 'bends back on', refers to, and affects the entity instigating the action or examination. Reflexivity is considered to occur when the observations or actions of observers in the social system affect the very situations they are observing. Reflexivity is another word for self-consciousness, that is to say, a consciousness that is directed towards examining its own operations, rather than external phenomena. Reflexivity is also found in philosophy, as in Descarte's famous cogito: I think, therefore I am. Reflexivity in art describes an artwork that flaunts its status as an artwork. Playwright and theorist Bertolt Brecht produced theatre that was purely 'theatrical,' in the sense that audiences could not help but be aware of the mechanics of theatre when they watched one of his plays. Brechtian theatre is characterized as having no sets, no costumes, and offered actors who would drop in and out of their characters as soon as they entered or left the area designated as the stage. A reflexive artwork is a text that openly displays the codes of its construction, thus, a prerequisite for an artwork to be interpreted as reflexive is that its spectators must also share an awareness of the codes. In cinema, a reflexive film employs cinematic devices that make its audience aware of the fact that they are watching a film. It is an awareness of film as a process and not just a finished product. One of the most denotative forms of cinematic reflexivity is *mise-en-abyme*, which means literally a film within a film.

signifying image – A frame, shot or scene from a film that can be isolated and explained as a key to part of the larger theme represented by the filmmaker and understood by the audience. In *Close Encounters of the Third Kind* (Spielberg, 1977), a young boy opens the door of his house to confront a bright and overpowering light to which he is drawn without fear, despite the trepidation of his mother. This represents the power of the inquisitive imagination in the youth that will bring him into contact with alien life forces and from which he will emerge transformed and enlightened, a major theme of the film evinced by this signifying image.

simulacra – The plural of simulacrum, from the Latin *simulare*, "to make like, to put on an appearance of." Notably used in a philosophical treatise by Jean Baudrillard. *Simulacra and Simulation* (*Simulacres et Simulation* in French), published in 1981. *Simulacra and Simulation* is most known for its discussion of images, signs, and how they relate to the present day. Baudrillard claims that our society has replaced all reality and meaning with symbols and signs, and that in fact all that we know as real is actually a simulation of reality. The simulacra that Baudrillard refers to are signs of culture and media that create the reality that we perceive. Baudrillard describes a world saturated by imagery, infused with media, sound, and advertising. This simulacra of the real surpasses the real world and thus becomes hyperreal, a world that is more real than real.

televisuality - John Caldwell defines televisuality as a historical phenomenon, an aesthetic and industrial practice and a socially symbolic act. It emphasizes extreme consciousness of style and visual excess on television. Producers and programmers use highly coded imagery and text to create textual borders around the program in order to stand out in the competitive flow of the media environment. Viewers are keenly tuned to the style of a given program and they identify with the coded visual elements it contains. So, a person might recognize in a split second that the images on the TV set correspond to an episode of *Baywatch* or *NYPD Blue* at the sight of yellow trucks and red swimwear, or claustrophobic squad rooms and hand-held camera work. This way, the producers create a border around the show that makes it easily recognizable and also creates a sharply defined visual context within which the narrative can unfold. Style and look serves to make it instantly identifiable.

Index